The
Kingmakers

VENTURE CAPITAL
AND THE
MONEY
BEHIND THE NET

Karen Southwick

John Wiley & Sons, Inc.
New York • Chichester • Weinheim • Brisbane • Singapore • Toronto

Published by John Wiley & Sons, Inc.
Published simultaneously in Canada.

Library of Congress Cataloging-in-Publication Data:
Southwick, Karen.
  The kingmakers : venture capital and the money behind the Net / Karen Southwick.
     p. cm.
  Includes bibliographical references and index.
  ISBN 0-471-39520-X (cloth : alk. paper)
    1. Venture capital.   2. Internet industry — Finance.   I. Title.
  HG4751. S66 2001
  332'.0415—dc21

                                                            2001017822

Printed in the United States of America.
10 9 8 7 6 5 4 3 2 1

CONTENTS

ACKNOWLEDGMENTS

I would like to acknowledge the cooperation of the dozens of venture capitalists, entrepreneurs, investment bankers, and others who gave me some of their most precious resource—time—so that I could complete this book. In particular, I'm grateful to Roger McNamee of Integral Capital Partners, who wrote the foreword and provided invaluable advice and insight into how the venture capital industry really works. I'd also like to single out entrepreneurs Hugh Martin of ONI Systems, David Roberts of Zaplet, and Glenn Kelman of Plumtree Software, who gave me unusual access to the inner workings of their companies' progress along the start-up trail. And *The Kingmakers* would not have been possible without the backing of John Wiley & Sons and my editor there, Matthew Holt. Finally, I must thank two people who provided absolutely critical support: editorial researcher Andrew Freiburghouse and content editor Eric Nee, who let me know, as always, what worked and what didn't.

Demystifying Venture Capital

O f the many economic innovations that emerged in this country in the years following the Second World War, few have had greater impact—or been less well known—than venture capital. The idea of marrying small amounts of capital with expert business advice in order to accelerate the development of new business ideas was not entirely new in the late 1940s, but it is from that period that today's venture capital industry traces its roots. From these roots, which were as much the product of accident as design, venture capitalists toiled in obscurity for 50 years. Thanks first to the proliferation of personal computers and then of the Internet, the technology funded by venture capitalists moved from a niche industry confined to Silicon Valley and Route 128 to an essential thread of the social fabric of American society. With the onset of Wall Street's Internet mania in the late 1990s, venture capitalists exploded into public view.

Thanks to the accompanying proliferation in media coverage of technology and Silicon Valley, the veil of obscurity has been lifted from venture capitalists. But not the mystery. In *The Kingmakers: Venture Capital and the Money behind the Net,* Karen Southwick provides a penetrating look at the venture industry, demystifying the people and processes of a tiny industry with enormous impact on our country.

While many Americans today know of venture capital and may even have a sense of what it does, few appreciate the strategic role that venture capital has played in the rejuvenation of the U.S. economy in the final two decades of the twentieth century. It is possible that the personal computer industry, biotechnology, and the Internet might have developed into growth engines for our economy without the assistance of venture capital, but there is no doubt that the process would have taken far longer and might well have produced less profound economic results.

Having lived and labored in Silicon Valley for the past 10 years as a cofounder of Integral Capital Partners and Silver Lake Partners—and having invested in technology at T. Rowe Price Associates for nine years before that—I have been privileged to observe venture capitalists and the results of their efforts firsthand. For me, venture capital is one of several instantiations of the unique nature of American culture. Unlike the European cultures that spawned us more than two centuries ago, ours is a culture that, when given a choice between optimizing the productivity of time or capital, chooses the former. Ours is a culture steeped in frontier values, where innovation and entrepreneurship are valued more than birth or status. Upward mobility is a way of life. We encourage risk taking and are uniquely charitable to those who fall short after fighting the good fight.

As a country, we love new economic opportunities. But just as important, we are never satisfied with the normal pace of development if the application of capital, brains, or policy will make it happen faster. We treat every new industrial opportunity as though it were the Manhattan Project, simultaneously funding multiple, mutually exclusive alternatives in the pursuit of a faster path to greatness. Thanks to the venture capital industry, our country has a novel mechanism to ensure that new technology—and new market opportunities—get the attention they deserve. Government policy, our financial markets, and the press are also important enablers of this national obsession with industrial innovation and development, but the cornerstone is venture capital.

When all of these forces—culture, capital, government policy, and innovation—come together behind a big new idea, greatness inevitably follows. More than 100 years ago, before the term *venture capital* was coined by Jock Whitney, the United States built a progression of great industries: Canals, railroads, petroleum, automobiles, telephones, electric power, and radio are among the most important examples. Each of these industries benefited from the interaction of great entrepreneurs, ground-breaking technology, and hordes of

cheap capital—often underwritten by stock and bond market ma-
nias—but even so, each took a generation or more to reach critical
mass.

Since the venture capital industry began to mature in the late
1970s, the pace of development in venture-backed industries has ex-
ceeded anything that came before it. New industries have emerged
seemingly overnight. While many forces contributed to this accelerated pace, the most important was professional venture capital. Venture investors leverage entrepreneurs with insights and experience, as
well as with access to business contacts and capital. Venture investors
were instrumental in helping entrepreneurs deliver on the vision of
personal computers, biotechnology, and the Internet. They played
major roles at groundbreaking companies such as Apple, Intel, Cisco
Systems, Juniper Networks, Amgen, and Genentech.

Now that Internet mania has come and gone, what will become of
the venture capital industry? I believe the prognosis is very good. It
may take time for the financial markets to return to equilibrium, but
that will not affect the pace of innovation in Silicon Valley and the
other centers of technology entrepreneurship. If you want to understand the role of venture capital in our economy—and get a glimpse
of what may be possible in the new millennium—read on. *The Kingmakers* will take you to the heart of one of the most important elements
of our economy.

Roger McNamee
Cofounder, Integral Capital Partners and Silver Lake Partners

Enabling the
Entrepreneurial Dream

Whenever we writers and storytellers look at the rise of a new age, the discovery of a new world, or the forging of a new industry, the first people we chronicle are the explorers and creators. That is as it should be. But then we realize that they couldn't have done it alone, and we look for the other essential contributors—the ones who made the exploration or the discoveries possible. Among them are the risk-taking financiers whose capital enables great achievements such as around-the-world voyages seeking out new lands or the invention of the printing press and the microprocessor.

The companies that are leading the technology revolution have become household names: Microsoft, Sun Microsystems, Cisco Systems, Yahoo, eBay, and so on. But the industry that made them possible—venture capital—is still, to a large extent, shrouded in secrecy. In this book I illuminate the real people behind the mythical figures who appear in newspaper headlines and explore how venture capital actually works at the nitty-gritty level of partnership meetings and entrepreneurial pitches. Venture capital is the fuel that turns entrepreneurial dreams into the companies just cited. Without this kind of risk investing, the New Economy would still be mired in the Old.

In just a few decades venture capital (VC) has become one of the most influential and important industries in the world, deciding what innovations and companies to fund. Small as it is—with just 620 firms registered as professional VC firms in the United States—the VC industry now extends its reach into virtually every nook and cranny of our economy. For as the Internet Age transforms our institutions the way the Industrial Age did 150 years ago, venture capital transforms the Internet Age. Venture capitalists—with their access to huge and growing sums of money, their knowledge, their strategic advice, and their choices—literally determine which new companies will live or die. Venture capital financed the development of high technology and biotechnology, the two revolutions that are shaping our future, for better or for worse.

Today, venture capital has become the accepted means of financing and nurturing innovation wherever it occurs. Corporations old and new, wealthy individuals, ordinary investors, governments, not-for-profits—all are getting into the act. The economic boom of 1999 and early 2000 largely rode on the back of venture investing; the bubble burst when the VC industry's excesses resulted in too many unprofitable, cash-burning companies. The professional VC industry is currently in a state of crisis—triggered, ironically, by its own success. The primary question: Can venture capital scale? Once a collegial fraternity, the industry has become a world-class financial power, but in the process it has both gained and lost: gained respect, unprecedented sums of money, and worldwide attention; lost some of its vitality and vision and willingness to bet the farm on a promising idea.

Kingmakers tells the story of this industry, from its roots to its tremendous flowering today. Included are tales of superstars like John Doerr, leading companies like Intel, entrepreneurs whose start-up companies may be the Intels of tomorrow, angels, accelerators, incubators, and a host of other new forms. This book explains what venture capital is, describes the key players, and forecasts how the industry might weather its crisis. Above all, it introduces a fascinating set of memorable people who are changing their world, and yours.

Chapter 1 opens with a bang: the initial public offering (IPO) of a venture-financed company. The IPO is the culmination of the entrepreneurial dream and the payoff for the VC partners whose skill and dollars turned that dream into reality. Chapter 2 details the workings of venture capital, what the industry is like today, and how it got that way. Chapter 3 goes back to the beginnings of venture capital to trace its evolution and the key patterns that persist today. Chapter 4 introduces the super-tier of venture capital, firms whose accomplishments and reputations make them the most sought-after financiers of entrepreneurial endeavors. Chapter 5 profiles some of the other VC players, ranging from mavericks to newcomers to struggling wanna-bes. Chapter 6 peels back the curtain even farther to look at the limited partners whose money fills the venture capitalists' coffers. Chapter 7 reveals the first phase of the often-rocky relationship between entrepreneurs and venture capitalists, the come-on for money known as "the Pitch." Chapter 8 chronicles the real-life travails of several entrepreneurial companies fighting to grow up, and the exasperating, invaluable aid provided by their VC mentors. Chapter 9 expands the picture to encompass investment banks, which step in to take venture-backed companies public or help them get acquired. Chapter 10 takes us inside actual VC partnership meetings, at which participants candidly discuss which companies to fund and which to cut off. Chapter 11 tells the story that venture capitalists would prefer to keep hidden: the "dark side" of risk investing, when companies fail and people lose their jobs and see their hopes dashed. Chapters 12 and 13 describe the continual entrance of new incarnations into the VC industry, ranging from angels and corporations to incubators. Finally, Chapter 14 ponders the future of venture capital, summing up the trends that drive the industry and what direction it might be headed.

Whether you're a would-be entrepreneur, an investor, an executive, or an employee in a New or Old Economy company, it behooves you to understand venture capital and why it may directly impact you and your future. Fortunately, the story of venture capital is so compelling in its own right that you may want to read it just for the fun of the unforgettable characters and their shenanigans.

CHAPTER ONE

The Grand Ritual

In the year 2000, a D day of sorts for the stock market came five days early: June 1, to be exact. On that day, San Jose, California–based ONI Systems, an optical networking company, was scheduled to offer its stock to the public for the first time in an initial public offering (IPO). Certainly, IPOs by technology companies were by then commonplace. In fact, both the previous year and the previous quarter had set records for numbers of IPOs and for the market valuations the companies had achieved (see Figure 1.1). But the markets, particularly Nasdaq, had been struggling for a couple of months. Nasdaq, where most technology issues are traded, had lost 25 percent of its value in a single week in April and was still seesawing in June, at a level far below its high. Many companies had been forced to cancel or delay their IPOs—only 23 companies went public in May, compared with 65 in March. The situation was grim, and investors were counting on ONI's sector, fiber optics, for salvation.

"If they can't go out then no one can," Roger McNamee, a general partner at Integral Capital Partners, and one of the savviest market observers around, confided to me. "ONI is the perfect company at the perfect time." From the VC capital of Sand Hill Road in Menlo Park, California, where Integral and dozens of other private investment firms

FIGURE 1.1   TECHNOLOGY IPOS (EXCLUDING BIOTECH)

YEAR	PROCEEDS ($MILLIONS)	NO. OF ISSUES	AVERAGE DEAL SIZE ($MILLIONS)	AVERAGE PERFORMANCE THROUGH YEAR-END (%)
1990	630.2	29	21.7	−5.0
1991	2,628.7	73	36.0	35.8
1992	4,395.0	98	44.9	44.3
1993	4,802.0	140	34.3	31.6
1994	5,210.0	138	37.8	37.7
1995	8,786.8	212	41.5	48.6
1996	18,065.0	271	66.7	22.1
1997	9,988.2	190	52.6	25.8
1998	8,291.5	126	65.8	66.8
1999	38,728.2	395	98.1	254.1
2000[a]	36,519.1	171	213.6	34.1

[a]Through close on July 10.
Source: Thomson Financial Securities Data

were headquartered, to Wall Street and other investment centers, people held their breath, waiting for the market's reaction to ONI's IPO.

Like an old-fashioned coming-out party for a young debutante, an IPO represents an entrepreneurial company's emergence as a public entity. The company has reached a certain maturity level and is ready to start existence on its own. The venture capitalists who invested in and nurtured the company from the time it was two or three people peddling a business plan detailed on PowerPoint slides are ready to let go. The company has navigated all the pitfalls that can befall fledgling start-ups and is supposedly on the road to sustainability, generation of revenues, a positive cash flow, and, ultimately, profitability.

That, at least, is the ideal. Subsequent chapters detail how the ravenous public appetite for entrepreneurial technology companies, particularly dot-coms, caused many to go public much earlier in their life cycles than ever before. That trend reached its peak in 1999 and early 2000 before subsiding later in the year. Meanwhile, though, the venture capitalists and start-up companies examined in this book had built a new model of entrepreneurialism—involving speed, branding, and market share—that is transforming the old, even as values such as a clear path to profitability have also re-asserted themselves. Give or take a few glitches, the new model worked well enough to make public entities of ONI and many other companies. In this book we also learn about the symbiotic relationship of entrepreneurs and venture capitalists, a relationship that reaches its highest fulfillment in the grand ritual of a successful IPO. "An IPO is part of the lore and the legend of Silicon Valley," sums up Jon Feiber, one of ONI's VC investors. "Nothing else is quite the same."

GETTING STARTED

During Christmas break of 1996 a young engineer who worked for Optivision of Palo Alto, California, decided to play around with some technology for optical switching buried deep within the 15-year-old company that did photonics work for the government. Infected by the entrepreneurial fervor of Silicon Valley, Rohit Sharma, a slight, intense man who had recently received his doctorate in electrical engineering, figured that there might be gold in this unharnessed technology immersed within an obscure little company. In February 1997, with the blessing of Optivision's management, he applied for patents on a metropolitan optical network that could deliver much faster access to the newly burgeoning Internet than could existing copper telephone lines. That summer he and a small team created a working prototype of the technology to demonstrate to long-distance provider Sprint.

"Optivision did not have the resources or understanding to go after the telecom area," Sharma recalls. Fortunately, he was in the right place at the right time. Not far away was Silicon Valley's famed Sand Hill Road, home to VC firms with interests in just about every emerging technology. Sharma began making presentations up and down Sand Hill. It didn't take the sharp-eyed venture capitalists long to spot an opportunity that would basically boost Internet bandwidth by some order of magnitude. "Everyone we talked to offered to fund us," says Sharma, including, as he notes, all the top firms. He narrowed it down to two, both of whom had extensive experience funding entrepreneurial companies: big kahuna Kleiner Perkins Caufield & Byers, "because of the muscle they bring to the table," and Mohr Davidow

Ventures, another highly regarded firm with a personal tie to Optivision. Cofounder Bill Davidow had gone to school with Optivision chairman Joe Goodman. The two venerable VC firms happen to sit across the street from each other on Sand Hill Road.

At Kleiner, Sharma met with the three partners who specialized in the Internet and networking: Will Hearst, who had recently joined from his family publishing firm; Vinod Khosla, cofounder of Sun Microsystems; and Kevin Compton, a former tech executive focused on telecom and software. "They were interested because we were in the right space and the ideas we had were not just incremental," says Sharma. With optical networking he could build a huge new market, *huge* and *new* being terms that elicit a Pavlovian response from venture capitalists. Later that same week Sharma went out to dinner with Mohr Davidow's partners, including Davidow, an early Silicon Valley executive turned venture capitalist, and Jon Feiber, like Khosla a former Sun executive. "We had a handshake deal [with Mohr Davidow] at the end of the meal," Sharma says.

Meanwhile, Kleiner was doing its own research into the company's prospects, a process known as *due diligence.* Khosla and Hearst came down to the Optivision facilities to watch a demonstration of an early optical switching prototype. Hugh Martin, who had been through the start-up experience several times and was now Kleiner's entrepreneur-in-residence, studied Sharma's business plan and talked to potential customers. The next Monday Sharma was invited to attend Kleiner's regular partners' meeting to pitch to everyone. After the presentation, one partner, an energetic, bespectacled guy named John Doerr (today the most famous venture capitalist on the planet), came out to talk to Sharma while the rest of the partners were thrashing over the deal. "I didn't really know who he was," Sharma confesses, "but he told me that even though he's not involved [in this networking space] he believes infrastructure will take off." Like Mohr Davidow, Kleiner was quick to offer a term sheet specifying how much it would invest for what percent of the company. Representing their respective firms, Feiber and Compton took seats on the new company's board of directors.

As a "very green entrepreneur," Sharma was excited to get two of the Valley's highest-quality VC firms. At the time, they each put in $4.5 million, for which they together received about a 30 percent stake in the as-yet unnamed company. "We had patents and a $500,000 contract with Sprint," says Sharma. "We had proven the basic technology with an early working prototype." All of that, combined with the "huge new market," made his venture capital foray a pleasant experience. For while venture capitalists are like sharks to blood in the water when they sense a big opportunity, they pass on probably 99 percent of the deals they're offered. When Sharma was pitching his idea in 1997, Kleiner looked at 50 business plans a day and might fund one of those. Today the ratio is worse, thanks both to the widespread availability of e-mail, which allows more entrepreneurial pitches to pour in, and to the increasing numbers of wanna-be entrepreneurs. In a survey of 12 big VC firms, the ratio of deals funded to business plans received ranged from 1 in 100 to 1 in 444.[1]

THE IPO EXPERIENCE

On the morning of June 1, 2000, Hugh Martin, now ONI's chief executive officer (CEO), got up early at his Silicon Valley home to scan the financial news channels and chat on the phone with Dan Deese in New York. Deese was the head of equity capital markets at Goldman Sachs & Company, ONI's lead investment banker, and would follow the IPO throughout the day. Everything looked promising, he told Martin, although ONI's stock had not yet begun trading. The night before, anticipated heavy demand from institutional buyers had caused Goldman to raise the ante on the 8 million ONI shares to $25 apiece, up from the previous range of $21 to $23 a share. Originally, the offering had been filed with the Securities and Exchange Commission (SEC) at $14 to $16 a share. This was all part of the elaborate staging that led to a hot IPO: In the first SEC filing, typically about 60 days before the offering, you set a modest price. Then you bump it up as the company goes through the "road show" and meets with prospective investors, fanning demand to a fever pitch. It was a tried-and-true formula perfected by entrepreneurial companies and their bankers over the last two decades of the technology revolution.

Martin was watching CNBC for the announcement that ONI had started trading when the phone rang. He picked it up. It was his wife Moira, who told him that their eight-year-old son Ryan had left his retainer on the kitchen table. He was supposed to wear it all day. Could Hugh take it over to the elementary school and find Ryan? The CEO obliged, driving to the nearby school and walking up and down the halls until he located the classroom where his son was. "Hi. How're you doing today?" the teacher asked casually. Martin was speechless.

"I didn't know what to tell her," he told me later that day. "But it sure put things back into perspective."

Martin drove down to ONI's headquarters in San Jose, just around the corner from one of the most valuable technology companies in the world—Cisco Systems, whose spectacular rise had become the symbolic target for ONI and a host of other entrepreneurial ventures. As Martin soon found out, ONI was on the right track: It had opened trading at $78, $53 above its offering price. It would close the day at $82.56, a 230 percent surge and the largest first-day gain for a new issue in more than two months, since the stock market's April doldrums (see Figure 1.2). ONI had a total market capitalization of $10.2 billion, roughly equal to Federal Express, a company with $18.3 billion in annual revenues. And Martin, who owned nearly 6 million ONI shares, was worth about half a billion dollars, on paper at least. By late June the stock was above $120. Another Silicon Valley shooting star was born, and at a most opportune time!

PARTY TIME!

ONI scheduled an IPO party for 4 P.M. Pacific Daylight Time, three hours after the official close of its first day of trading. It was an exclusive affair: Only ONI's four hundred employees were invited. Press were not allowed because the SEC's "quiet period" restrictions limit the amount of publicity leading up to and immediately following an IPO. In an attempt to keep a lid on stories that might unduly influence investor interest, the federal agency's policies often unwittingly spawn rumors that lead to even more excitement. For instance, the day before ONI's scheduled IPO, one of the biggest players in the networking arena, Lucent Technologies, had purchased a small Israel-based competitor of ONI's, Chromatis, for $4.5 billion in stock. Now Chromatis, unlike ONI, was what is termed in industry parlance a *prerevenue company;* that is, it had not yet shipped a single product, although it did have at least a couple of "firm" orders. That price tag for a zero-revenue competitor who had maybe two customers definitely didn't hurt ONI's chances, nor did a published report that ONI itself was be-

FIGURE 1.2   TOP 20 IPOS IN 2000 (THROUGH DECEMBER 14; RANKED BY POST-OFFER VALUATION)

COMPANY	OFFER AMOUNT ($MILLIONS)	POST-OFFER VALUE ($MILLIONS)	AGE AT IPO (YEARS)
Corvis	1,138.5	3,348.1	3.2
Transmeta	273.0	2,682.8	5.8
Storage Networks	243.0	2,390.2	1.9
UTStarcom	115.2	2,340.3	8.8
Avanex	216.0	2,251.1	2.3
Mediacom Communications	380.0	1,710.0	4.6
Buy.com	182.0	1,678.8	3.4
Handspring	200.0	1,676.6	NA
Niku	192.0	1,657.1	2.2
Onvia.com	168.0	1,655.8	3.0
Silicon Labs	99.2	1,443.9	3.2
Sonus Networks	115.0	1,386.4	2.8
Blue Martini	150.0	1,348.5	2.1
Avenue A	126.0	1,336.2	3.2
Marvell Technology Group	90.0	1,233.2	5.4
VIA Networks	150.2	1,198.4	2.7
Capstone Turbine	145.5	1,173.4	2.5
Tanox	213.8	1,163.5	14.3
ONI Systems	200.0	1,073.6	2.7
IBEAM Broadcasting	110.0	1,061.5	2.4

Source: Venture Economics/National Venture Capital Association.
Note: Post-offer valuation represents the value of all shares outstanding (primary shares, management shares, etc.) at the offer date.

ing eyed as takeover bait by Juniper Networks. In fact, ONI's offering had been delayed for more than a week because of minor snags in dealing with the SEC—time enough to fuel widespread speculation as to the cause, ranging from the stock market's lukewarm response on new offerings to concerns that ONI had not properly accounted for all the shares it handed out to customers and partners.

I'm able to attend the party because I signed a nondisclosure agreement (NDA) stating that this book would not be published until 2001. On a warm spring day, I drive down Highway 101 to ONI's headquarters, arriving a few minutes early. The receptionist, a heavyset African American woman, is giggling on the phone with a friend: "I've been tracking this since last night. I've had the calculator out." Neither she nor any other employee will be able to sell stock until after the six-month "lockup" period that prevents insiders from flooding the market with shares and precipitately driving down the price. And employees will also have to wait until they're "vested"—that is, take ownership—in their shares, which depends on the length of time they've been with the company. Still, the receptionist's anticipatory calculation on the day of her company's IPO is typical and entirely understandable.

The lobby is cool and spacious, decorated in aqua and maroon. I sink into one of the black leather chairs, watching the blurry reflections of people walking through as they appear in the ceiling of mirrored tiles. There's a Robotron video game in the corner behind me. As I wait, one young, red-headed guy tries his hand. "You feel lucky today?" I ask him. "After the IPO anything else would be gravy," he responds.

Larry Loper, ONI's corporate communications guru, bounds down the stairs and offers to give me a tour of ONI's new facility across the street, which will be filled as soon as it's ready. In Silicon Valley, space, like time and people, is a resource in short supply. ONI is currently subleasing from neighboring JDS Uniphase, but that company wants the space back for its own growing workforce. The hallway of the new facility has curvy sculptured walls and decorative black lights, Martin's idea of how to represent optical networking, Loper tells me. "He better keep his day job," I reply. Part of the facility is already occupied by an engineering division. The adjoining kitchen is stocked with boxes of breakfast cereal, loaves of bread, and other snack foods, delivered by Webvan, the struggling online grocery service that is a surefire hit with Silicon Valley engineers, who work all sorts of crazy hours and don't have time to run to the grocery store. Actually, the new facility won't last long. Martin has just agreed to move ONI further south, to far cheaper land in South San Jose, although the employees don't officially know this yet.

ONI doesn't have a room big enough to house all its employees, so it has rented space for the party in a temporarily empty building down the street. To get there, I drive by Cisco's imposing stretch of buildings and then past a lemon grove and processing plant: the new and old Silicon Valley, cheek by jowl. Within the building is a large open room where folding chairs have been set up in front of a podium. The food, catered by the ubiquitous Webvan, includes shrimp platters, cold cuts, strawberries, beer, and champagne. A couple of Loper's assistants hand out blue T-shirts emblazoned with "Team ONI" on the front and "GET LIT!" on the back. The mood is festive, yet restrained. There is still much to do; this is, as Martin emphasizes, not an end but a step along the way. Technology officer Hon Wah Chin is talking on his cell phone as he gets ready to leave for an important trade show the next day. I overhear three workers discuss their stock-vesting schedules: One receives ownership of the first set of his shares in November, the others the following March. One of the latter comments, "You'll have a very happy Christmas; we'll have a very tense Christmas."

As Martin enters, wearing a "GET LIT!" T-shirt and his customary jeans, employees surround him, slapping him on the back and getting their photos taken with him. One photo grouping sandwiches Martin, who is tall and imposing, with short curly brown hair, between a guy with green hair and another with a long purple ponytail. One thing not much in evidence is gray hair. Like much of Silicon Valley, ONI's employees are young, mostly in their twenties and thirties. Martin and other members of the management team are past 40, but they look like just about the only ones.

At 4:30 P.M. Martin starts asking people to sit down and steps behind the podium as the clapping and cheering swells up. It surges as the CEO holds up a hand-scrawled sign, "82+," and sets it down in front of the podium. The CEO puts on his glasses, blue eyes peering over the top of the gold frames: "I have an important announcement to make," he says solemnly, as the room quiets down. "Two-for-one split" comes from the back of the room. Martin waits for another burst of cheering to subside, and continues: "The last time we were in this building I was getting hoarse from giving the first version of the road-show pitch. Since then we've given 86 of those around the world. From those meetings we had a hit rate of 100 percent. Every single buyer we met with put in an order for our stock."

ONI sold 8 million shares, raising $200 million at the initial $25 price, but generated demand from institutional investors for 165 million shares, Martin reports. From the individual investor side came another 40 million shares of demand, in large part from Silicon Valley itself, a testament that insiders know when a stock will be hot. The ONI offering was roughly 25 times oversubscribed, in a market that had recently been cool to IPOs. One mutual fund, Janus, had declined to invest in any more IPOs for about two months, but temporarily suspended that decision when it came to ONI, he says: "For us they made an exception." And despite the 230 percent increase, Janus is sitting tight on its shares. "It's really congratulations to all of us," the CEO tells his crew. "There are so many nights and weekends when our parking lot is full. I feel like I'm the front man you trot out every once in a while."

The casual, jeans-clad audience is a far cry from Hollywood and the elegant Academy Awards, yet Martin's thank-you list is long enough that it could have come from an Oscar acceptance speech. He praises ONI's lawyer and accountant for putting up with the SEC accounting guys, "who spend their lives torturing entrepreneurs." Goldman Sachs' bankers get to take a bow, including a 26-year-old team member whose youth and competence earned him the nickname "Doogie Banker." Martin also singles out Andy Page, the young vice president of corporate development who had to double as chief financial officer (CFO) for about a month while ONI did a frenzied search to fill that critical position. Martin recalls meeting a very enthusiastic investor in Boston who pumped his hand and told him, "I'm just real excited to be here." Then the man added, "My son's name is Andy Page." Others singled out include founder Rohit Sharma and new CFO Chris Davis, who came on board a week before the road show. "The hardest part of her job, she had to listen to me 86 times," Martin jokes.

From the easy camaraderie he has with the crowd, you can see that the tall, buoyant CEO provides a good public persona for his company. He tells another story about dealing with the SEC: In anticipation of the IPO, which was expected on May 23, Loper had scheduled Martin to appear on several of the major financial news stations, including CNBC, CNNfn, and Bloomberg. CNBC had been trumpeting the appearance on its Website. What Martin refers to as the "voice of God," meaning an SEC regulator, got on the phone the next morning with ONI's attorney: "What in the hell are you guys doing? You're violating the law. Your CEO was on CNBC last night." A frantic half hour ensued during which it's verified that Martin did not make the appearance on CNBC, despite the publicity, because the IPO was delayed. Out of this came an order from the SEC that Martin must sign, in which he agreed not to appear on television for 25 days after the IPO.

Finally, Martin asks for questions from the employees. Several people shout out, "When are we moving to South San Jose?" Obviously, the secret has leaked. Martin levels with them: ONI has signed a deal on a facility in South San Jose. For the first time, boos mingle with the cheers. Some people's commutes will undoubtedly be more arduous in car-choked Silicon Valley. Martin insists that the majority will have a shorter commute and adds that the space is much cheaper, $1.87 per square foot compared with $4.25 to $4.50 where they are now. "To have the same level of profitability, we'd have to sell $65 million more product a year," he points out. "I'd rather put $65 million toward the bottom line." He promises that ONI will build a gym, fitness facility, and cafeteria, because there's no place to eat nearby, and the company expects people to be putting in a lot of hours. The move is expected by the first quarter of 2001.

When he gets no further questions, Martin concludes on a serious note: "Though the shirt says 'get lit,' please don't. We need all of you."

THE ROAD SHOW

It's hard to compare the period immediately preceding an IPO to anything else, except maybe a football team preparing for the Super Bowl or a troupe of actors rehearsing for a Broadway opening. The IPO road show—an entrepreneurial company's presentation to the all-important mutual funds, pension funds, money managers, and other institutional investors that will buy its stock—happens only once in a company's lifetime, and everything depends on it. If a road show doesn't generate enthusiasm for the planned offering, a company might still go public, but then languish in the ghetto of unfulfilled expectations.

Case in point: On the same day that ONI had its public offering, so did CrossWorlds Software, a Burlingame, California, software company that I profiled in my first book, *Silicon Gold Rush*. Unfortunately, CrossWorlds never executed on its early promise, and its IPO was lackluster. The shares were priced at $10 apiece, below the original range of $14 to $16. In first-day trading, investors bid up the price only 12.5

cents. CrossWorlds' problems extended far beyond the road show, of course, but its situation demonstrates that if the CEO and other senior managers making the presentation don't (or can't) effectively communicate the strategy and positioning of the company, its IPO can be DOA.

Martin and CFO Chris Davis were determined that that wouldn't happen to ONI. Davis joined the company the first week of May, literally the week before the road show, replacing Terry Schmid, who had been Martin's CFO at his previous company. About five weeks earlier, Schmid told Martin that he was having doubts about how long he wanted to stay with the company. Martin responded, "We should change now because we're going to be introducing you to 80 institutional investors," who would be counting on Schmid to be their liaison both before and after the IPO. Schmid's departure forced ONI to do a stressful search for a CFO just weeks before the road show.

Davis came on board from Gulfstream Aerospace, where she had handled a turnaround, an IPO, and a buyout. Before that, she had spent 17 years at General Electric. "My number one priority was making sure I spent enough time jumping into the business, understanding it so I could represent the company and myself in the IPO process," says Davis, who has light brown hair cut in a neat pageboy, high cheekbones, and a no-nonsense approach. "I wasn't about to go out there and bullshit people." She didn't have to, because ONI had impressive credentials—credentials that brought Davis on board in the first place. It was backed by blue-chip venture capitalists, and a gold-standard investment bank was going to take it public. In addition, says Davis, "this was in an exciting space with a leadership team that wanted to build a business for the long term."

How ONI was going to build that business was detailed in the actual road show pitch, accompanied by painstakingly assembled PowerPoint slides. The pitch to investors was designed to be finished in 30 minutes, about 25 minutes by Martin on the company's strategy and market positioning and five minutes by Davis on the financials. In a typical hour meeting, that left investors plenty of time for questions. Recalls Martin: "Chris [Davis] and Rohit [Sharma, the founder, who joined the road show in its New York City leg] would take bets on how fast I could do it. If I did it in 25 minutes they'd give me $1. I only collected $1 the whole road show."

   Martin's central message was that ONI was delivering the infrastructure and services to power the Internet. He would explain that
technology was in one of those periods of "discontinuity"—in this case
the shift from electrons (conventional networking) to photons (optical networking). "Whenever there's a discontinuity, there are tremendous opportunities," he explained. "There's also going to be a $1
trillion buildup of the Internet over the next 10 to 15 years." After this
promise of a megamarket, Martin would describe where ONI is posi-
tioned: offering optical networking and services within metropolitan
areas and then connecting to long-haul carriers. Already, ONI,
though still a small company, had major customers and impressive
partners such as Sun Microsystems, Juniper Networks, Brocade Communications, and JDS Uniphase. After Martin introduced the ONI
team, Davis would go through the financial milestones and income
statement. During the road show, which spanned 17 cities in 12 days,
the two of them did this 86 times, both to groups and in one-on-one
meetings with more than 100 investors and funds (see "Red Eyes and
Exhaustion").
   In between appointments within a city, like athletes during a time-
out, Martin and Davis would fortify themselves with bottled water,
snacks, and Powerbars that were always on hand in their stretch limo.
They'd also make phone calls and catch up on what Nasdaq was doing. What kept Martin going through the strenuous road show was his
belief in ONI's mission. "This wasn't hawking something you don't believe in," he says. "For every single investor I wouldn't let them go until I had won them over. We had a 100 percent hit rate." To Davis, it was
like being in the movie *Groundhog Day,* reliving the same experience
over and over. "You have to remind yourself that even though you
might have done the presentation seven times already that day, the
people you're meeting with have never seen it before," she says.
   For both of them, the road show has now become such a blur of
presentations, people, and pitches that it's hard to single out memorable moments. Martin does remember being told by one investor, a
woman, "Forget the presentation and tell me why you're building this
company." He doesn't remember what he told her. "What I would say
now is that I want to build something I can look back on and say, 'I
made that,'" he says. "This is a very special time we're living in, and I
don't want to look back someday and say, 'What did I do?'"

RED-EYES AND EXHAUSTION

For an entrepreneurial company's top executives, the IPO road show represents perhaps the most incredibly intense couple of weeks in their business lives. Here, thanks to a diary kept by ONI Systems CEO Hugh Martin, is the actual schedule of its road show, which usually included Martin, CFO Chris Davis, and two representatives from Goldman Sachs & Company, the lead banker on the deal. Founder Rohit Sharma joined the team during the New York leg. After it was over, Martin summed up the road show this way: "It gets to be nothing but a blur." Once you read the schedule, you can see why.

Wednesday, 5/3/00. Pitch to the Bank of America sales force. BofA is one of four investment bankers who will handle the IPO. [Educating the sales forces is critical because they will in turn sell to investors. If the investment banks' sales forces don't love the deal, the IPO is dead.] Fly to New York that night to meet with Goldman the next day.

Thursday, 5/4. Pitch to Goldman Sachs' sales force. Goldman says the presentation is the best dry run they've seen. Fly home.

Friday, 5/5. Morning—present to Chase H&Q and FleetBoston Robertson Stephens, the two remaining investment bankers, in San Francisco. Afternoon—two meetings with investors.

Monday, 5/8. Presentation to about 200 people at the Chase H&Q high-technology conference, the largest and most important in the world. Numerous meetings with investors in San Francisco for the event. That evening, take private jet to San Diego.

Tuesday, 5/9. 6:30 A.M. meeting at investor's home in La Jolla, California. Drive to San Diego for another meeting, fly to Pasadena for a meeting, then fly to Portland, Oregon, for a meeting. That evening, fly to Houston, arriving at 12:30 A.M.

Wednesday, 5/10. Four meetings in Houston starting at 6:30 A.M. Fly to Chicago midday for three meetings in the afternoon. Take the 6:50 P.M. red-eye flight to London.

Thursday, 5/11. Land in London at 10 A.M., go to a meeting at 11 A.M., followed by a lunch meeting and four meetings in the afternoon. At 7 P.M. take a private plane to Frankfurt, Germany, arriving at 9:30 P.M.

Friday, 5/12. 7:30 A.M. breakfast meeting in Frankfurt with 15 investors. Take 10:30 A.M. flight to Paris for lunch meeting, followed by three meetings in the afternoon. Take 5:30 P.M. flight from Paris to San Francisco.

Sunday, 5/14. Catch 2:25 P.M. flight to Kansas City, Missouri.

Monday, 5/15. 7 A.M. three morning meetings in Kansas City. Fly to Denver for four meetings. Then fly to New York City, arriving at midnight.

Tuesday, 5/16. 6:30 A.M. take private helicopter from New York to Plainsboro, New Jersey, for 7:30 A.M. meeting. Fly back to New York for two meetings, followed by lunch at the Metropolitan Club with 150 people. Four afternoon meetings, plus a dinner meeting. Fly to Boston, arriving at 11:30 P.M.

Wednesday, 5/17. 7 A.M. start of four meetings in Boston. Lunch with 30 people at the Boston Harbor Hotel, followed by four afternoon meetings. Fly to Baltimore, arriving at 12:15 A.M.

Thursday, 5/18. 7:30 A.M. meeting in Baltimore. Take train to Philadelphia, and do two meetings downtown and three meetings in the suburbs. Take train to New York, arriving at 7 P.M.

Friday, 5/19. Nine meetings in New York. Take evening flight to San Francisco, arriving at 10:30 P.M.

Sunday, 5/21. Fly to Minneapolis.

Monday, 5/22. 7:30 A.M. start of two meetings in Minneapolis. Fly to Milwaukee, Wisconsin, for lunch meeting and three afternoon meetings. Then fly to New York, with pricing of the offering planned that evening and start of trading on Tuesday, May 23. [Actually, trading was delayed and Martin flew home to the San Francisco Bay Area on May 24.]

OVERCOMING AN SEC SNAG

The preparation for the IPO had split off into two legs, the first with Martin and Davis on the road, and the second with ONI's lawyers and accountants working to satisfy all the SEC queries. Martin had launched the road show without finishing up on the SEC end because the agency's early questioning had been very light. So he'd expected a quick resolution of all the paperwork that had to be done before the final prospectus was issued. But it wasn't to be. The SEC had unexpected questions about ONI's handling of its stock warrants, and the IPO got delayed again and again.

When the road show ended, Martin was in New York at Goldman Sachs' offices, expecting to price the issue on the evening of Monday, May 22, and then start trading on Nasdaq the following day. But the SEC still wasn't satisfied. With no resolution in sight, on May 24, Martin, who had intended to be in New York for the first day of trading (and appear on the financial news programs), flew home. The SEC finally cleared the offering more than a week later, on May 31, the following Wednesday, and trading opened on June 1.

The week and a half of waiting, although it left Martin and the ONI team twisting in the wind, wound up having a silver lining. After weeks of seesawing, Nasdaq managed to turn in a couple of strong days. In a June 1, 2000, online story by CNNfn, pundit Ben Holmes, president of ipoPros.com, commented on ONI's offering: "This is an example of an experienced underwriter timing the deal.... They held back until they knew it was a good market to launch the IPO."[2] That kind of speculation amuses Martin and Davis, who were frantically trying to get the IPO off the ground whenever they could. "With the delay, all the excitement and buildup gets yanked away from you," says Martin. To ease the disappointment of each day's agonizing postponement, he and other members of the management team forced themselves to adopt the attitude, "I won't believe it until it happens."

"Those extra days were extraordinarily painful," the CEO adds. "If I had to do it again, I wouldn't start the road show until after the SEC comments." Davis notes that while in hindsight the unusually long delay didn't hurt, no one knew that at the time. "After the successful road show, we were working very diligently to maintain the credibility of the company through the delay," she says.

ONI Systems' moment in the sun proved that the public offering window was still open, at least for companies with champion pedigrees, and gave hope to investors that the incredible run of 1999 and early 2000 was not entirely over. But investors were becoming far more discriminating. "Optical networking is the gold standard in the IPO market," wrote Holmes of ipoPros.com. "Nothing is garnering more interest or getting higher premiums."[3] The previous hot sectors, dotcoms, and business-to-business (B2B) exchanges were yesterday's news. In mid-2000, fiber optics ruled the day.

BEHIND THE SCENES

Almost unnoticed in the hoopla surrounding ONI's IPO were the venture capital firms whose cash and strategic advice propelled the company from its founding in 1997 to the momentous "going-out" day. After their initial funding of the spinout from Optivision, Mohr Davidow and Kleiner had continued to invest as the company grew and met designated milestones. Each VC firm wound up putting in about $23 million, and each had come out of the first day of trading with more than $1 billion worth of stock, which would later be distributed to the two firms' own investors. "It was the biggest single IPO for us so far this year," recalls Mohr Davidow's Feiber.

He'd had no doubts that ONI would be able to complete its IPO, given that its positioning as an Internet infrastructure play made it virtually market-proof. *Infrastructure* refers to a manufactured product—software or hardware—that provides the underpinning of the Internet, allowing it to be accessed faster and better. Infrastructure is the refuge when markets go south, because although you don't need another jewelry or pet store on the Web, everyone needs infrastructure. "Even though the overall market for IPOs has been slow, communications infrastructure IPOs have remained very hot," said Tim Savageaux, senior research analyst at W. R. Hambrecht & Company, the day after ONI's offering. "Maybe they're not as hot as they would have been two months ago [before the market crash], but they've still been extraordinarily successful."[4]

ONI netted $186 million in capital from the IPO (the other $14 million went to its investment banks), to continue building its business and possibly look for takeover candidates. The amount would also balance out about $90 million in accumulated losses. "The rest of [the surge in price] was gravy," says Feiber. "The company achieved its objective in raising the capital." By the way, the "gravy," as he calls it, goes entirely to investors, not to the company itself. ONI reaps only the capital raised from selling shares at the announced initial price.

However, the so-called IPO "pop"—the 230 percent gain in the opening day of trading—provides another type of reward for ONI: It puts the company on the map. "In a very short order, ONI has changed its stature to be one of the three or four leading companies in its sector instead of one of the mighta-bes," says Feiber. Competitors that go public in the future will aspire to ONI's offering-day performance. Its highly valued stock now becomes currency for acquiring smaller ventures with innovative technology. With only a small portion of the total number of shares (123 million) in public hands, ONI can contemplate a secondary offering to raise more money. Or it might do a debt financing, an option not usually available to a nonpublic company.

ONI also gave a boost to the entire technology arena. Because of the Nasdaq gyrations that preceded its offering, ONI wound up as a kind of bell cow, very closely watched to see which direction the IPO market was heading. ONI had all the elements to succeed: a good story in an important and emerging market, a respected management team, prestigious partners and investors, and so on. "When [public] investment gets constricted, there are inevitably one or two early companies that help to redefine the market," says Feiber. In a serendipitous way, ONI achieved that redefinition.

BACK TO THE FUTURE

Another common outcome for an entrepreneurial start-up like ONI is to be acquired by a larger, public company, which can result in the same economic returns to investors and executives as an IPO, but not the same emotional satisfaction. ONI explored, and continues to explore, buyout options, Martin acknowledges, but he insists that the intent is to remain independent. CFO Davis is with him on that: "I've already been at the top of a public company that got bought by somebody bigger. It's not where I want to be again," she says.

Some observers think of the IPO as an exit strategy or a liquidity event, allowing early investors, and even executives and employees, to cash out at significant premiums. However, the lockup and other restrictions don't allow any of these people to get out quickly. It will take at least a year, in most cases. For Martin, the IPO is an important event, to be sure, but only one in what he vows will be a long chain of important events. "For a company sitting here with $3.6 million worth of revenue in one quarter, to be worth $10 billion says we have a bright future. We have to make that happen," he says.

Feiber seconds him, saying that the IPO is a balancing act between recognizing its significance as a milestone and realizing what still must be accomplished. "I don't think we're so blasé we'd say the IPO has become a routine event," he says. "It's always thrilling when a company goes public." Employees deserve the chance to celebrate, but the hard work resumes very quickly. And because the company is now public, there's even more scrutiny and more pressure to achieve more milestones and move toward profitability. "ONI had a tremendous IPO, and follow-up was strong, but the real measure of a company is extended performance," notes Feiber. "What will the company be worth in a year, in five years?" He hopes that ONI will have other memorable days, like crossing the $100 million threshold in sales, growing to 1,000 employees, or recording its first profit.

Indeed, a couple of weeks after the IPO, ONI had its first board meeting as a public company, and it was business as usual. One change was that only the six actual board members, consisting of Martin, Feiber, Compton, and three outside directors, were present. The observer seats granted to late-stage investors and corporate partners disappear after an IPO. The board meeting included a review of the IPO, a status update on the company's progress in areas such as sales and marketing, and an update on engineering ONI's next product. The roles of Feiber and Compton, who remain on the board, will change, as they're now public rather than private investors. "Before, they were on the board because they wanted to watch over their investment," says Martin. "Now they're on the board because we want them there; they add value. Both of them are terrific advisers and consultants. As long as we continue to be a high-impact player, we're someone they want to be involved with."

To be that high-impact player, ONI had taken one major step forward. At the end of the day, the company pulled off such a successful IPO because it had a compelling story for a market soured on the empty promises of far too many dot-coms whose business strategy was spending to buy market share, with profitability never in sight. ONI also had astute VC backing, a seasoned CEO, and, after some initial flailing about in search of its market niche, a well-executed business plan. None of these things happened by accident. The coming chapters reveal how venture capitalists work with entrepreneurs to orchestrate all the elements that create a company like ONI.

CHAPTER TWO

The Venture Capital Way

It's a testament to the success of venture capital that it barely needs a definition today. If this book had been written even 10 years ago, it's questionable whether many people outside entrepreneurial strongholds like Silicon Valley and Route 128 in Boston would have known how this form of investment worked and why it was important. For up until the early 1990s and the advent of the Internet, venture capital remained a rather collegial industry (see Chapter 3) whose small number of practitioners clustered in a few locations—primarily Silicon Valley, Boston, and New York—and drew a shroud of secrecy over what they did. Without venture capital, however, it's doubtful whether we'd have such now-taken-for-granted advances as the microprocessor, the personal computer, the browser, genetically engineered drugs, or Web portals.

Venture capital is private investment capital offered by professional firms to entrepreneurial start-ups in which the firms exchange cash for an equity stake in the company. By defining the participants as *professional firms,* I'm excluding the wealthy families who have invested in new companies in a rather hobby-like fashion for centuries, up to and including today. But as a formal entity, venture capital is a relatively new industry, becoming a recognizable niche in the late

1960s to early 1970s and growing up side by side with the creations it enabled: high tech and biotech. In fact, some of the practitioners—men like Alan J. Patricof, Arthur Rock, and Don Valentine—have been in the industry almost since its inception.

Because venture capital (VC) is private and largely unregulated, the methods by which it operates have developed organically. Venture capitalists have a complex set of relationships on both sides of the money. It starts with the limited partners who invest in VC funds in "silent" fashion, in exchange for returns that are expected to be better than what the public markets offer. Traditionally, VC investments are considered riskier than those in the public market because entrepreneurial companies are unprofitable and have an unproven business model. (For a time, in 1999 to early 2000, that risk/reward ratio briefly reversed itself because of the huge public appetite for all things Internet, but the anomaly had subsided by mid-2000.) These limited partners include university endowments, foundations, pension funds, and wealthy people. Key attributes are the ability to commit millions of dollars for up to 10 years (the length of time of a typical VC fund), long-term investment perspective, tolerance of risk, and trust in the VC firm that will manage the money. The latter is particularly crucial today because the VC firm has almost complete discretion over what to do with the money. In the early days of venture capital, the limited partners had more power because money was harder to come by. But now, thanks to their unprecedented success, especially in the late 1990s, the best VC firms turn money away.

In turn, VC firms take their increasingly large pools of money—the biggest funds today are between $1 billion and $2 billion—and pour them into entrepreneurial companies, hoping that some of them will be incendiary successes like Genentech and Intel, Cisco and Netscape, Yahoo and Amazon.com. As noted in Chapter 1, the ideal is to grow the start-up into a public company that can stand on its own and no longer needs venture capital, because it can access the stock market and debt instruments; it has achieved capital self-sufficiency. Another common outcome is for the start-up to be acquired by a larger public company in exchange for stock, or to be merged with a competitor. In an analysis by McKinsey & Company's San Francisco office, about 27 percent of VC-backed start-ups launched in 1995 were able to achieve either an initial public offering (IPO) or be acquired within three years, a ratio the consulting firm expected to decline as VC firms' tremendous successes caused them to fund too many companies of mediocre quality (see Chapter 11). Another study, by Horsley Bridge Partners, an investor in VC funds, demonstrates both the risky nature of venture capital and its potential for huge payoffs. Of 61 funds in which Horsley Bridge invested between 1985 and 1996, 28 percent of the money was written off, while 5 percent of the money generated 68 percent of the eventual return. Overall, those 61 funds invested $6 billion, creating more than $60 billion in value, a tenfold multiple!

THE GOLDEN ERA

Like everything else in Silicon Valley, nostalgia develops rather more quickly than in most other places. Already, in mid-2000, as people began to reflect on the period from 1999 through the first quarter of 2000, it took on the shimmer of a golden era when venture capital investors, it seemed, could do no wrong. Unprecedented sums flowed its way: More than $64 billion poured into U.S. VC funds in 1999, according to Venture Economics Information Services—more than double the previous year's commitment of $30 billion. From January through mid-December 2000, another $75 billion was committed to venture capital (see Figure 2.1). Put another way, 1999 and 2000 together accounted for more than half of all the venture capital ever raised since Venture Economics began keeping records in 1982. In each of those years, the industry raised more cash than it had in its entire lifetime from inception until the mid-1990s. In the beginning of that decade, all the professional venture capital raised in a year did not equal one large fund raised in 1999 or 2000.

"The last year [1999] was one in a million," proclaims Roger McNamee of Integral Capital. "We were lucky to be here for it because we won't see another like it." At the 2000 Chase H&Q Investment Conference (where, coincidentally, ONI started its road show), McNamee was warning investors that venture capitalists would never be able to duplicate 1999. "It was a speculative blow-off of world-class proportion."

You can gauge the success of venture capital by its imitators of every ilk. As previously noted, venture capital has never been a large industry. Even today, only about 620 professional VC firms are regis-

FIGURE 2.1   AMOUNTS RAISED BY U.S. VENTURE
CAPITALISTS, 1982–2000

YEAR	NO. OF FUNDS	SUM RAISED ($MILLIONS)	AVERAGE PER FUND ($MILLIONS)
1982	76	1,563.0	20.6
1983	138	4,246.5	30.8
1984	120	3,477.3	29.0
1985	140	3,492.2	24.9
1986	121	4,694.4	38.8
1987	131	4,607.3	35.2
1988	117	4,041.0	34.5
1989	123	6,134.4	49.9
1990	110	3,902.0	35.5
1991	59	2,338.9	39.6
1992	88	5,246.1	59.6
1993	115	5,139.9	44.7
1994	162	10,457.5	64.6
1995	186	9,661.0	51.9
1996	197	12,098.6	61.4
1997	292	20,675.3	70.8
1998	348	36,812.1	105.8
1999	417	55,096.3	132.1
2000[a]	409	75,341.3	184.2

Source: Venture Economics/National Venture Capital Association.
[a]2000 figures are preliminary, through December 13.

tered with the National Venture Capital Association. Once upon a time, brash young business school graduates went into investment banking or climbed the corporate ladders at major U.S. corporations. No longer. "Everybody today wants to be a VC or an entrepreneur," says Ann Winblad, a veteran venture capitalist and cofounder of Hummer Winblad Venture Partners in San Francisco. As an example, prestigious Harvard Business School, whose graduates have been chief executives of companies such as IBM, Merck, and Procter & Gamble, is reinventing itself around entrepreneurialism. Instead of general management, once the school's signature course, first-year students must now take a class called the Entrepreneurial Manager. Instead of looking at case studies focused on Caterpillar, Colgate-Palmolive, and General Electric, students follow entrepreneurial companies like Bitstream and Intuit, as well as VC firms like Onset Ventures.[1]

Old Economy companies like Wal-Mart, Toys R Us, Procter & Gamble, and Nordstrom have all teamed up with VC firms in an effort to get their dot-com entities off the ground. American corporations routinely have internal VC arms. From professional athletes to consulting firms to California's largest electric utility, Pacific Gas & Electric, everyone, it appears, is jumping on the VC bandwagon—even the U.S. Central Intelligence Agency (CIA).

In late 1999 the CIA established a VC arm in Silicon Valley, later named In-Q-Tel (the abbreviation for intelligence sandwiched around the *Q* that identified James Bond's high-tech whiz). "In-Q-Tel, by design, is about as outside the box as government gets," wrote the *Wall Street Journal.* "And the box, in this case, is none other than the CIA, which wasn't even hooked up to the Internet until a couple of years ago and remains woefully behind the high-tech curve." Nonetheless, In-Q-Tel's mission is the same as that of any other VC firm on Sand Hill Road or in Boston or New York: Invest in leading-edge technology, find the best teams, and build companies to bring the technology to market. The CIA, of course, is after stuff that can help its covert missions, such as improved computer security and smaller sensors.[2] Meanwhile, Newt Gingrich reportedly ponders moving to California and becoming a venture capitalist, because it's so much easier to get things done in entrepreneurial companies than in government.[3] And *Time* magazine proclaims that the era of "venture-capital politics" has arrived because wealthy candidates like Jon Corzine and Steve Forbes spend their own money to try to win elections.[4]

The venture capitalists themselves have become trendy and cool. Kleiner's John Doerr made it onto *Vanity Fair*'s list of the top 50 leaders of the information age, part of the magazine's 1998 New Establishment.[5] *Business Week* named Ann Winblad, the best-known female venture capitalist, as one of Silicon Valley's top 25 power brokers in its August 25, 1997, issue.[6] Even crusty old veteran Don Valentine is heralded as a "silicon patriot," whatever that is, by *Worth* magazine.[7] What gives? Why this sudden boost of popularity for an arcane industry run like a benevolent oligarchy out of country clublike settings in Menlo Park and Palo Alto?

INTERNET-FUELED TRANSFORMATION

Venture capitalists almost universally point to the emergence of the Internet in the mid-1990s as the seminal event that transformed their industry, for better or for worse, from a narrowly defined regional specialty into a global powerhouse. Before that, they had helped to fund technologies like the microprocessor, gene-splicing, the PC, and software, but none of these had reached out to both the public and the business sector the way the Internet has. For consumers, the Internet connected PC users and enabled a brand-new world of interactivity. It also spawned the creation of thousands of new start-ups and forced every existing company to rethink its strategy and its place in the new Internet world. "We're seeing the cumulative effects of technology," says Dick Kramlich, the veteran investor who cofounded New Enterprise Associates on Sand Hill Road. "There's a continuum of ever-enlarging opportunities."

Andy Rappaport, a partner with August Capital on Sand Hill Road, has an eclectic background that spans consulting, journalism, and research physics. Bearded and bespectacled, the shaggy Rappaport looks like he'd be right at home in a college classroom, and indeed he has lectured extensively on his areas of expertise, including semiconductor design, computers, and telecommunications. For more than 17 years, Rappaport has been active in technology consulting and investing, so when he says the Internet Revolution is going to outdo the Industrial Revolution in impact by an order of magnitude, you listen.

"We're talking about a major change in the way humans live their lives and create societies and interact," says Rappaport. "The Industrial Revolution was the last period that did that. We haven't had one of those yet in technology, but the magnitude of what we're dealing with now could reach beyond the Industrial Revolution." That's because the Industrial Revolution took a century or so—from 1750 to 1850—to play out, giving the generations time to adjust. "The Net revolution may play out in 10 years," notes Rappaport, "so time frames are incredibly collapsed. We've never seen this magnitude of societal and cultural change in such a short time."

What's different from previous technologies is that the impacts of the microprocessor, PC, and software industries were largely self-contained within the workplace. They changed the way we work. The

Internet is changing the way we live. Technology has moved from the back office to the forefront of the way companies conduct their business and the way people conduct their lives, says Geoff Yang, a partner and cofounder of Redpoint Ventures, one of Sand Hill Road's newest firms. Redpoint was formed in the fall of 1999 from two older firms in order to concentrate on the Internet. As Yang sees it, from its introduction in the 1970s through the early 1990s, technology for companies represented back-office cost displacement—better ways of managing accounting, communications, human resources, and the like. But with the introduction of Netscape's popular browser in late 1994, the Web changed the front-office part of doing business—the way you interact with people, deal with suppliers and partners, and even organize your executive suite.

The Internet forces everyone from the Global 500 to your neighborhood flower shop to consider how to compete in the era of e-tailing and e-commerce. If Webvan will deliver groceries to my door for the same amount it would cost me to go down to Safeway and buy them myself, what do I need Safeway for? What's the fate of my neighborhood bookstore if I have a choice of millions of volumes at my fingertips on Amazon.com? EBay has created whole new communities of people buying and selling artifacts, baubles, and junk online. Technology has moved from being a tool for improving workplace productivity to being a tool for restructuring the economy, society, and just about every other human endeavor. If the Web isn't in your future, do you have one? The Internet is collapsing traditional hierarchies, stripping out geographical boundaries, and allowing overnight formation of new competitors and new business models.

It's this type of sweeping change that causes Vinod Khosla, one of the most visionary venture capitalists around, to peer into the future and see vast opportunity. Khosla, an Indian immigrant who is now a partner with Kleiner, previously cofounded Sun Microsystems, one of Silicon Valley's most successful companies (and the topic of my previous book, *High Noon*). The Fortune 500 companies, says Khosla, are worth $10 trillion, give or take a trillion or two. From 1981 to 1990 the PC created $100 billion in market capitalization in new companies, he says. The Internet is doing the same thing at one to two orders of magnitude greater. "In the next decade we'll see at least a dozen companies with market caps greater than $100 billion starting from scratch," he says. And he intends to get his share.

"ALL THE WORLD'S A STAGE"

The explosion in opportunity fostered by the Internet has allowed venture capitalists to play upon a much larger stage. Instead of being confined to high tech and biotech—both of which were science-oriented, research-driven fields that most of the general public knew little about—venture capitalists could now invest in everything from pet food to chemical exchanges, groceries to jewelry, bookstores to airline bookings. The sea change represented by the Internet makes new companies possible in just about every niche you can think of. "Once, if you were a technology investor, you were investing in things like plumbers and carpenters, providing services to companies," says Ann Winblad of Hummer Winblad. "Now you're starting new businesses that compete with all those companies you used to service." Hummer Winblad has invested in fields as diverse as online pet sales (Pets.com), allergies (Gazoontite.com), and the new musical exchange format called Napster. As we'll see, the first two companies are now defunct, and the third is fighting to stay alive, so it's debatable whether venture capitalists' expanding scope is entirely a good thing. Winblad sighs, looking back over her career spanning two and a half decades, first as an entrepreneur, then as a venture capitalist. "Did I ever think I'd be in the mortgage industry, or transportation, or pets? . . . Never."

This type of investing caused the venture capitalists to shift their emphasis from something they'd gotten very good at, establishing a technology, to something they would have to learn, building a brand. The former meant doling out money carefully to an engineering-driven organization, which was running lean and mean, hitting technological benchmarks, convincing customers one-on-one, and finally launching the product. The latter meant gorging the company on cash, pushing it to grow fast, hiring not only engineers but also sales and marketing people as quickly as possible, expending massive amounts on advertising, and swiftly pulling off the all-important IPO, which had now in itself become a "branding event."

Indeed, the new VC firm Redpoint wouldn't even exist without this Internet-based business model, predicated on branding and momentum. "We formed Redpoint with the theory that we could establish a major brand and be a force right away," says Yang. How to do that? By picking six strong partners well versed in the Net from two existing firms and then counting on "increasing returns" and the "network effect" to goose their business. That is, Redpoint intends to grab enough high-profile Internet deals that other top start-ups will be compelled to at least consider the firm. It's an economic theory that has worked in technology markets. Whether it will succeed in venture capital remains to be seen. "We're trying to redefine the industry, create this buzz and perception of a franchise out of the box," says Yang.

On the other end of the spectrum you find Sequoia Capital's legendary Don Valentine, of the iron-gray hair and steely eyes, whose career in VC investing is now in its fourth decade. Venture capitalists "don't understand brand development," he maintains. From 1970 to 1995, venture capitalists weren't interested in retail businesses or branding. In fact, "until the Internet came along, the word *brand* was almost never mentioned," he growls (perhaps because the VC industry's previous foray into branding, in the form of specialty retailing in the mid-1980s, was a disaster). Today, the Net-based business model, especially in e-commerce, forces him and other veteran venture capitalists into a world they're not quite comfortable with. "It's a very difficult and expensive proposition to develop and maintain brand recognition," Valentine says.

Yet another important impact of the Internet has been on the nature of public investing in technology. In its early days, technology was so complex and arcane that investing was largely confined to specialists who could devote the time to understand it. Thus, the major brokerages and mutual funds recruited analysts who would delve deeply into the scientific breakthroughs and advances in semiconductors and computers. But it doesn't take any deep knowledge of chip manufacturing or Moore's Law to figure out what Pets.com or Webvan is trying to do. Besides, the Internet has democratized research that used to be reserved for selected high-paying clients and has allowed the formation of chat sites and bulletin boards devoted to all the New Economy stocks. The unprecedented public demand for these stocks caused venture capitalists and their limited partners to open up the financing tap to create new companies that met that demand.

Because this tremendous public appetite for entrepreneurial companies coincided with the explosion in opportunities enabled by the Internet, the result was an outpouring of start-ups, particularly technology start-ups. "An unprecedented number of new companies have been made possible by the advent of the Internet, the tremendous influx of capital, and the performance of the public market," sums up Tim Haley, a Redpoint partner who had a lengthy previous career in executive search. In 1998 the U.S. VC industry invested in 2,004 deals, of which more than half were in information technology (IT) and the Internet, according to VentureOne, a VC tracking firm in San Francisco. (Other investment segments included health care and conventional consumer products and services.) In 1999 the number of deals jumped 57 percent to 3,153, with 1,656 of those in IT. In the first half of 2000, venture capitalists invested in 2,138 deals, including 1,043 in IT. That represents thousands of new companies in two and a half years! (See Figure 2.2.)

WHAT VENTURE CAPITALISTS WANT

The closed deals are only the tip of the iceberg when it comes to the total number of business plans that venture capitalists must peruse. Remember, they invest in less than 1 percent of what they see. "Most of our business is about saying no rather than yes," notes another Sequoia Capital partner, Michael Moritz, a former journalist who joined the firm in 1985. Compared with the stocky, down-to-earth Valentine, the tall, thin Moritz comes off as a bit of a snob, with his dark hair, glasses, and clipped Welsh accent. Like Valentine, however, he knows a good idea when he hears it. What Moritz zeroes in on is the clarity with which the entrepreneurs can communicate what they intend to do. In 1987 Sandy Lerner, the cofounder of Cisco Systems, had a three-word summation of what her company did: "We network networks," she said in a presentation to Sequoia's partners, including Moritz and Valentine, who decided to invest almost immediately. "It was crystal clear," Moritz recalls. No doubt they felt chills down their spines. "Fourteen years later," he adds, "Cisco's business model has changed, and its product lines have expanded into areas no one contemplated, but the core business of networking networks is still there."

Traditionally, VC investors have concentrated on three primary components: the team of people who propose to start the company, the potential market in terms of size and competition, and how well the technology or product involved serves that market. However, the emergence of a new Internet business model, which demands speed to market and branding rather than pure technology innovation, has tended to downplay the significance of the actual product and accentuate the importance of the team and market size. "All I care about is a passionate entrepreneur and a big opportunity with unlimited upside," proclaims Tim Draper, a partner and cofounder of Draper Fisher Jurvetson in Redwood City, California. Draper, who's tall, dark-haired, and cheerful, has VC investing in his genes: both his grandfather and father were involved in the industry. Draper Fisher uses market size as a screen: If the market is too small, usually under $1 billion in today's environment, the firm will pass. "We do market size checks before we even meet the people," says Draper. "If they pass that barrier, then we want to see if they have the passion."

It's Valentine who is the undisputed king of market investing. If he can find the right market, he'll come up with the people to run the company. That's exactly what he did at Cisco, bringing in veteran management to replace the founders, who were forced to leave. "Neither of the founders knew anything about sales, marketing, manufacturing, or running a business," says Valentine. "The understanding was that we'd find people who were functionally expert in those areas." However, Valentine acknowledges that he's in conflict with some of his peers for his devotion to the market over people. "Arthur Rock [another old-line venture capitalist] and I have disputed this for 30 years," says Valentine. "Arthur looks for fabulous people. He's a fairly rare person who has the ability to find a great person. Most of us can't do that. It's much easier to pick a great market. I left the great people-picking to Arthur and went after businesses that had huge markets. I found at least one of those every decade: Apple, Cisco, and Yahoo."

So what does Rock, whose investments in Fairchild and Intel spawned today's Silicon Valley (see Chapter 3), have to say for himself? Shier and harder to draw out than Valentine, Rock is still investing his own money from a one-man (plus an assistant) office in San Francisco. When I met with him, he was courtly and apologetic for making me wait. Slightly stooped, with thinning brown hair and glasses, he had on a white shirt and tie, one of the few ties I saw in 200 or so interviews. "I had no technical background and still don't quite understand all the technologies," Rock admits. "You have to know the players and what's happening. You have to find the people. To do that you need to be networked in." In the early days of VC investing, the relationship with companies and people was like a courtship followed by a long, stable marriage. "When I was doing investments, we cared more about the

FIGURE 2.2 VENTURE CAPITAL INVESTMENT BY SECTOR, 1997–2000

INDUSTRY	1997		1998		1999		2000 (FIRST HALF)			
	NO. OF DEALS	AMOUNT INVESTED	NO. OF DEALS	AMOUNT INVESTED	NO. OF DEALS	AMOUNT INVESTED	NO. OF DEALS	PERCENTAGE OF TOTAL	AMOUNT INVESTED	PERCENTAGE OF TOTAL
Information technology	1,070	$6667.70	1,165	$8,687.86	1,656	$20,662.97	1,043	49%	$19,321.65	55%
Communications and networking	247	$2,380.48	295	$3,105.05	386	$8,191.74	267	12%	$8,232.71	23%
Electronics and computer hardware	87	$506.70	83	$478.32	74	$723.06	30	1%	$389.02	1%
Information services	142	$775.45	191	$1,458.81	430	$4,660.10	275	13%	$4,121.27	12%
Semiconductors	66	$457.96	72	$513.49	89	$905.28	58	3%	$824.10	2%
Software	528	$2,547.11	524	$3,132.19	673	$6,163.47	412	19%	$5,751.95	16%
Other information technology	0	$0.00	0	$0.00	4	$19.33	1	0%	$2.60	0%
Percent change from previous year			9%	30%	42%	138%				
Healthcare	418	$2,802.05	413	$2,809.13	414	$3,381.44	247	12%	$2,785.84	8%
Biopharmaceuticals	112	$792.01	136	$990.53	118	$1,227.71	81	4%	$1,097.85	3%
Healthcare services	108	$821.25	84	$628.33	57	$403.73	28	1%	$116.68	0%
Medical devices and equipment	140	$777.74	129	$811.88	170	$1,211.04	71	3%	$601.14	2%
Medical information systems	58	$411.05	64	$378.39	69	$538.96	67	3%	$970.18	3%
Percentage change from previous year			-1%	0%	0%	20%				

	1997		1998		1999		2000 (First Half)			
Industry	No. of Deals	Amount Invested	No. of Deals	Amount Invested	No. of Deals	Amount Invested	No. of Deals	Percentage of Total	Amount Invested	Percentage of Total
Products and services	315	$1,812.38	395	$2,826.71	1,059	$13,148.84	829	39%	$13,139.44	37%
Consumer and business products	49	$297.79	35	$226.92	35	$288.41	21	1%	$348.67	1%
Consumer and business services	188	$966.64	271	$1,979.07	847	$9,188.75	744	35%	$11,706.61	33%
Retailers	78	$547.95	89	$620.73	177	$3,671.68	64	3%	$1,084.16	3%
Percentage change from previous year			25%	56%	168%	365%				
Other	35	$194.36	31	$180.70	24	$153.58	19	1%	$121.50	0%
Percentage change from previous year			-11%	-7%	-23%	-15%				
Stage—All industries										
Start-up	132	$360.39	179	$636.41	276	$1,190.99	140	7%	$992.61	3%
Product development	568	$3,435.46	597	$4,431.95	865	$9,144.22	607	28%	$9,828.42	28%
Shipping product	1,036	$7,044.95	1,135	$8,696.30	1,911	$26,073.67	1,351	63%	$23,895.35	68%
Profitable	100	$632.20	90	$720.24	96	$922.78	39	2%	$645.55	2%
Restart	2	$3.50	3	$19.50	5	$15.17	1	0%	$6.50	0%
Total	1,838	$11,476.50	2,004	$14,504.40	3,153	$37,346.83	2,138	100%	$35,368.43	100%
Percentage change from previous year			9%	26%	57%	157%				

Source: VentureOne.

companies," Rock maintains. "I was on the Teledyne board for 33 years and the Intel board for 32 years. Today there's a much greater need to show results very quickly. VCs don't have the time to spend with their companies."

Dick Kramlich, who was Rock's partner in the early 1970s, tries to strike a balance between the two opposing views. "I'm always asking three questions," he says, which are, *How is this going to change the way we do things? Is this a group of people who can get through thick or thin? How can the market become open-ended and not just a little niche?* "If it passes those tests, then you get all the nitty-gritty stuff about the numbers."

Jon Feiber's decision to invest in ONI Systems synthesizes the gut feeling that really drives most VC decisions. ONI was a little different because it was spun out as a research group from an existing company, but the issues were the same: Could the team carry it through? Was this a market that could take off? Were optical switches the right product for that market? It was obvious that optical switching was going to be an important step forward in networking, Feiber says. "We liked the people, so we made the investment. In hindsight it was a bet on faith that we could build a company." Rohit Sharma's original research, he says, was only a "distant cousin" of what eventually became ONI's first product. But that's nothing new. "The number of companies who follow the strategy we outline the day we fund them is small," Feiber says. What was present was the "right primordial soup" for ONI to emerge: "There were a set of key people and a passionate belief that optical equipment would be important. That was enough of a spark."

EMERGENCE FROM THE "SOUP"

In Chapter 1 I skipped from ONI's founding in 1997 to its IPO in 2000, but there was enormous effort in between. The management team, led from early 1998 on by CEO Hugh Martin, had to figure out which market to attack in the many-faceted optical networking space and with what products. "We spent a lot of time brainstorming with Kleiner and Mohr Davidow," recalls founder Rohit Sharma. ONI eventually zeroed in on metropolitan area networks, which connect urban areas with long-haul transmission. Meanwhile, a more recently founded start-up, Sycamore Networks, zoomed past ONI. Founded in February

1998, Sycamore brought out its optical networking product in March of the following year and had an impressive public offering in October. It wasn't until April 1999 that ONI introduced its first product, a networking platform/operating system that allows metropolitan networks to deliver Internet and broadband services to businesses and consumers.

Martin, the Kleiner entrepreneur-in-residence who had handled the due diligence research into ONI, quickly became the obvious CEO-designate for the new company. In a pattern very typical of entrepreneurial companies, the board of directors, dominated in the early stages by VC investors, brings in an experienced executive to run a company as it gathers momentum. "The very first meeting I had with Hugh, he didn't quite say [that he would become CEO], but it was clear that's what the setup would be," Sharma recalls. He was comfortable with that. "I'm an instinctive person when it comes to people," he says. "Right from the beginning we got along very nicely. Hugh and I had a very informative, informal talk about the assumptions of how people were going to use the Internet. I could tell he was good at spotting what gives a quantifiable benefit to the consumer." Sharma and Martin have complementary strengths. "Hugh has this ability to connect with whoever is on the other side of the table, whether it's a technology or business person," says Sharma. His own strength is connecting ideas to actual applications: "I can identify needs and address them."

Martin has a sterling pedigree for an entrepreneurial CEO: previously, he had held high-ranking executive positions at 3DO Company and Apple Computer. Before that, he cofounded and served as vice president and chief development officer of Ridge Computers. When he left 3DO in 1997, Martin flirted for a time with Microsoft, which wanted to start a company to compete with Kleiner's @Home (later Excite@Home). Instead, Kleiner persuaded Martin to join the VC firm as an entrepreneur-in-residence, where he could do consulting and jump into any Kleiner company that interested him. "In late 1997 [Kleiner partner] Will Hearst told me, 'I think we've found a perfect company for you,'" Martin recalls. This was a spinout that intended to compete with Ciena, whose spectacular IPO occurred on the back of a networking technology called dense wavelength multiplexing. After talking to customers and studying the business plan, Martin told Kleiner, "You should invest in this company, and I'll run it."

Martin joined ONI, formerly called Optical Networks, in January 1998. The following April, networking king Cisco Systems invested $4.5 million in the start-up, which then consisted of "a bunch of research contracts and 18 Ph.D.s," Martin recalls. "We were still figuring out what we were going to build." The original idea was to make an optical interface box that would connect routers, Cisco's primary product, and networks. "It was clear to me that we would end up being bought by Cisco if we did that." But Martin's vision, shared by Sharma and others at ONI, was to go for the grand slam, building another Cisco rather than becoming part of it. That meant finding a greenfield market that ONI could develop instead of working on incremental technology. Looking at the market for optical networking, which offered far greater capacity than traditional copper, ONI's management concluded that long-distance buildup of fiber optics was well underway, but the metropolitan areas were still ripe. "We picked a tough challenge," says Martin. "We had to build a very advanced optical technology, along with an operating system and the tools to run it." Telecom transmission was not a West Coast expertise, "so we recruited out of Lucent and Nortel."

With two decades of experience in the entrepreneurial world, Martin has come up with a formula for creating a successful new company:

1. Take advantage of discontinuity. ONI is exploiting two ongoing discontinuities: the need to rebuild the aging telecom infrastructure to accommodate the demands of Internet and broadband, and the accompanying switch from electrons to photons.

2. Have a vision that allows you to attack the market in a strategic place. By picking transmission in metropolitan areas, "we're much closer to the user than long-distance companies," says Martin, which gives ONI leverage in negotiating with potential customers much bigger than it is.

3. Secure access to capital from high-quality sources. "The fact that we're a Kleiner company tells our customers and our employees that we're going to win," says Martin. Having Kleiner and Mohr Davidow onboard enabled ONI to raise money from other investors on favorable terms. "People were killing themselves to get into our deal."

4. Put in a management team that's capable of going all the way and won't take the easy way out, such as selling to Cisco.

In October 2000 ONI followed up its IPO with a secondary offering that combined equity and convertible notes, raising $896 million, just before the technology downdraft of late 2000 pounded even infrastructure and optical companies. (In March 2001, ONI was trading around $19 a share, compared with a high of $142.) "The difference between the offerings is that you give away money in the IPO, but in the secondary you're selling at the market rate, minus a small discount," Martin notes. For the secondary, he undertook another exhausting road show, and lost his voice for part of it. "I was squeaking into a microphone at Fidelity because I could hardly speak," he recalls. "One investor told me, 'Just shut up and we're in.'" Following on the heels of its IPO, the completion of the secondary demonstrated ONI's staying power in an increasingly skeptical market.

HOW VENTURE CAPITAL WORKS

Although the decision to invest may be an intuitive one, the processes by which venture capitalists work after that have become relatively standardized. As one entrepreneur told me, "You have all the power [to select the firm] until you take the check." Then the power shifts to the venture capitalist. Generally, VC firms have split into two types: early stage and late stage. Early-stage VC firms concentrate on finding companies just as they're forming, or sometimes take an idea and build a company around it. By investing at that point, they're able to exact a good-sized piece of the company—25 to 30 percent is preferred. The logistics—size of the investment in exchange for what percentage of the company, board seats, voting rights, and so on—are outlined in an extensive term sheet proffered by the VC firm to the entrepreneur. The company will then go through a series of funding "rounds," called Series A, B, C, and so on. The amount of money raised in each of these rounds has gone up sharply in recent years. The median first round per company was $3 million in 1995 and had doubled to $6 million by 1999, according to VentureOne. The second round increased even more, from $4 million in 1995 to $10.8 million in 1999, whereas later rounds moved from $5 million to $12 million in the same period (see Figure 2.3).

FIGURE 2.3 MEDIAN AMOUNT OF VENTURE CAPITAL RAISED BY ROUND, 1999 AND 2000 (IN $MILLIONS)

	1999					2000				
	1Q	2Q	3Q	4Q	1999 TOTAL	1Q	2Q	3Q	4Q	2000 TOTAL
Seed	$1.30	$1.40	$1.50	$1.50	$1.50	$1.50	$1.74	$1.20	$1.07	$1.50
First	$5.00	$5.00	$5.00	$6.68	$5.25	$8.00	$7.50	$7.50	$7.50	$7.60
Second	$8.70	$10.00	$9.94	$12.39	$10.30	$15.00	$15.00	$15.00	$14.00	$15.00
Later	$10.00	$10.00	$14.90	$17.00	$12.00	$17.00	$18.05	$21.45	$19.94	$19.00
Grand Median	**$6.00**	**$6.00**	**$6.50**	**$8.50**	**$7.00**	**$10.00**	**$10.00**	**$10.20**	**$10.50**	**$10.00**

Source: VentureOne

The very earliest round, called *seed*, may be raised from the entrepreneur's friends and family rather than from a venture capitalist. Seed money, which in 1999 and 2000 averaged $1.5 million per company, is used to develop a business plan, perhaps build a product prototype, and gather a small team. After that the early-stage venture capitalists typically step in. Early-stage venture capitalism is where the glory is: All the famous names like Kleiner, Sequoia, Mohr Davidow, Benchmark, and the like, have established their reputations by being able to pick an Amazon or a Yahoo or an eBay before it was recognized by anyone else. This is where the emotion and the intuition come into play, where the risk is the highest, but where the payoff could be 10, 50, or 100 times the initial investment. With later-stage investing, the calculations are more cut-and-dried: Has the company met its benchmarks, gotten the product developed, wooed a few important customers, and filled in the management holes?

The early-stage VC firms continue to invest through subsequent rounds of funding, although their percentage of the company gets diluted as other investors come in. For instance, corporations usually invest during later rounds. In the ideal situation, each subsequent round of funding is done at a higher valuation. Pre- and post-money valuations refer to the value assigned the company before and after a funding round. If an early-stage investor buys 30 percent of a company for $3 million, in VC-speak, that investor put in "$3 million at a *post* of $10 million." As the company progresses, the next round might "step up" to a valuation of $25 million to $50 million or more, depending on how heated the market is. With ONI, its third-round, post-money valuation of $80 million in mid-1998 ballooned to $825 million in its final round in December 1999, at the height of the Internet bubble. The last round, completed just before an IPO, is referred to as *mezzanine* and is intended to give the company enough money to bridge it through to the public offering.

Venture capitalists make their money in two ways. They take a generous portion of the payoff that occurs through a liquidity event, either an IPO or a merger. Top-tier VC firms like Kleiner and Sequoia now demand a 30 percent carry, basically a portion of the profit made through the liquidity events. The remaining 70 percent goes to the limited partners who put up the money in the first place. If Kleiner, for example, made $1 billion on its ONI investment, it could keep $300 million of that while $700 million is returned to the limited partners.

There are complicating factors. Kleiner cannot sell its ONI shares all at once because of rules on insider trading (more on the complex process of distribution in Chapter 6), but you can see the gigantic rewards that a VC investment can reap—better than the California lottery. Only Kleiner and a few other top firms are at a 30 percent carry, according to several limited partners I spoke with. Most VC firms take a 20 percent or 25 percent carry.

In addition to the carry, VC firms also charge management fees of 2.5 percent annually, based on the amount of the fund raised. Although VC firms are continuous entities, they raise discrete funds (Sequoia 1, Sequoia 2, etc.) every couple of years. A $1 billion fund generates $25 million annually for the VC firm, before any payoff from the carry. Because the firms are usually running several funds simultaneously, they're also collecting multiple fees. The management fees represent the VC firm's operating budget, and they are used to pay salaries and expenses for partners, entrepreneurs-in-residence, associates, and secretaries, and to run the office. In addition, partners split up the carry among themselves, and often coinvest their own money with the firm's, so the best venture capitalists have become just about as wealthy as the entrepreneurs who hit it big. For example, Arthur Rock ($2 billion) and John Doerr and Vinod Khosla (both of Kleiner, and both at $1 billion) were on the 2000 *Forbes* 400 list of the richest people in America.[8] The industry's unreal attitude about money is evident in the following conversation, which occurred about four years ago at a conference. Several young venture capitalists were discussing an entrepreneur who had just sold his company. "It's unbelievable," said one. "He took out $100 million." But another replied disparagingly, "Big deal. That was pretax!"

NOT JUST THE MONEY

To a man or woman, venture capitalists insist that they're not in this just for the money. It's to build great companies, create new industries, and work with brilliant, energetic people. Here's what Pierre Lamond, another veteran partner at Sequoia whose hawk-like appearance reminds me of his fellow Frenchman Jacques Cousteau, has to say: "What keeps me coming in is the fun of working with the upper 5 percent of the population—intelligent entrepreneurs who are go-getters. Being involved with young people keeps me young. I have the body of a 45-year-old. I think I'm going to go on working for a long while." Lamond, by the way, is pushing 70.

But, of course, the money is at the root of it. Sure, the venture capitalists get off on the adrenaline rush of building a company from that "primordial soup" that Feiber talked about, but in the end what validates the company's and the venture capitalist's worth is the money. And the price that the company fetches in an IPO or a high-profile merger. And the return to the limited partners and the VC firm. And being able to brag that the IPO is a "10-bagger or 100-bagger," which refers to the ratio of the IPO valuation to the VC firm's initial investment. After all, they don't call it *venture capital* for nothing. Who's going to complain about becoming a multimillionaire or even a billionaire essentially by playing with other people's chips? Not these guys. They're too smart for that.

As subsequent chapters show, however, venture capitalists do bring a lot of value to the table: their industry knowledge, contacts, strategic advice, and, sometimes, just sheer bullying of a reluctant entrepreneur to think bigger. Without the alchemy of venture capital, the technology revolution might not have happened, and certainly would have been a very different animal indeed. The Fairchild Eight would have had no one to fund their critical research into the semiconductor, the cornerstone technology of Silicon Valley. Herbert Boyer could have stayed happily in his University of California laboratory experimenting with gene-splicing. Sandy Lerner might still be wiring networks for Stanford University. And Steve Jobs and Steve Wozniak would be entertaining their grandkids with their quaint invention.

The venture capital industry's raison d'être is the same one that drives many an entrepreneur they fund: Find a need and fill it. Chapter 3 will go back and look at how the pioneering venture capitalists found a gaping hole in the traditional funding structure and filled it, in the process creating a new industry that shook the world.

CHAPTER THREE

The Beginning

Even in the fast-changing Internet world described in Chapter 2, to figure out where you're going, it helps to know where you've been. This book does not purport to be the whole history of venture capital, but rather to offer a snapshot in time of what it's like today and, in this chapter, a snapshot of what it was like in the beginning. While in some ways venture capital has been radically changed by the Internet and by its own success, in many important areas its practices trace back several decades to the pioneers. It was they who formulated such things as seed capital, funding rounds, and pre- and post-money valuations. They also developed the symbiotic, occasionally exultant, often exasperating, always fascinating relationship with entrepreneurs that became the foundation of the technology revolution.

Of course, long before formal venture capital existed, adventuresome individuals found ways to get the financing they needed for bold projects. The Medici family in medieval Florence underwrote much of the art and architecture that graced the forthcoming Renaissance. As every schoolchild knows, Christopher Columbus had to go from his native country, Italy, to Spain to seek financing from Queen Isabella for his famed 1492 excursion to the New World and for later expeditions. Much of the exploration of the Americas was funded by the church (Catholic clergy) or the state (monarchs like Isabella and England's Queen Elizabeth). During the Industrial Revolution, wealthy families in Europe, the United Kingdom, and the United States provided investments that financed the high-tech industries of yesteryear, like railroads, oil, steel, and banking. But no formal institution was as yet helping the little guy tinkering in the barn, or later, the garage. Inventors of this sort still had to depend on the kindness of friends and relatives.

It wasn't until the mid-twentieth century, before and after World War II, that some families, like the Rockefellers and Whitneys, began to hire professional managers to look for promising new companies as potential investments. After his prewar success in companies like Eastern Air Lines (with Eddie Rickenbacker) and McDonnell Aircraft Corporation (with James S. McDonnell Jr.), Laurance Rockefeller assembled a staff that invested in military science such as jet engines and helicopters. According to one source, it was Rockefeller's peer Jock Whitney, in the process of setting up a $10 million investment firm called J. H. Whitney & Company, who came up with the term *venture capital*, which combined the notion of risk with the notion of adventure.[1]

ENTER GENERAL DORIOT

Most experts identify the first modern venture capital (VC) firm as American Research and Development (ARD), formed in 1946, not in Silicon Valley, but in Boston, which was heir to a longtime tradition of patronage by rich individuals. For instance, when Alexander Graham Bell needed money in the late nineteenth century to complete product development on what would become the telephone, he turned to a local merchant and lawyer for help.[2] Following World War II, the leaders of three venerable institutions, the Massachusetts Investors Trust, the Federal Reserve Bank of Boston, and the Massachusetts Institute of Technology, teamed up to create an organized source of capital for the science-based entrepreneurialism springing up in Boston. They tapped General Georges Doriot, the War Department's deputy director of research and development (R&D) and a part-time instructor at Harvard University, to run it.[3]

Doriot, now regarded as the father of venture capital, didn't have an easy time raising money to finance his "Dream Factory," as one magazine dubbed it. The three backers of his fund had gotten pledges for $2.5 million, en route to what they hoped would be $5 million (less than an average first-round investment in a single company today!). Doriot managed to get the fund up to $3 million, proving that it was possible to raise money privately in an organized fashion. The general (everyone who mentioned him to me always called him "General Doriot," as if General rather than Georges was his first name) ran ARD until it was acquired in 1972. His goal was not profits but financing "noble" ideas, like one early investment in a company developing X-ray technology to fight cancer. However, when that company, High Voltage Engineering, went public in 1955, ARD's $200,000 investment was worth $1.8 million.[4] Veteran venture capitalist Bill Davidow remembers visiting once with Doriot: "He talked about how every one of his companies had had a crisis, and he would sit with the [affected] entrepreneur and talk for hours while listening to music." Ah, the good old days!

In 1957 Doriot made the investment that would validate his vision and establish a pattern for a successful VC fund that holds today. He put up $70,000 for a 77 percent stake in a new company, Digital Equipment Corporation (DEC), founded by a feisty engineer from MIT, Ken Olsen. Despite Doriot's disdain for making money, ARD's stake in DEC was worth about $350 million at its peak and accounted for the majority of the VC firm's assets and half its profits. This convincingly demonstrated that it took only one "home run" in a VC fund to have the endeavor pay off for shareholders.[5] That mentality of going for the home run—swinging for the fences rather than pecking away with a series of singles and doubles—continues to prevail.

THE GOVERNMENT STEPS IN

Ironically, despite the libertarian, hands-off mentality toward government that is predominant in entrepreneurial circles today, especially in Silicon Valley, the U.S. government was an important player in the establishment of venture capital as a real industry. Not only did Doriot and other practitioners get their training in assessing R&D in the military, but the government became the prime VC lender for a time in the 1960s and early 1970s, with the formation of the small business investment companies (SBICs) under the auspices of the Small Business Administration (SBA). On the East and West Coasts, a number of prominent venture capitalists, among them Alan J. Patricof (Patricof & Company Ventures Inc. in New York), Rick Burnes (Charles River Ventures in Boston), John Mumford (Crosspoint Venture Partners in Woodside, California), Pitch Johnson (Asset Management Company in Palo Alto, California), and Tim Draper (Draper Fisher Jurvetson in Redwood City, California), all got their start in SBICs.

The career of Patricof, the patrician New Yorker who now runs an immense patronymic fund with global reach, parallels the course of the industry in many ways. He started off in the mid-1960s managing money for wealthy families. "These families would casually put in $100,000 or $500,000 in these private fundings," he recalls. The investment banks were also key because they would sponsor start-ups and encourage their clients—the same high net worth individuals—to invest, cobbling together funds of $1 million to $2 million. Patricof became increasingly involved with the small companies he invested in, including New York Magazine, Datascope Corporation, and Lin Broadcasting. "I was involved in the decision making. It was much more interesting than investing in public stocks," he says.

So, in 1970 Patricof approached about 10 of his clients and suggested establishing a formal fund for investing in new companies. He would charge a retainer—in effect a carry—on the investments. In this way he raised $2.5 million, which he disbursed to about 15 companies. "After several years of doing that, I realized you had to have a more permanent base of capital," he says, and his company became an SBIC in 1974. Under its rules, the SBA would give you a loan to match what you raised privately. Patricof raised $4.5 million and wound up with a $9 million pool of capital. He remembers that the percentage of losses was much higher than today because it was difficult to find later rounds of financing and many companies failed for lack of capital.

Unlike today's VC firms, which specialize, "we invested in whatever passed our door—plated wire, memory, electronic components, even publishing," Patricof recalls. His first deal as an SBIC was with a company called Revere Smelting Refining (RSR), which was in the lead smelting business and wanted to buy scrap operations around the country. Patricof invested $265,000. "We did it all by ourselves," he says. "There was nobody to syndicate [coinvest] with." The company went public for $2 million in 1972, an impressive sum at the time, and subsequently did a leveraged buyout. Another investment of the SBIC was Apple Computer. Patricof put in $250,000 and reaped around $12 million. But in 1980 he decided the SBIC was too limiting and raised his first institutional fund of $22 million. His sixth and most recent fund was $1 billion.

You can tell that Pitch Johnson, now a partner at Asset Management Company in Palo Alto, has enjoyed his nearly 40-year career in venture investing. Jovial, white-haired, and heavyset, Johnson loves to tell stories from the old days. In 1962 he founded Draper Johnson with Bill Draper, with whom he had worked at Inland Steel in the Midwest before returning home to California. Draper already had VC experience, because he had worked for his father, also named Bill but referred to as General Draper because of his military background, at Draper Gaither & Anderson. Draper Johnson started with a measly $150,000 in capital and then became an SBIC, eventually raising a $1.2 million fund. Johnson recalls doling out about $60,000 at a time, because government rules limited the percent of total capital one could invest in any one deal. Eventually, he and Bill Draper sold their portfolio, which included investments in programmed learning and instrument companies, and went their separate ways.

Bill Draper, meanwhile, gave what was left of the SBIC investments to his son Tim to run when the father took a government position in 1981. "I'd kept the SBIC to leverage my own private investments," Bill says. The portfolio wasn't doing particularly well; the SBA valued it at about $2 million. But Tim, with a freshly minted Harvard MBA, was eager to prove himself in the family business. "The greatest thing I did for Tim was leave him alone," says Bill. His son managed to borrow $6 million against the SBIC portfolio in 1985. "I took that $6 million and invested it in Parametric Technology, which is now an $8 billion company," Tim Draper says proudly. With that experience behind him, he later founded and currently runs his own firm, Draper Fisher Jurvetson.

The SBIC, dependent on government loans, gradually faded as other sources of capital became the preferred financing instrument in the mid-1970s and later. This was propelled by the rise of the institutional investor, due to both the attractive returns that venture capital was generating (about 20 percent, according to one study by General Electric Investment Corporation) and a change in the law that made it easier for pension funds to invest in private equity.[6] In 1978 the U.S. Department of Labor issued a ruling that allowed pension funds to have more of their assets placed into risky investments with higher rates of return. The pension funds were joined by university endowments as the two largest sources of VC funding, replacing the government's SBICs. By the late 1980s, SBICs accounted for just 7 percent of VC financing, compared with 75 percent a quarter century earlier.[7]

ROCK-SOLID FOUNDATION

As the institutional VC fund became the norm, the industry continued to expand nicely in New York and Boston, the latter funding the emerging minicomputer industry kicked off by DEC. Meanwhile, as a new decade approached, venture capital was just venturing forth on the other coast. General Draper's Draper Gaither & Anderson, set up on the Stanford campus in 1959 to exploit ideas coming out of the university, was one of the earliest VC firms on the West Coast. The older Draper had been with the Marshall Plan in Europe after World War II and thought the same kind of self-help idea would work in private investing. He and two partners raised a $6 million fund, keyed by an investment from the Rockefellers. Bill Draper, working for his father, remembers knocking on doors trying to explain what it was all about. "My wife would tell people that we were in the banking business," he says, and, if pressed, she would explain that it was the private banking business. At the time, no one in what would become Silicon Valley had a clue about what venture capital meant.

The seminal event in the history of West Coast venture capital—and, indeed, in the history of technology—was Arthur Rock's effort to aid engineer Eugene Kleiner and a group of six other employees who wanted to leave Shockley Semiconductor Laboratory and form their own company. In a story that has justifiably become part of the Silicon Valley legend, Kleiner in 1957 wrote a three-page letter explaining why he and his peers wanted to break away from William Shockley's "confusing and demoralizing management" and start their own semiconductor company. The initial products would be silicon-based integrated circuits. To set up the company, Kleiner sought $750,000 to $1 million from a family friend at the New York investment bank Hayden Stone & Company. The letter wound up on the desk of the 31-year-old Rock, who, along with a colleague, went out to California to investigate.[8]

After meeting with the Shockley defectors, now joined by an eighth colleague, Bob Noyce, Rock approached more than 40 prospective corporate partners for funding. They all turned him down. Finally, he found Sherman Fairchild, who ran two patronymic companies that made cameras and aircraft. Fairchild, interested in moving into a new arena, was willing to put up $1.5 million to do it. Thus, Fairchild Semiconductor came into existence, and Rock wound up moving to the San Francisco Bay Area to run Hayden Stone's West Coast office and look for other investments in emerging technology. "The companies here were much more enterprising than those on the East Coast, but all the money was there," he recalls. "What I tried to do was bring East Coast money here." But this kind of investing would be no sure thing, he warned the investment bank. "We figured one year out of five would be a loss year."

In 1961 Rock left Hayden Stone to form his own VC firm with Tom Davis, a California land attorney who had become part of Rock's network. The firm Davis & Rock started with $5 million, which they invested in increments of about $300,000. "We did mostly seed investing," says Rock, "but that $300,000 had to last until the company got profitable." The first investment was Scientific Data Systems (SDS), an early computer maker that grew swiftly and even surpassed Doriot's DEC for a time. Xerox bought out SDS in 1968 in a stock transaction, and Davis & Rock reaped $60 million on their $300,000 investment. At Davis & Rock, "we had the luxury of learning as we went and correcting our mistakes," Rock recalls. "Now you're through if you can't go fast and understand the technology." With characteristic modesty, he confides, "If I were running a VC firm I wouldn't hire anyone like me today. When we started you just had to understand the people, not the technology."

After Davis & Rock distributed their fund in 1968 and disbanded the partnership, Rock was again on his own. Two of the Fairchild Eight, the group he had financed earlier, came back to seek funding to leave Fairchild and start their own company. The two, Gordon Moore and Bob Noyce, were going to call it Intel. Rock, as always going on his trust in people, raised $2.5 million in funding, including $300,000 of his own money. A second round would raise another $3 million. It took only $5.5 million in venture capital, a small sum by today's standards, to finance one of the world's most important companies, Intel, which manufactures the bedrock technology that gave

Silicon Valley its name and made the PC and the Internet possible. Rock's experience with Intel also established a crucial pattern in the history of venture capitalism: would-be entrepreneurs leaving companies time and again to form new ventures, and returning to the moneymen who had funded them before. This was the oft-repeated sequence that would make Silicon Valley the most fertile region ever for the creation of new, innovative, cutting-edge companies.

HOW THE WEST WON

With its free-wheeling, swing-for-the-fences mentality, the West Coast eventually trumped the East Coast, where venture capital had originated, and became the undisputed leader in this new investment medium (see Figure 3.1). Indeed, the Horsley Bridge study revealed that, of the $6 billion invested by the 61 VC funds it tracked between 1985 and 1996, half of the total went to 604 companies in northern California, generating $44.5 billion in value, for an impressive 14.8 : 1 ratio of value to cost. Boston was a distant second, with the funds investing $519 million in 129 companies there, generating $3.3 billion in value, or 6.4 : 1 (see Figure 3.2). The ascendancy of Silicon Valley was aided by a number of factors that have been well explored else-

FIGURE 3.1   VC INVESTMENTS BY REGION, SILICON VALLEY VS. BOSTON (1995–2000, IN $MILLIONS)

	AMOUNT INVESTED	
YEAR	BOSTON	SILICON VALLEY
1995	423.1	1,115.4
1996	924.9	2,571.7
1997	2,237.7	3,469.0
1998	2,176.8	3,998.0
1999	4,899.0	11,937.0
2000[a]	8,161.7	19,259.0
Total	18,823.2	42,350.1

Source: Venture Economics/National Venture Capital Association.
[a]2000 figures are preliminary, through December 14.

FIGURE 3.2 INVESTMENTS BY LOCATION

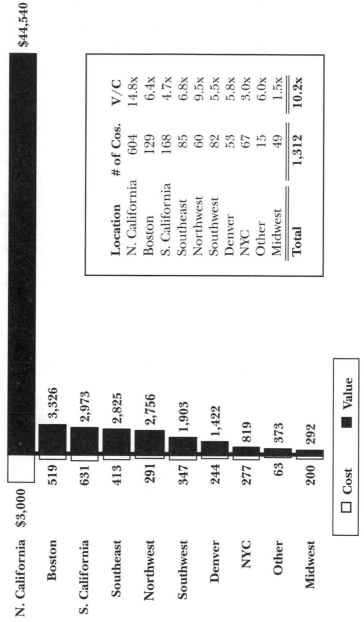

Location	# of Cos.	V/C
N. California	604	14.8x
Boston	129	6.4x
S. California	168	4.7x
Southeast	85	6.8x
Northwest	60	9.5x
Southwest	82	5.5x
Denver	53	5.8x
NYC	67	3.0x
Other	15	6.0x
Midwest	49	1.5x
Total	**1,312**	**10.2x**

Source: Horsley Bridge Partners' analysis of 61 VC funds invested in between 1985 and 1996.
Note: Dollar values are in millions.

where, including a greater willingness to cannibalize existing companies, less reliance on traditional management thinking, the presence of great universities that provided the needed talent, technology paradigm shifts that created unprecedented opportunities for the formation of new companies, a critical mass of expertise in companies like Hewlett-Packard, and the continual accretion of money and talent that built up the premier West Coast VC firms.

For example, Eugene Kleiner, one of the original Fairchild Eight, teamed up with fellow entrepreneur Tom Perkins, who had taken classes from Doriot at Harvard, to form Kleiner & Perkins, which raised its first fund of $8 million in 1972. They would be joined by Brook Byers, who served his apprenticeship with Pitch Johnson, and Frank Caufield, a Harvard MBA who had been with Oak Grove Ventures, another early Silicon Valley firm. Reid Dennis, who ran a mutual fund for Fireman's Fund Insurance, expanded into VC investing, eventually morphing into Institutional Venture Partners, from which Redpoint later split off. After he left Rock, Davis cofounded Mayfield Fund, while Rock teamed up with Dick Kramlich, who would later start New Enterprise Associates. Don Valentine, a marketing director at National Semiconductor by way of Fairchild Semiconductor, began what would become Sequoia in 1972, the same year that Kleiner & Perkins was founded. These two firms would wind up as great rivals and VC exemplars.

Parallel to the entrepreneurial world that venture capitalists were helping to create, the VC industry was formed by small teams of people who knew each other well and, at first, all sprang from a few common sources (i.e., Fairchild Semiconductor spawned much of the early microprocessor industry in Silicon Valley, while Rock and his associates were at the basis of several VC firms). Again paralleling entrepreneurial companies, which are renowned for their turnover at the top, the early VC partnerships were creatures of their founders. In fact, one hallmark of a great VC firm is recruitment of a new generation that allows the firm to survive the founders' retirement. But once VC partnerships have overcome this generational transfer, they're difficult to dissolve, in part because of the complex financial relationships involved but also because of their consensus-driven decision making (see Chapter 4 for more discussion of the VC hierarchy).

While a number of the original VC funds, like Rock's, were located in San Francisco's financial district, in the early 1970s key venture capitalists began moving about 30 miles south, to Sand Hill Road, which had recently been built out by enterprising developer Thomas Ford. Silicon Valley had by then received its name from *Electronic News* editor Don Hoeffler in 1971. The signature buildings of Sand Hill Road are low-profile, no more than a couple of stories high, and scattered amid native groves of pine and redwood. It is a bucolic setting for this adrenaline-stoked industry. Among the early group that embraced Sand Hill Road were Reid Dennis and Don Valentine. Valentine broke the mold in another way as well: Whereas venture capitalists like Rock, Kramlich, and Dennis came from the financial world, Valentine had real operating experience, as, incidentally, did Kleiner and Perkins. That dichotomy—venture capitalists with either operating or financial backgrounds—persists today.

SHORT ON CASH

As Rock noted, most of the available money in these early days of venture capital was still on the East Coast. Venture capitalists on the West Coast had to improvise. Dick Kramlich, the genial, laid-back veteran whom several people called the "nicest guy in venture capital," remembers those days all too well. Rock had persuaded Kramlich to move west from Boston and join him as a partner in 1969, just in time for a long dry spell in the VC industry that would last until the early 1980s. Kramlich started out investing money for wealthy families at a private investment firm in Boston but found the atmosphere stultifying. "The average age [in the office] was about 68," he recalls. "It was very structured, and I am not a structured kind of person." He happened to read a *Forbes* article featuring Arthur Rock, who was looking for a new partner, and contacted him. After about a year of fencing, Rock and Kramlich met in New York. "We each had a list of 10 priorities in organizing a venture business," Kramlich recalls. "We took an hour-and-a-half walk in Central Park and found that our lists were very similar."

Rock and Kramlich were partners for about eight years. In that entire period, they "had commitments for $10 million and actually invested $6 million," Kramlich recalls. The partnership distributed around $40 million, not a bad return in those years. "The rule was that Arthur and I had to agree before we invested in anything," says Kram-

lich. Such democratic decision making is still the norm at VC firms. As
an individual investor, Rock had been involved in funding both Intel
and Apple Computer. Now he and Kramlich invested in a grab bag of
companies like Xynetics, which did access-linear positioning systems,
and Autotronic Systems, which offered gasoline self-service. All of
them were acquired, notes Kramlich, because the new issues market
was not very active. "Maybe two companies went public in the mid-
seventies out of the whole industry," he says, with only slight exagger-
ation. Not being able to raise enough money in the United States,
Kramlich made a trip to Japan to raise additional capital for the partnership's struggling portfolio. "Nobody really had any money then,"
he says. "The pension funds weren't investing yet, because the law
didn't change until 1978. The stock market was dead. There was a
little money from insurance companies. It was like Death Valley with
no oasis in sight."

He and Rock used to hike home from San Francisco's downtown
financial district to the outlying areas where they lived. "We were
talking about doing a second fund," says Kramlich, but Rock was getting burnt out. "He really didn't want to build or do anything."
Kramlich, on the other hand, felt that the field needed more per-
manence than partnerships that existed for one fund and then ex-
pired. "I wanted to be part of a VC organization that would last for a
hundred years," he says. In 1978 he left Rock to form New Enterprise
Associates (NEA) on Sand Hill Road. "With great difficulty we raised
$16 million in six months," he says. NEA had offices in Silicon Valley
and in Baltimore, where one of the partners lived. "We were the first
firm to have offices on both the West and East Coasts," says Kramlich.
However, that was one innovation most of his peers in Silicon Valley
did not adopt until very recently, preferring to keep all their partners in one place.

Valentine, who became a formal venture capitalist in the early
1970s after investing privately for a few years, has memories similar to
Kramlich's. "Thirty years ago, the venture community had only a few
practitioners in northern California," he says. "The amount of money
available was so small it took everyone together to finance one company." The atmosphere was collegial and noncompetitive because it
had to be. "As George Quist [of Hambrecht & Quist] put it to me
once, 'Look, kid, if you want to invest in anything just let me know. Any
amount of money.'"

Valentine's new firm managed to raise $5 million in 1972, targeting institutional investors like university endowments and foundations. Kleiner & Perkins was doing the same thing. "Our respective firms were among the first to organize around institutional investors," says Valentine. "Before that it had been SBICs and individual investors." In 1972, he estimates, the total amount of organized venture capital in the United States was less than $50 million from these institutional sources. Now a single limited partner can put that amount into a fund that totals $1 billion.

Three decades ago, the VC investing process was ad hoc and leisurely. There was no need to hurry because no other firm would step in and take the deal away. When venture capitalists invested together, referred to as *syndication,* the one who knew the most about a given field, such as semiconductors, was assigned to do the lead due diligence and usually wound up on the board. "A lot of this stuff happened over a monthly lunch in the basement of a fairly nondescript restaurant in San Francisco or Menlo Park," Valentine recalls. Although the preferred locales have changed over the years (right now it's Buck's, a homey, western-themed restaurant in Woodside just a freeway exit away from Sand Hill Road), deal making over a meal is a tradition that remains firmly intact.

BACK IN BOSTON

The VC community in Boston, though it did eventually cede leadership to Silicon Valley, remains an important center for risk investing. The legacy of General Doriot and ARD was carried on in firms like Greylock, Matrix Partners, TA Associates, Charles River Ventures, and, later, Battery Ventures and Highland Capital Partners. Boston had most of the ingredients that Silicon Valley could also boast: availability of capital, great universities, and a critical mass of technology companies like DEC and Prime Computer. But Boston, with its well-entrenched industries and proud culture, did not adapt as readily as Silicon Valley to the go-for-broke mentality that proved to be the winning strategy in high-tech investing. Despite Doriot's DEC "home run," Boston's technology and VC industries favored a more conservative, incremental strategy than did the West Coast, one that may have cushioned them in bust times but hurt them in boom times like the ones spawned by the PC and the Internet. Silicon Valley venture capitalists exploited the boom times with big bets that allowed them to pull into a commanding lead.

Greylock probably personifies as well as any firm the conflict between Boston's conservative culture and Silicon Valley's flamboyant risk taking. Greylock sprang directly from ARD. It was founded in 1965 by ARD graduate Bill Elfers, along with money manager Dan Gregory, and soon recruited Charles Waite out of ARD as well. ARD was wrestling with the issue of generational transfer that would plague the VC industry to this day. At 65 Doriot showed no signs of retiring, so Elfers, who was 47, bolted to start his own fund, according to Henry McCance, who joined Greylock four years later. "By the time I came along, they thought they might survive," he says. McCance, a respected, gentlemanly man with sparse, dark hair and a wizened face, doesn't want to repeat Doriot's mistake. He is now searching for a way to pass the baton to younger partners at Greylock.

In the mid-1960s, McCance was an eager young economics graduate with a Harvard MBA. He did systems analysis for the U.S. Department of Defense, earning a deferment from Vietnam, but did not enjoy working for a government bureaucracy. "I was lucky enough to land my first and only job at Greylock in April 1969," he says. "I have a couple of classmates who went into venture capital after me, but nobody in my Harvard class of '66 even knew what it was yet." Greylock was still investing its first fund of $10 million, raised from six wealthy families, when McCance signed on. The partnership didn't raise its second fund until 1973. "Venture capital was a buyer's market in the 1960s and '70s," McCance recalls. "There weren't a lot of alternatives for capital, so you could be quite opportunistic. You could wait until the company got to a certain level of development before you invested," reducing the VC firm's risk. Greylock, consequently, did not get involved in start-up financing.

Instead, start-ups at the time raised money from friends and family and had to get cash flow positive very swiftly. "Those companies worried about their burn rate [the rate at which they consumed capital before profitability]," McCance says. "Projects were not capital intensive, and companies had to use their wits to generate early cash flow." They got products out into the marketplace as soon as possible, and then turned to the venture capitalists. "Many times when we invested, not only was the product established and revenue ramping, but the companies were already profitable," he says.

With the initial public offering (IPO) window virtually closed throughout the 1970s, the role of venture capitalists was to provide expansion capital, usually in the range of $1 million to $3 million, in order to allow these growing companies to accelerate marketing and add new products. Greylock investments of the period included Teradyne (semiconductor test equipment), Prime Computer (minicomputers), New England Business Services (business forms via mail order), American Management Systems (formed by a group who left the Pentagon), and life sciences companies such as Cobe Labs (artificial kidney and dialysis) and Stryker Medical (orthopedic equipment).

By the early 1980s, however, the VC industry's returns and dramatic investing style were beginning to receive some notice, and money was flowing in. According to Venture Economics, venture capitalists raised $4.2 billion in 1983, compared with only $1.6 billion in the previous year. Faced with all this new capital, Greylock had a choice. It could continue to do safer, later-stage investments—and pay a higher valuation for the lower risk—or it could move into the arena that the West Coast venture capitalists were playing so effectively: early stage. "We decided we wanted to become company builders by doing seed and start-up investments," says McCance, "and we changed the mix of our business dramatically." An accompanying step was to narrow the focus to high technology because investing "in two guys and a sheet of paper" required a much greater level of participation and knowledge on the part of the venture capitalists. Reflecting a philosophy of "if you can't beat 'em, join 'em," Greylock also opened a West Coast office in Palo Alto.

Over at Matrix Partners, Paul Ferri followed a similar path. Like most early venture capitalists, Ferri had stumbled upon the career. He studied electrical engineering and then worked at a big aerospace company for six years and hated it. "I realized I had to do something else." He got his MBA from Columbia University, became a securities analyst, and discovered that he had a real interest in small companies. "That led me to venture capital in 1970," he says. At that time, "there were probably only 40 or 50 professional VCs in the entire United States." As Ferri admits, "I knew nothing about the business, but I quickly realized no one else knew much either. You began by learning from your mistakes, what to do, what not to do." He was with WestVen Management for eight years, before founding Hellman Ferri in 1978 and Matrix in 1982. "When we started Matrix, we invested across a variety of industries and a variety of stages."

Then, like McCance, Ferri realized that the world was changing, with a lot more money coming in. What that meant was that venture capital was no longer really about just money, but rather about offering the needed expertise and focus to build companies from scratch. "Up until the 1980s, having money was a distinguishing characteristic," Ferri says. But by the end of that decade, that was no longer true. "For Matrix to do better than others we had to have a very clear focus." Consequently, Matrix also moved into early-stage investing and concentrated on technology, with a mix of investments in New England and the West Coast. Ferri's new goal: "I decided to try to be the best VC firm for start-ups in New England."

BOOM-BUST CYCLES

You can't talk about the history of venture capital without discussing its notoriously cyclical nature. As NEA's Kramlich points out, most of the 1970s was a "Death Valley" for venture capital "with no oasis in sight." Rick Burnes, a cofounder of Boston-based Charles River Ventures in 1970, remembers scraping to find willing entrepreneurs during that decade. In New England, "there were disk drive and minicomputer companies, but there weren't entrepreneurial companies," he says. What few entrepreneurs there were came out of places like DEC and IBM and lacked start-up or management expertise. "We were backing technically skilled people, but they didn't have much managerial experience," says Burnes. Charles River's first fund of $6 million was invested in 20 companies over several years, including home runs Computervision and Storage Technology. Now Burnes sometimes invests just about that much in a single day.

In the early to mid-1980s, the industry began to pick up, spurred by the successes of such companies as Intel and Apple, and, on the biotech side, Genentech. In Silicon Valley and in Boston, there were enough big-name firms—like Intel, Hewlett-Packard, National Semiconductor, DEC, Computervision, and Prime Computer—to provide a breeding ground for would-be entrepreneurs. A pattern was established: A series of spectacular IPOs by venture-backed companies leads to an inflow of investment. The VC business then winds up funding too many companies, returns go down, IPOs dry up (this coincides with a down public market), and available capital shrinks. For example, after the market upturn in the early 1980s, Battery Ventures raised its first fund of $34 million in 1984, according to cofounder Bob Barrett. "There were 30 to 40 small venture firms, and people were crowding into computing," he recalls. "Everybody was doing the same thing: disk drives and memory chips. The industry was very narrow in terms of what was getting funded." During the bad times that followed, the ranks of disk drive and memory chip companies shrank dramatically.

It happened again after the 1987 market crash, which firmly shut the IPO window. Kevin Landry, who joined TA Associates in Boston in 1968, vividly remembers that era. "The VC business wasn't a lot of fun in the late '80s," he says. "You'd come in on Monday [the traditional day for the partnership meeting] and figure out which companies do I keep alive and which ones do I shut down." The industry recovered when connectivity—networking—became the rage, fueled by investments like Cisco Systems. "Connectivity had a great run in the early '90s," he says. This was followed by another, briefer dry spell in the 1991–1993 era. By 1994 it was obvious that the Internet, which Landry calls "the ultimate connectivity play," was going to create multiple opportunities. "With each of these cycles the amplitude has been bigger than the last one," he says. And the amount of time between boom and bust cycles has diminished. "There are now enormous capital flows looking for investment opportunities," Landry notes. "It's still going to cycle, but that trend [of large investments in venture capital] will continue."

Kleiner's Vinod Khosla, widely credited with being one of the shrewdest venture capitalists around, sees the industry oscillating between greed and fear. In the greed cycle the industry always funds far too many companies. In the fear cycle a lot of those companies end up starving to death for lack of later-stage funding. From 1999 through early 2000, the industry was in a greed cycle of unprecedented proportions, one which led to a plethora of unprofitable dot-coms, followed by a fear cycle in mid-2000 in which many of the dot-coms closed their doors (see Chapter 11 for more).

Venture capitalists don't like to admit it, but most of them have a herd mentality, which causes them to get hit by the same seemingly bright idea at the same time. This can exacerbate the ups and downs in an industry that is, by its very nature, bound to be cyclical. Thus, we've had periods when every VC partnership had to have a workstation maker or a disk drive manufacturer or a gigabit ethernet company or an e-tailer in its portfolio. By late 2000, the rage was Internet infrastructure, including optical networking companies like ONI Systems, and wireless connectivity. As we'll see in the next chapter describing the VC hierarchy, one proof of a great VC partnership is its ability to be a contrarian, to make investments that stand out from the crowd and take technology to the next level rather than merely offer incremental improvements. Another proof of greatness is being able to survive in bad times and triumph in good ones, to establish a track record of excellence regardless of whether it's "nuclear winter," or, as one wag described early 2000, it's "fall out of the boat and hit the water time."

The Venture Capital Hierarchy

The venture capital (VC) industry is still small enough that it reminds me of one of those aristocratic societies described by novelists like Edith Wharton or Jane Austen. Everyone knows everyone else and has a pretty good idea of who's at the top of the heap and who's not, except when it comes to his or her own firm. A venture capitalist's own firm is always either top tier or aiming for top tier. When you ask people to specify what they mean by top-tier firms, the first answer you get usually mentions IRR, or internal rate of return. That's the annualized profit that goes back to the limited partners, except for the 20 percent to 30 percent carry reserved for the VC firm. IRR is indeed one important indication of quality, but it's also a fungible number that varies depending on what year a fund was raised and invested (i.e., in a good cycle or a bad one) and can be drastically affected by one big hit. Remember that General Doriot's Digital Equipment Corporation (DEC) home run accounted for most of American Research and Development's (ARD) success as a VC firm. Besides, IRRs are jealously guarded bits of information that can be twisted or interpreted as the VC firm sees fit. Another measurement is the annual number, and value, of initial public offerings (IPOs) of the companies funded by a VC firm, but that has some of the same problems as IRR. Consequently, I'm not using IRR or IPOs as my sole determinant of top-tier firms (see Figure 4.1).

What I'd put at the top of my list for determining a great VC firm is consistency. Through good times and bad, through fads and fashions, these firms have been able to attract high-quality entrepreneurial deals and to pick the winners. And not only to pick winners, but also to nurture those winners in a way that allows them to succeed big-time! Kleiner Perkins has a dozen Forbes 500 firms to its credit, while companies funded by Sequoia Capital account for roughly 20 percent of the entire value of the Nasdaq stock market. Indeed, many an entrepreneur told me that but for their venture capitalist's strategic advice, the company would have foundered. So a great VC firm must have a track record that demonstrates both consistency and big winners, which will be reflected in the IRR.

A second important factor is the same one that determines success in entrepreneurial companies: keeping the best people. A great VC

FIGURE 4.1   LEADING VENTURE INVESTORS, BY NUMBER OF IPOS, 1999 (PROFESSIONAL VC FIRMS)

FIRM	NUMBER OF IPOS
New Enterprise Associates	19
Kleiner Perkins Caufield & Byers	18
Sequoia Capital	17
Benchmark Capital	15
Norwest Venture Partners	14
Vulcan Ventures	14
Integral Capital Partners	13
Technology Crossover Ventures	13
Accel Partners	12
Draper Fisher Jurvetson	11
Greylock	11
Patricof & Company Ventures Inc.	11
Softbank Venture Capital	11
Oak Investment Partners	11
Amerindo Investment Advisors	10

Source: Thomson Financial Securities Data.
Note: Firms exclude corporate investors and investment banks.

firm is truly the sum of its partners: the John Doerrs, the Don Valentines, the Paul Ferris, the Dick Kramlichs, the Henry McCances. VC partnerships stay small for a reason: They're like a family that has its share of bickering leading up to a decision but pulls together once the investment has been made. Don Valentine may not like all of Sequoia's dot-com investments, but he doesn't bad-mouth them publicly.

Yet a third factor is one that many of the old-timers profess to despise: branding. In the early days of the industry, it was enough to have capital. No longer. As this chapter makes clear, money has become a commodity, and the venture capitalist's value added is dependent to a large extent upon his or her reputation. Like it or not, a reputation as a VC rock star, with press citations in the likes of *Vanity Fair* and *GQ*, enhances deal flow, aids in recruitment, and rubs off on the associated entrepreneurial firms. Even the quieter VC firms worry about their images and what they can do to improve them. Up until the last couple of years, it was almost unheard of for a VC firm to have a formal public relations (PR) entity. Now, a number of firms have hired internal PR specialists, including Bessemer Venture Partners, Crescendo Ventures, Draper Fisher Jurvetson, InterWest Partners, Mayfield Fund, Mohr Davidow, and Sequoia Capital. Several had outside PR help—for example, Accel Partners, Benchmark Capital, Doll Capital Management, and Redpoint Ventures—and many more were thinking about it.[1]

THE NEW VALUE ADDED

As the history of venture capitalism presented in Chapter 3 demonstrated, the greatest value added of a venture capitalist when the industry started was to write a check, pure and simple. Venture capitalists invested across the board, in companies that did everything from chips to industrial manufacturing to publishing, so they brought no specific experience of their own to bear. Venture capital was a generalist industry in which raising money took a lot of energy and concentration, and investing it was a matter of finding any available deals. As one venture capitalist notes, "Venture capital was the easiest job in the world. Anybody with a checkbook could be a VC." That's why many of the early practitioners were financial types—because they had connections on the money side.

Today the value added has flip-flopped. Raising money is easy, and finding *prospective* deals is easy. What's difficult is picking the quality deals at a very early stage and then painstakingly working to build the companies and the entrepreneurial teams. "Early-stage venture is hard work," says Tom Dyal, one of the younger partners at Redpoint. "It's not about investing and watching the company grow. It's put your money in and now the work begins." From being a fairly laid-back profession that attracted semiretired executives, venture capital has become labor-intensive. With a typical venture capitalist deeply involved with the firm's companies—sitting on 10 to 12 boards—"no longer do you work 40 hours a week and play golf on the weekend," says Dyal. Instead, you take business plans home to read in the evenings and on weekends, and get on the phone at 6 A.M. with an East Coast CEO you're trying to recruit.

When I met with Hummer Winblad's Ann Winblad, she described one recent, hectic day in her life. The day began with an 8 A.M. board meeting in which she participated via teleconference while driving from her house in San Francisco to a 9 A.M. board meeting in Cupertino about 60 miles south. (Venture capitalists had better hope California doesn't pass a law outlawing talking on your cell phone while driving.) In rush-hour traffic Winblad's drive takes close to two hours, which is why she left her house shortly after 7 A.M. After the board meeting, she heads north again to give a speech at a noon meeting in Palo Alto, where about 700 people show up. She's besieged by several would-be entrepreneurs who will be e-mailing her their business plans. Then she drives to a law firm handling an IPO filing by another portfolio company so she can skim the 200-page document and offer any suggestions. Back on the freeway, Winblad heads north again to Burlingame for a publisher's dinner at *Forbes* magazine. At 9:30 P.M. she gets home in time to do another teleconferenced board meeting. She returns phone calls and answers e-mails until 1:30 A.M.

Let's look at all the different roles Winblad played during that single day: board member, mentor, speaker, interviewer, strategic adviser, deal assessor, and on and on. The venture capitalists who fund early-stage companies nearly always take a board seat and are active in formulating and adjusting the company's business strategy. In fact, they may even step in temporarily to run a company if no experienced CEO is available, as Winblad's partner Hank Barry did with Napster when it was struggling with legal issues related to online music-swapping. As one of the few successful women in venture capital, Winblad has become a public figure in her own right, which means giving speeches and participating in events like the *Forbes* dinner. She tries to pick forums in which she can promote her companies, Winblad says.

Where a venture capitalist's value is really apparent is not so much with the home run investments, but in helping a company that is just barely getting by to make it. Kevin Landry, of TA Associates in Boston, recalls working very hard with companies that may return only one or two times the investment (barely a bunt single in today's environment). "We just sold a little software company and got back 97 cents on the dollar," he says. "It was a company on the verge of bankruptcy. The old product fell off, and the new product wasn't ready, but we stayed with it." TA provided additional capital and hand-holding while the company, which was trying to introduce a new product that turned out to be riddled with bugs, underwent a change of management and a repositioning. At last, it managed to turn a profit and negotiate a buyout by a competitor. "Nobody cares because it wasn't a big hit, but it was nice," says Landry, with satisfaction. A hallmark of great venture capitalists is that they're able to salvage some sort of win from their train wrecks, often by merging several struggling companies or selling outright. They also learn from their mistakes. In the mid-1990s, Kleiner's John Doerr poured $75 million into Go, a disastrous foray into handheld computing, but then recouped himself with Handspring, a 1998 start-up by the former founders of Palm Computing. In a tough market, Handspring's June 2000 IPO managed a 35 percent gain on the first day of trading. By late 2000, it had claimed more than one fourth of the handheld computing market for devices of its type, mostly taking share away from Palm.

Interacting with companies and the public is only half of a venture capitalist's job. The other half is generating deal flow, reaching out to would-be entrepreneurs in forums ranging from college business school competitions to casual lunches to conversations at the supermarket. "The best firms don't wait for the phone to ring," says Kathryn Gould, a partner with Foundation Capital in Menlo Park, California. "The best firms have relationships with entrepreneurial companies where we work with people for years." Even as they're funding a company, venture capitalists will identify young, eager, talented people within it who may someday want to split off on their own. When a young marketing vice president inside a Foundation company gets a hot idea and is ready to start a company, "he'll come to us," Gould says.

One of a venture capitalist's most critical value adds is recruitment. Several people told me that Doerr probably has the biggest Rolodex in the industry, a tribute to his networking ability. But the recruitment effort doesn't stop there. With the creation of more companies than ever, the search for management talent has become an unending battle, even for a highly regarded firm like Kleiner Perkins. Gordon Eubanks, who founded Symantec and has been in the software industry for 35 years, didn't really need another gig when Kleiner Perkins came calling in early 1999 looking for an experienced CEO to run Oblix, an Internet software company in Cupertino, California. Kleiner partner Ted Schlein, who had worked for Eubanks at Symantec, came over for dinner to broach the idea. Another partner, Will Hearst, lobbied to accompany Eubanks on a skiing trip to Utah. Then the firm sicced top dog John Doerr on him. Doerr had funded Symantec, so Eubanks had to listen. "They're relentless," he says of Kleiner. "They kept ratcheting up the attention, dropping in at my house and at my place in Monterey. They called me every day." In the end, he agreed to take the job, appearing with Doerr at the press event to announce the recruiting triumph.

WANTED: GREAT VENTURE CAPITALIST

All the venture capitalists I interviewed agreed that the important ingredients of their jobs now constitute everything but the money: strategic advice, industry knowledge, recruiting ability, people smarts, and so on. But where they didn't agree was in pinpointing how you get to be a good venture capitalist. Although the skill set may be obvious, the background and character that produce those skills are far more elusive. "I don't know what it takes to be a successful VC," confesses Sequoia Capital's Mike Moritz, who was a *Time* magazine correspondent before joining the industry. "You can't predict it from a résumé." Some firms, like Foundation Capital and Crosspoint Venture Partners, emphasize operating experience, whereas others, like Accel Partners and Draper Fisher Jurvetson, have a preponderance of "career venture capitalists," who get an MBA and jump almost directly into the financial industry.

The first generation of venture capitalists, like General Doriot and Arthur Rock, of necessity had to come from somewhere else. They were accidental venture capitalists. The second generation, personified by Don Valentine and Eugene Kleiner, had operating backgrounds at some of the early entrepreneurial companies. Then, in the 1980s, with venture capital established as a career choice, a wave of people came along, such as Draper Fisher's Tim Draper, Redpoint's Geoff Yang, and Accel's Jim Breyer, who learned the industry from the ground up, by doing it. This generation of career venture capitalists also ratcheted up the competitive intensity in the industry, as opposed to the collegial cooperation of the early years.

Today the pendulum has swung back toward operating experience at companies, in part because the VC firms tend to pick niches and specialize, rather than do deals across the board, so deep domain knowledge is preferred. Kleiner partner Ted Schlein first decided he wanted to be a venture capitalist upon meeting Arthur Rock as a senior in high school. Schlein's father, Phil, was on the board of Apple, and Ted accompanied him to a company plant opening in Cork, Ireland. "Here I am, this punky little high school student, asking Arthur Rock what he did," says Schlein, "He told me, and I thought, 'Wow, to take a thing that's nothing and turn it into something, I want to do that.'" However, Schlein realized later that he had to learn the industry before turning to venture capitalism. After college, he joined Symantec and entered his chosen career only after 10 and a half years in industry.

Similarly, Redpoint's Tom Dyal spent nine years in operating roles before moving into venture capitalism in his early thirties. "The career VCs were very successful in an age when specialization wasn't as important as it is today," he says. In the new environment, with a mandate to move as quickly as possible, the value of operating experience is elevated. After all, in a crisis situation, who would you rather get advice from: someone who has been through it or someone who has merely observed it? In the newest generation of venture capitalists, of whom Dyal counts himself as one, "you're starting to see a compromise." People who have been engineers and product managers spend five or ten years in industry and then move into venture capitalism. "This group has good knowledge about a particular business, but they can still change careers and have a lot of value to offer," says Dyal.

Among Dyal's generational peers is Steve Jurvetson, who beat out more than 250 applicants for a position with Draper Fisher and has since become a partner with his name alongside the two senior guys. The light-haired, slightly goofy-looking Jurvetson, who is so energetic that words flow out of him in bursts, fits Dyal's description of today's venture capitalist to a T: He designed chips at Hewlett-Packard, did management consulting at Bain & Company, got an MBA at Stanford, and moved into venture capital. "No one knows for certain what makes a successful VC," Jurvetson says, echoing Moritz. What happens, he adds, is that the older partners tend to hire people whose backgrounds resemble theirs. "Kleiner Perkins thinks you need 10 years of operating experience," says Jurvetson, "but to me, having breadth of experience—working with six different start-ups—is more important than depth. To be a successful board member, you're a confidante, a cheerleader, and a coach." Jurvetson can take what he's learned from numerous companies, aggregate it, and apply it: "I understand entrepreneurs' fears and concerns. I can see early warning signs and bring perspective. The most valuable thing to the entrepreneur," he maintains, "is cross-company aggregation."

Foundation Capital's Gould, whose glam L.A. good looks (long blonde hair, blue eyes, lots of jewelry) are coupled with thoughtful analysis of the VC industry, says that having a "feel for what's bullshit and what's not" is the highest priority for a successful venture capitalist. Other qualities include being an omnivore about technology, understanding market opportunity and what people will buy, and possessing that hard-to-define notion of "creativity," since a venture capitalist is building something, not just assembling a by-the-numbers kit. "You need operational chops because something always happens after you've made the investment," she says, "and you have to cajole the founders to change their course," as Kleiner and Mohr Davidow did with ONI Systems.

Arthur Rock, whose unparalleled investing career has just entered its sixth decade, sums it up simply: The key to being a successful venture capitalist is having the right instincts. "After a while it doesn't make any difference what your background is, if you have the right instincts about people and ideas."

OPENING THE DOERR TO THE SUPER TIER

Nearly everyone I interviewed, both inside and outside the VC industry, cited three VC partnerships as a super tier: Kleiner Perkins, Sequoia Capital, and Benchmark Capital, all Sand Hill Road firms and all among the few who command the coveted 30 percent carry from their limited partners. The three present an interesting contrast. Although they share the qualities of excellence I've already cited—including consistency, superstar venture capitalists, high recognition, and top-quality returns—they are very distinct in style and philosophy.

Let's start with Kleiner, whose best-known venture capitalist, John Doerr, has become synonymous with the Internet revolution. Among the firm's investments are America Online, Excite@Home, Amazon.com, Healtheon, Homestead.com, Cerent, Juniper Networks, ONI Systems, and, most famous of all, Netscape. But Kleiner's instinct for good companies spans other important technologies as well. In its almost 30-year history, it has backed Compaq Computer, Genentech, Lotus Development, Sun Microsystems, Cypress Semiconductor, and Intuit. As of late 2000, Kleiner had invested nearly $2 billion in entrepreneurial start-ups, creating 250 public companies with a market cap exceeding $724 billion, 75 private ones, and 252,000 jobs.

The firm is also renowned for the so-called Kleiner *keiretsu,* an interwoven network of portfolio companies that are strongly encouraged to do business with each other and pool shared expertise, promotional opportunities and the like. One thing strictly forbidden is one Kleiner company's recruiting from another. But if a person has already announced that he or she is leaving, that person is fair game. "We live and breathe the *keiretsu,*" says Schlein. "We call upon companies to help other companies and foster relationships. We can't make anybody do anything, but we can open doors." The *keiretsu* also encompasses influential entrepreneurs whom Kleiner funded, like Andy Bectolsheim and Bill Joy, who become important filters in originating and assessing deal flow.

Kleiner has not one but two superstar venture capitalists. The energetic, charismatic Doerr is the "Michael Jordan of VC," one of the many accolades that pour forth from his peers. Previously a sales executive at Intel, Doerr is an awesome recruiter who "works his butt off" for his companies; he's "the ultimate salesman and promoter"; he's a "world-class magician" who makes you believe he can pull off any deal. Doerr hardly looks the part of a legend; he has a rather mousy appearance, with receding blond hair, a pale complexion, glasses, and reputedly the same silver-and-blue tie at every meeting. In a way, the cloud of myth surrounding him is a self-fulfilling prophecy. Being funded by Kleiner and having John Doerr on your board proclaim to the world that your company has cachet: "You better take notice, because the current god of venture capitalism has given me money." Nonetheless, to a person Doerr's peers credit his extraordinary abilities and hard work, more than the media's ravenous interest in Silicon Valley and technology, as the basis for his success.

Then there's Vinod Khosla, an Indian immigrant who conceived of Sun Microsystems and was its first CEO. "To have Doerr and Khosla together in the same firm is unbelievable," says a colleague from another VC firm who has worked with them both. "Doerr has extreme charisma and is a great team builder. Khosla is very much a deal guy but has tremendous connections." In 1999 Khosla probably had the best year of any venture capitalist. Two of his investments alone reaped Kleiner at least $8 billion. One was Cerent, a telecommunications equipment company bought by Cisco. The other was Juniper Networks, in the same arena as Cerent and Cisco, whose June IPO was one of the biggest in a big year. "You don't do a year like that. It happens by luck, although you do a lot of smart things to prepare," says Khosla, whose looks match his intensity: dark circles underscore penetrating eyes, and there are only a few wisps of black left among the full head of gray hair. He jiggles his foot as he talks, very rapidly, and every once in a while emits a high-pitched nervous giggle. "I don't believe in brilliant VCs," he maintains. "It's a lot of grunt work and hoping for the best."

Khosla, who is known for focusing on a single sector and building it out with several companies, says his focus is on value to the customer rather than on catering to the IPO market. "I consider myself a venture assistant, not a venture capitalist. I don't care one hoot about Wall Street," he says. "If you can find areas where there is fundamental change going on and build a company to service that, then all that's left is the execution." He adds that Kleiner's success speaks for itself and doesn't require any boost from a PR specialist. "We [the partners] represent ourselves," says Khosla. "We've never had PR, either internal or external, and we never will."

One rap against Kleiner is that Doerr, and to an extent Khosla, put everybody else in their shadow. It's also widely rumored, although not confirmed by anyone at Kleiner, that they get more of the carry than some other partners, which can lead to friction. Schlein says he has no ego problem working with Doerr and Khosla. "I benefit from being in John's shadow. I get to work with, and learn from, two of the greatest VCs of all time, both from a reputation and return standpoint."

Schlein is free, he adds, to pull what he likes and discard what he doesn't like in terms of their styles. Kleiner's 11 general partners typically form groups of three to work with a particular company, although only one will serve on the board. "We invest in relatively few companies—two, three per partner per year," says Schlein. "We put the time and energy into these companies and approach them as a team. Vinod and John's deals are held up to the same level of scrutiny as anyone else."

Among the two, Doerr gets the lion's share of press attention, but Khosla insists that that doesn't bother him. "Doing the press rounds isn't my style," he says, telling me dismissively about "some reporter who wants to write about my dogs." He prefers talking about investing. "John and I are both looking for the big place," says Khosla. "We tend to sync up a lot in terms of our vision of the future. We don't sit on boards together, but we work very closely, brainstorming ideas—both with respect to new opportunities but even more often for strategies, alternatives, and deals for our existing companies." He and Doerr may have some competition for the limelight in the future. In August 2000 yet another high-visibility technology executive, former Oracle president Ray Lane, joined Kleiner as a partner, calling the firm "the New York Yankees" of the venture business. As a Kleiner partner, he'll be working with other former executives like Tom Jermoluk from Excite@Home, Floyd Kvamme from Apple Computer, and Will Hearst from Hearst Corporation.

And yet, the designation "Kleiner company" can be a two-edged sword. "If you become a Kleiner company, you've got to do exactly what they want," says the same colleague who praised Doerr and Khosla so highly. "That's why not every one wants to go to them." Khosla especially is known for his attention to detail and for wearing down founders with a barrage of suggestions until they follow his course, which they concede usually turns out to be right. "Our reputation is for being very active investors," says Schlein. "You don't come to us because you just want a check." He says that Kleiner, as a minority shareholder, doesn't really manage companies, although it will define who the management will be. "We're active board participants. Some would allow we're the loudest board participants," he says. Khosla insists that Kleiner's reputation for telling company executives what to do "is a rap that the other venture firms push because they can't compete against us." He adds, "For high-tech start-ups we're the equivalent of what McKinsey is to the Fortune 500. We get involved in the details and give recommendations, but we never override management."

Khosla can be defensive when charged with being too controlling. "I have many an entrepreneur who walks in with a couple of gaping holes in his [business] plan," he says. "I give people the bad news they don't want to hear." There is a definite logic to his argument that he forces entrepreneurs to focus on the holes rather than the good points. For example, he says, he got e-mails from a customer calling one CEO of a Kleiner company an "arrogant jerk." Khosla phoned the CEO, read him the e-mail, and asked him what the problem was. "He got really mad at me," says Khosla. The venture capitalist asked the CEO if he would have preferred not to get the feedback at all. "Couldn't you put it more mildly?" the CEO asked. Khosla responded, "I'm just reading you what I got." He professes not to understand why people avoid honest criticism. "The best thing that has ever happened to me is great criticism," Khosla says.

SEQUOIA THE BULLDOG

If Kleiner could be likened to a sleek racing greyhound, Sequoia is a street-fighting bulldog. You feel the difference just walking into the lobbies of the two firms, which are only a stoplight apart on Sand Hill Road. Kleiner's spacious, well-lit lobby has high-pitched ceilings and worn, but comfortable, gray leather chairs you can sink into. Every weekday, the firm brings in a decent catered lunch—consisting of a hot dish like pasta plus salads, desserts, and breads. Everyone there (even journalists doing interviews) can help themselves to the meal, served buffet-style from a central table. Go over to Sequoia, climb the wooden stairs up to its second-floor office, and there's barely room to sit down in the narrow lobby. You face a huge wall with the framed IPO announcements for Sequoia's companies. Such a panoply is common among all the firms I visited, but Sequoia's lineup reflects almost the entire history of Silicon Valley: Apple, Oracle, Cisco, Yahoo, and dozens of others. As you wait, you overhear the partners' assistants, wedged into tiny open cubicles along the wall opposite the framed ads, deflecting calls from eager entrepreneurs, journalists, and others. If you wind up at Sequoia for lunch, you get what one entrepreneur called "those ratty sandwiches" in plastic containers.

Sequoia's reputation matches its hard-edged, unpretentious lobby. "With Sequoia it's my way or the highway," says one peer. Although Don Valentine, who founded Sequoia, is semiretired, his formidable personality continues to permeate the firm. Valentine "eats people for lunch," says entrepreneur and admirer Trip Hawkins, whose Electronic Arts was partly funded by Sequoia.[2] When *Forbes ASAP* compiled a list of the top venture capitalists for its May 29, 2000, issue, Valentine was named to the list by virtually every person interviewed, including competitors, outside observers, and entrepreneurs. He is justly renowned for his ability to pick niches that will blossom, like he did with Cisco in networking. But Sequoia has also been good at bringing in capable younger people as Valentine and his contemporary, Pierre Lamond, gradually fade out. It was the only firm with three partners on the *Forbes ASAP* list: Valentine, Mike Moritz, and Doug Leone.[3]

Valentine's corner office has no door. Everyone walking by can see whom he's meeting with and hear snatches of the conversation. "I don't believe in doors or window coverings," he tells me. "It's easier to have an open-door policy." And an open-mouth policy. Valentine doesn't mind sharing his opinions. For instance, when I ask him why Sequoia doesn't have any women as partners (nor do most VC firms), he says bluntly, after offering me some tea, "Women don't go to engineering schools, so the start-up community in Silicon Valley has developed very few women entrepreneurs. The venture community matches up with the entrepreneurial community."

Valentine is famous for a lot of things, including his fierce devotion to markets over people and his willingness to dump original CEOs in favor of ones with more experience or different skill sets. Several people repeated a favorite quote from Valentine: "I never fired a CEO too soon." When I raise this issue, he replies, "When companies fail, it's always for the same reason: Management execution stinks." So Sequoia has to deal with this imperfect execution, "which puts us in the mode of changing the people," he adds. "We've never invested in a company where the science has failed. It's always the people who fail." Valentine's list of affiliations starts with Fairchild and National Semiconductor, where he served on the executive teams, and goes on to encompass funded companies such as Apple, Atari, Oracle, and Electronic Arts. With Cisco, he discovered a husband-and-wife team connecting networks on the Stanford campus, and, after ousting them for veteran management, used their technology as the foundation of what temporarily became the most valuable high-tech company in existence. In 1987 Valentine invested $2.5 million for 30 percent of Cisco Systems. In mid-2000 that stake in Cisco, which went public in 1990, would be worth more than $100 billion! No one has a better instinct for huge nascent markets.

He may be willing and able to fire founders, but Valentine also has an appreciation for talent wherever it originates. In 1997 Sequoia founded an affiliate partnership, Sequoia International Partners, which was the first in Silicon Valley to invest exclusively in immigrants and first-generation Americans. Says Valentine: "We have armies of companies where you're hard-pressed to find an original citizen." At Sequoia itself, "we have Pierre from France, Doug Leone from Italy, and Mike Moritz from Wales. This has always been an equal opportunity place." Over the years, Sequoia's list of immigrant-founded companies reads like a Who's Who of high tech: LSI Logic, C-Cube Microsystems, 3Com, Yahoo, Crescendo Communications, Altos Computer, and so on.

Not surprisingly for two firms that grew up side by side and are now at the top of the heap, Sequoia and Kleiner are cutthroat competitors, although they occasionally invest together. Khosla and Lamond have done several joint deals, including Abeona Networks, a Web appliance company, whereas Doerr and Moritz teamed up on Google, a high-profile Internet search-engine company. The younger partners at each firm, however, are more aggressive about seeking to take a commanding stake in a company and be the lead strategist, which tends to rule out collaboration on early-stage deals. Valentine, reflecting back on the days when venture capitalists almost always worked together, pronounces being competitive "stupid." "If we invested together, we would be able to share the workload. We could be on six boards each instead of 12 and do a better job." However, he admits, with regard to Kleiner and Sequoia, "we have partners with competitive personalities on both sides who have recognition needs. We just don't seem to get it [coinvesting]done."

Despite his towering presence, Valentine says Sequoia is far more of an equal partnership than, say, Kleiner. Some firms, he suggests without naming names, "have become too much the cult of the individual." Sequoia is a partnership that makes decisions unanimously, he says. "When you have a pyramid with one person on top, you have a structure that's vulnerable to one person being wrong." Moritz and Leone are proof that Sequoia's greatness is not confined to a single generation. Moritz took another pair of Stanford graduate students, who had a little search engine, and helped create Yahoo. Leone, who specializes in software and communications, has invested in Broadband, Alantec, and Assured Access.

The investment philosophy at Sequoia, according to Valentine, is, "We start companies. And we start industries. We're focused not on how much we can invest but on how much we can make. And we're not going to change." As someone behind many of Sequoia's significant Internet plays, including PlanetRx, Webvan, and Google, Moritz seconds Valentine's investment strategy. "It hasn't changed with the Internet," he says. "What we look for in our next investment in the year 2000 are the same [market] opportunities that Don looked for 25 years ago. What the Internet has done is open up the aperture" into industries like financial services, media, retailing, and even oil services. Across all of those, "what we have is an appreciation for the impact that technological change can wreak." While Sequoia no longer invests in medical fields, "we'll never become a single-sector fund," asserts Valentine.

One requirement for working at Sequoia seems to be having an acerbic tongue and the willingness to wield it. Those with Valentine, Moritz, and Leone were among the most candid of my VC interviews, even though Sequoia's recently hired marketing guy, Mark Dempster, sat next to me when I interviewed Leone. Of medium height and build, Leone smiles a lot but is constantly watching you. A fellow venture capitalist noted that Leone is aptly named—his name means *lion* in Italian—because he eats five pounds of meat for breakfast. He starts off our meeting by sketching out Sequoia's investment strategy on a whiteboard. Unlike later VC firms, which concentrate on sectors of the Internet like business to business or business to consumer, Sequoia "has always invested in the gamut," which to Leone stretches from semiconductors at the bottom, through hardware systems, operating systems, and applications, to services at the top. The advantage of "looking at the whole food chain" is that it gives Sequoia "impressive visibility into the future."

Echoing Andy Grove's oft-repeated "only the paranoid survive," Leone insists that he and his partners "don't feel like we're in the super tier [of venture capitalists]. We're consistently insecure about what we've done." He remembers one week in which Sequoia had five companies that went public, generating a $2 billion payoff for the firm. "But on that Friday afternoon we missed a deal that we really wanted. That was what stands out about the week. There's a great sense of paranoia that we're missing opportunities." They haven't missed much. At Nasdaq's peak in early 2000, Sequoia was the only VC firm whose companies were approaching a combined market capitalization of $1 trillion, Cisco being almost half of that by itself.

BENCHMARK, THE NEWBIE

Benchmark is the odd one out among the super tier. Founded in 1995, it makes its fortune in part by being the Not-Kleiner, Not-Sequoia. "Benchmark has been able to soar by offering an alternative" to Kleiner and Sequoia's control model, says a venture capitalist who specializes in seed funding. For follow-on financings, "we like to promote our companies to Benchmark first." While adjectives like *controlling* and *abrasive* are tossed about by colleagues and entrepreneurs when they talk of Kleiner's Khosla or Sequoia's Valentine, Benchmark's star venture capitalist, Bob Kagle, is described by one peer "as a nice guy with a wonderful personality." In a world of super-inflated egos, Kagle is relatively modest. As he told the *New York Times,* "Some venture capitalists see themselves as the center of the universe. We see it as a service business."[4] Named to *Forbes ASAP*'s list of top venture capitalists, Kagle confided that his hobby is collecting antique fish decoys from Michigan, that he owns a 1957 Corvette, and that his wife threw him his 39th birthday bash at a bowling alley. "I guess you can take the boy out of Michigan, but you can't really take Michigan out of the boy," he observes.

Kagle is not Benchmark's only star. What all seven of Benchmark's partners have in common is credentials. The founding partners came from either Technology Venture Investors (TVI) or Merrill Pickard Anderson & Eyre, two respected, albeit aging, Silicon Valley VC firms. Kagle spent 12 years with TVI, whereas Benchmark cofounder Andy Rachleff had a decade with Merrill Pickard. They left with several others to found a firm that would target Internet investments, particularly in the consumer sector in which Kagle had built up an expertise, and offer each partner an equal share of the carry. This democratic ideal is trumpeted on Benchmark's Website, which boasts that "we rewrote the book on venture capital . . . We have seven equal general partners, all working together . . . Each portfolio company has access to the combined resources of our entire firm."

Those resources are impressive. There's David Beirne, a superb headhunter at Ramsey/Beirne who signed on with Benchmark to add venture capital to his own résumé. Beirne's connections are legend: He recruited, among others, Jim Barksdale as CEO of Netscape, Bob Herbold as chief operating officer of Microsoft, Tom Jermoluk (now at Kleiner) as CEO of @Home, and Eric Schmidt as CEO of Novell. There's also Rachleff, who keeps a lower profile than Kagle or Beirne but made the *Forbes ASAP* list (unlike Beirne) for his quality list of investments, including America Online and LoudCloud, the start-up founded by Netscape's Marc Andreessen that was one of the hottest VC deals of 1999. Rachleff, wrote *Forbes ASAP,* "is simply a solid, reliable, no-flash sort of guy . . . refreshing in this age of VC superstardom."[5] Another partner, Bruce Dunlevie, combines those "operational chops" that Gould talked about with a solid financial background. He worked in systems design with Andersen Consulting and in investment banking with Goldman Sachs, founded and led the PC division of Everex Systems, and was a venture capitalist for six years with Merrill Pickard. Finally, there's Kevin Harvey, an entrepreneur turned venture capitalist, and Bill Gurley, who was a top-ranked research analyst with Credit Suisse First Boston and spent two years at Hummer Winblad before joining Benchmark. Newest partner Alex Balkanski was the CEO of C-Cube Microsystems. It all gives Benchmark a well-rounded, highly regarded team to woo entrepreneurs.

What propelled Benchmark into the super tier was financing Internet auctioneer eBay. In 1997 Benchmark bought 22 percent of eBay for $5 million. Two years later, that stake was worth $2.5 billion, a whopping 49,900 percent return that is still the largest ever so quickly in VC history. As one Benchmark investor commented, "They've had an immediate impact in Silicon Valley and are already among the very top tier."[6] If eBay was Benchmark's lone home run, however, the firm wouldn't make the super tier. It was the lead investor in helping Palm Computing spin out of 3Com, and again led the funding, joined by Doerr, when Palm's founders started Handspring. In just a few short years, Benchmark has funded Ariba, Critical Path, E-Loan, Juniper Networks, Kana Communications, Red Hat, Scient, and

1-800-Flowers.com. Although overshadowed by eBay, Ariba, which sells electronic procurement tools to businesses, was another tremendous success. In its June 1999 IPO, Ariba shares soared 290 percent on the first day of trading to close at $90. "Ariba perfects the modern IPO," trilled Redherring.com.[7] The incentives of eBay and the other big deals like Ariba and Scient puts pressure on all the partners to shoot for the best, says Gurley. "Everyone gets to pitch in on every deal, which means you've got a lot of work to do to keep up with the peer pressure."

Gurley left Hummer Winblad to join Benchmark because "the guys here just fit like a glove." Indeed, the first six partners, including Gurley, are all very tall (over six feet) white males in their thirties and forties. Balkanski broke the mold at least on height. But Gurley says it's more than physical similarities. The partners are truly egalitarian and, unlike nearly every other VC firm, have no associates to do the due diligence investigations into companies for them. "We chose not to have staff underneath," says Gurley. "We don't believe in having a 26-year-old MBA doing the work of venture capitalists. When you sign on with Benchmark, you get a partner." The partnership's top priority is to be "100 percent referencible" with the entrepreneurial community. That is, every entrepreneur who does business with Benchmark would come back for funding and would recommend the firm to others.

"No one is anyone else's boss," adds Steve Spurlock, a corporate attorney who joined Benchmark in 1999 as its operating partner, running the office and providing legal expertise to the general partners. "Equal shares in the carry take internal politics away." He says the hierarchical structures of the predecessor firms TVI and Merrill Pickard, which weighted the compensation in favor of senior partners, helped lead to their demise. "The founders of Benchmark chose the equal partnership model, not just for them but for everyone else they bring in. There's an incredible incentive to pull your weight because you don't want to let your partners down." By enlisting the entire partnership in every company, "we've adopted a labor-intensive approach to helping these companies succeed," says Spurlock. "We'll help them recruit, refine their strategy, wash their car, whatever it takes."

But the problem with Benchmark's full-bore approach is that, with little underlaying structure to do the detail work, the partners are spreading themselves really thin. The most common criticism I heard about Benchmark is that the partners are rapidly running out of bandwidth and have taken on far too many companies—an average of 13 apiece in mid-2000. That leaves them with limited time to return phone calls and e-mails from all those inquiring entrepreneurs. One colleague who did a joint deal with Benchmark says that the load fell upon him when the company ran into trouble and needed more help than the overtaxed Benchmark partner could provide. Then too, the difference in style between the flamboyant Beirne and the lower-key Kagle and Rachleff could flare up into outright friction during difficult times.

Benchmark also stubbed its toe with the unraveling of the Toys R Us deal, a highly publicized partnership to create the toy firm's online entity. Benchmark was supposed to invest $10 million in Toysrus.com for a 10 percent stake, but the deal fell apart over disagreements between the two principals and problems in recruiting a CEO. Softbank Venture Capital later stepped in and concluded a separate deal with Toys R Us. Says Spurlock, "There are significant, inherent problems in dot-coming the Fortune 500. You've got to get existing management to sign up to cannibalizing their existing business." In the case of Toys R Us, that didn't happen. He says Benchmark never wrote a check to the toy firm, but only had a "handshake deal."

Like a professional athlete who pulls off an awe-inspiring triumph early in his or her career, Benchmark also faces the inevitable question of what's next after eBay. Ariba proves that Benchmark is not a one-trick pony, but it may be pushing too hard to score other Internet hits. In mid-2000, Benchmark sent letters to its limited partners in two funds, asking them to make supplemental cash investments of up to 20 percent of their original stakes, raising about $50 million to $65 million. "Benchmark, which became the poster child of dot-com venture capital by snacking huge home runs with eBay and Ariba, apparently finds itself a little light in the wallet these days," wrote Barron's. "Even highly successful venture firms such as Benchmark may have been overzealously swept up in Internet mania."[8] But the firm was hardly alone in that; VC-backed dot-coms were falling like flies in late 2000.

Benchmark is diversifying its investment reach by expanding into Europe, where it raised a $750 million fund in mid-2000. Gurley says that the European fund will be run by partners in London who have their own incentive structure, so it won't cut into the U.S. partners' time. "We feel pretty comfortable serving the U.S. from here [on Sand Hill Road]," he says. "We have investments in Silicon Valley, Atlanta, Seattle, Chicago, and Madison, Wisconsin. We haven't been the arrogant VCs who say they'll only do deals close to home."

Of the three in the super tier, Benchmark's hold on the top is the most tenuous because its track record is the shallowest and its focus the narrowest. To become a franchise the way Kleiner and Sequoia have, Benchmark must do two more things: continue to produce top-tier returns in tough times and recruit a follow-on generation of partners who will carry on the quality tradition. Chapter 5 will look at some top firms who aspire to the super tier, firms whose reputations have diminished somewhat, and new entrants scrambling for a place at the table.

CHAPTER FIVE

The Venture Capital Hierarchy
The Other Guys

N ot every venture capital (VC) firm can, or even wants to be, in the super tier described in Chapter 4. With more than 600 VC firms in existence, the vast majority are obviously not going to be in the super tier. Below is a handful of firms whom peers describe as being very close to the super tier in quality, consistency, and great venture capitalists, including Accel and Crosspoint in Silicon Valley and Matrix in Boston. Redpoint, a firm formed in 1999, is an energetic wanna-be whose partners believe that they have the credentials to one day be super-tier. And a dozen or so other firms with long-established reputations, such as New Enterprise Associates and Mohr Davidow, have remained in the top tier (defined as being in the top quartile of returns) but have never quite reached the super tier.

Knowledgeable entrepreneurs have a list of about 20 VC firms, either in Silicon Valley or Boston, where they go first for funding. It's only after they're turned down by these firms that they move on to other tiers. "If you work with the top-tier venture capitalists, they're willing to get behind a major concept and push it," says Gaurav Garg, the founder of Redback Networks. "They don't like getting involved in anything unless it can be real big."

This chapter looks at a variety of firms that span the gamut from old-line to new-entrant, from top-tier to slipping. First up will be firms that are close to the super tier—some of whom want to get there and some of whom don't. I also profile some older firms and how they're trying to maintain their reputations amid increasing competition, and then finish with a description of three newcomers and what it might take for them to achieve lasting success.

ACCEL: THE JIM BREYER SHOW

Several sources suggested that Accel Partners is already among the super tier, although it was not picked as regularly as Kleiner, Sequoia, or Benchmark. That's because the 17-year-old firm, which focuses on communications and the Internet, is dominated by a single partner, the engaging, photogenic Jim Breyer. Accel has yet to build the kind of strong internal teams with multiple stars that are the hallmark of the other three. But it does have former McKinsey consultant Breyer, whom one entrepreneur described as having "the highest ratio of IQ to ego around."[1]

In his forties, Breyer is a world-class venture capitalist who has made his mark recently by tapping his consulting background to help Old Economy companies figure out what to do in the Internet age. In his highest-profile deal, retailing giant Wal-Mart picked Accel as its joint venture partner in the online world. Says Breyer, "The world's best retailer could be the single best brand in the Internet space. Our challenge is to build a truly independent Silicon Valley start-up." Walmart.com was deliberately located in California instead of Arkansas, with its headquarters initially on the second floor of Accel's facility on University Avenue, downtown Palo Alto's main drag. Breyer insists that Walmart.com will succeed where other Fortune 500 dot-coms might not because it is not afraid to cannibalize Wal-Mart's traditional business. "We will compete fiercely with Wal-Mart stores if necessary."

Breyer followed up the Walmart.com deal by partnering with Kohlberg Kravis Roberts (KKR), of leveraged buyout fame. Accel-KKR will focus on creating companies with an online and offline presence, similar to Walmart.com. The process will be via "corporate carve-outs" in which an online entity is spun out from the parent, such as BrassRing. com from the *Washington Post*. "We are not doing buyouts," Breyer emphasizes, "but starting new companies." In doing such joint ventures, Accel is not forgetting its roots: early-stage investing in entrepreneurial companies. Breyer has invested in more than 20 companies that have completed successful IPOs or mergers, including Redback, Agile Software, Macromedia, and RealNetworks. "We measure ourselves by whether we get the first phone call when entrepreneurs start their next company," says Breyer. "If we're not getting 99 percent of those first calls, we're falling short."

CROSSPOINT VENTURE PARTNERS: THE QUIET FIRM

On its Website (www.cpvp.com), the question is posed, "What's special about Crosspoint?" The answer: "The ratio of success to humility." Crosspoint was founded in 1970, initially as small business investment company (SBIC), by Stanford graduate student John Mumford, a dedicated, practicing Christian who combines "commitment and propriety."[2] Crosspoint eschews the Sand Hill Road fishbowl in favor of less frenzied Woodside, California, where the VC firm has taken up residence on the second floor of the old Pioneer Hotel. Instead of framed initial public offerings (IPOs), photos on the walls depict historic scenes from the area's past, such as logging and deliveries by an ice truck. The Crosspoint lobby makes you feel like you're in a nineteenth century hotel, with hardwood floors, throw rugs, and comfortable chairs. Both partners I interviewed, Seth Neiman and Bob Lisbonne, emphasized that Crosspoint is not about flash, but about producing dependable results and caring about the entrepreneurs it funds.

Over lunch at Buck's, the hangout that is a block away, Lisbonne, in his late thirties and the youngest partner at Crosspoint, describes the team. "Between the six partners, we have 100 years of operating experience," he says. "We've each spent 10 to 20 years running companies." In a separate interview, Neiman stresses the same point. Mumford, he says, was one of the first to recognize how venture capitalism was changing, so he focused Crosspoint on early-stage investing and brought in partners with "deep operating experience." Crosspoint doesn't seek publicity because "we don't think of ourselves as a financial institution that needs to promote itself," says Neiman. "As ex-entrepreneurs, we recognize that it's the entrepreneurs who make the companies."

As for investment strategy, Crosspoint doesn't sound that much different from its peers. "We look for places where there's a very large new market and an opportunity for new companies to become dominant," Neiman adds. This is hardly unusual, but Crosspoint has been one of the best at carrying it out. In 1999 five of the ten biggest IPOs were Crosspoint companies. Although Benchmark racked up points for cofunding Ariba, the company was actually incubated at Crosspoint, as was another major success story that year, Brocade Communications, which makes fiber optics networking products. In a happenstance that in hindsight looks prescient, Crosspoint largely missed the short-lived dot-com boom because of its insistence on old-fashioned values like making money. Instead of funding companies selling pet supplies or jewelry on the Web, Crosspoint stuck to infrastructure (Covad, Juniper Networks), business to business (Ariba), and Internet market exchanges (National Transportation Exchange, RapidAutoNet). Says Neiman, "Maybe we should be a little more aggressive [in public relations], but we just haven't gotten around to it. We've been too busy building companies."

THE BEST OF BOSTON

Boston, the number two center for venture capital, boasts a number of high-quality firms, including Battery Ventures, Charles River Ventures, Greylock, Highland Capital Partners, and TA Associates. But the firm that many singled out as the best of Boston is Matrix Partners, whom one peer described as New England's super tier. The reason it's not as well known as the Sand Hill Road super tier is a deliberate difference in philosophy. Paul Ferri, who cofounded what became Matrix in 1978, is unapologetic about not following the California tradition of making big bets and boasting about growing brand-new industries. "We're not visionaries the way some people on the West Coast are," he says. "We don't stick our necks out. We try to back people who have had good careers at good companies, understand competitors and markets, and want to do something on their own relevant to their background." Ferri says he wouldn't have backed either Steve Jobs or Bill Gates because they didn't have that kind of experience: "We stick to our knitting." However, Matrix measures its success against its Sand Hill Road counterparts and hasn't been found wanting. "I would put my returns against anyone's over the last 10 years," says Ferri.

One of Matrix's biggest deals was Sycamore Networks, a maker of optical networking components that at its peak yielded $8 billion on a $10 million investment. In early 2000 Forbes.com said of Matrix, "The quiet, publicity-shy firm is hitting more home runs than the home-town team, the Boston Red Sox."[3] That's because, as Ferri says, Matrix works hard at cultivating relationships with budding entrepreneurs— "90 percent of our deals come from prior relationships." Sycamore was founded by a group that came from a previous Matrix investment, Cascade Communications. With locations on the East and West Coasts, Matrix focuses on networking and bandwidth, although it also does deals in unglamorous, yet still-profitable sectors such as semi-conductors and storage. Besides Sycamore, other Matrix hits—all in the communications/networking space—include Grand Junction Networks, PSINet, and, more recently, Copper Mountain Networks and Phone.com. "Amazingly enough, over the last 10 years we have not had a huge flop," says Ferri. "If we lose money on two out of 35, that's unusual."

Matrix's eight partners, based in Boston and in Menlo Park, Cal-ifornia, bring complementary skills in financial and operating spheres. Besides Ferri, who has been a venture capitalist for 30 years, Tim Barrows and Michael Humphreys also have multiple years of ex-perience in the industry. As for partners with operating backgrounds, Andrew Marcuvitz cofounded Apollo Computer, an early minicom-puter company; David Schantz helped start Cadia Networks after stints at Bay Networks and Bell Labs; and Andrew Verhalen was with 3Com and Intel. The two newest additions are Mark Vershel, who came from PeopleSoft, and Edgar Masri, formerly president of 3Com's venture investing arm. You can see from these résumés why Matrix is particularly strong in networking and connectivity. Ferri's first big hit was a modem maker called Codex, later acquired by Motorola.

Close behind Matrix in quality is Charles River Ventures (CRV), which now focuses on just two sectors: e-commerce and data commu-nications. Rick Burnes, who cofounded the firm in 1970, says venture capital has become far more professional in his three decades in the business, requiring more focus. "For most of my career it was an arti-san business where we sat around trying to figure out which way the wind was blowing. Today, because of the specialization you have to have real deep knowledge of an industry." Over CRV's long history, it has invested in major players in various technology arenas, including Sybase (databases), Parametric Technology (computer-aided design software), Cascade Communications (networking), Excite (search engines), and Vignette (online customer relations management).

In 1997 Jonathan Guerster joined CRV after four years at one of the early Internet companies, Open Market. "Most venture firms are like rich dysfunctional families," says Guerster, who did a survey of firms before deciding which one to join. "Every firm has two great people, two people who do other stuff like medical devices, and two people who are arrogant assholes. Charles River was different because Rick Burnes hires people who aren't egocentric." Guerster got promoted to general partner within two years, entitling him to the same salary and carry as every other partner, regardless of seniority. That egalitarian attitude has allowed CRV to decentralize decision making. In each of its two focus segments, "our two teams [of partners] act independently in making deals," says Guerster. "The old-world venture model was 'everyone's opinion matters'. The new-world is 'only informed opinions matter.'"

Greylock's veteran Henry McCance represents Boston's enclave of gentleman venture capitalists at its finest: polite, self-effacing, and very effective in an understated way. "We've spent 31 years building a culture here of great respect for the entrepreneur," he says. "As venture capitalists, we need to build sustainable, long-term companies rather than one-iteration product companies." Here's an example: In the late 1970s, McCance was an investor in Tellabs, anticipating all the infrastructure investments of today. Tellabs, which now has a market cap of $20 billion, makes sophisticated switches and other telecom equipment. When McCance wound up on the *Forbes ASAP* list of top venture capitalists (as selected by peers and knowledgeable observers), it was somewhat of a surprise. "McCance is a bit mysterious," wrote the magazine. "It's difficult to find information about this guy. His work is always done behind the scenes, with nary a press appearance."[4] And McCance is scaling back an already low profile by handing off duties to younger partners: "One of our goals has been to push responsibility down to younger partners and put every incentive possible for people with a career here."

HOLDING THE LINE ON SAND HILL ROAD

The penchant for flash displayed by the likes of Kleiner and Benchmark has relegated some solid, old-line Sand Hill Road firms to the ranks of, well, solid and old-line. Firms like New Enterprise Associates (NEA) and Mohr Davidow are still in the top tier and continue to get their share of good deals, but they sometimes lose the really hot deals to the really hot deals to the really hot VC firms.

The most infamous example of this occurred when Kleiner and NEA dueled over Netscape. NEA's founder Dick Kramlich, whose roots in Silicon Valley venture capital go back nearly to the beginning, had a longstanding relationship with serial entrepreneur Jim Clark. NEA had funded Clark's first company, Silicon Graphics Incorporated (SGI), which certainly led Kramlich to believe he'd get in on whatever Clark chose to do after leaving SGI. "Jim Clark was an adviser to NEA when he got into a real tiff at SGI with [then CEO] Ed McCracken," says Kramlich. Clark wanted to start a company in interactive TV, but Kramlich was reluctant because the costs would be so high. "Then Jim came to us and said he'd met this guy [Marc Andreessen] and was interested in the Internet." Clark would invest $3 million of his own money to start this Internet company; Kramlich proposed that NEA would come up with another $3 million for 50 percent. Clark wanted double the $6 million valuation. In that era (1994), "we'd never pay $12 million premoney because that didn't meet our valuation formula," Kramlich says. So he took Clark over to John Doerr. "That was the biggest mistake I ever made," Kramlich says now. Kleiner put in $6 million at a then-astounding premoney valuation of $18 million and snatched the deal away from NEA. "I'd approach it in a different way today," says the mild-mannered, likable Kramlich. "I'd lock up the deal first. No more trust your neighbor—we learned that from John Doerr."

But NEA has had its share of successes. In his interview with me, Kramlich could tick off eight companies that had gone from zero to a $1 billion–plus market cap with NEA as an investor: Macromedia, Ascend Communications, Dallas Semiconductor, Immunex, Healtheon (another Jim Clark company), Juniper Networks, 3Com, and SGI. The most recent, Juniper Networks, "has the makings to be the best of any of them," says Kramlich. "In every one of those cases I had a feeling they were absolutely pure quality plays into an unlimited space. That was what resonated with me." NEA's reputation today is going after quantity rather than the highest-quality deals; as a result, it usually places high on lists of top VC firms as ranked by number of IPOs. In late 2000 it closed the largest VC fund ever raised: $2 billion. That fund will be invested over three years in NEA's focus areas: networking, infrastructure, and life sciences.

Mohr Davidow Ventures has supplemented its small group of general partners—just seven—with so-called venture partners who offer specialized knowledge in selected areas such as consulting and public relations (PR). The general partners, including veterans Nancy Schoendorf and Jon Feiber, do the deals and sit on boards, but they can turn to people such as famed consultant Geoff Moore, author of *Crossing the Chasm,* and marketing specialist Donna Novitsky for applied expertise. "Geoff gives a day or two of time to each Mohr Davidow company," says Feiber. "Every one of our companies needs to be 'Geoffed' once a year." For Moore, it's a chance to keep in touch with the start-up world, since his consulting practice, the Chasm Group, is devoted to larger companies seeking to remake themselves. "What I do with start-ups is now focused exclusively within Mohr Davidow," he says. "I want to be active in creating the next round of metaphors [in the technology industry]. It's all just an ex-English teacher on steroids."

Novitsky, who is full-time with Mohr Davidow, helps its portfolio companies polish their images and achieve that all-important branding. In some cases, she will join a company temporarily as marketing vice president. Likewise, another venture partner, Randy Strahan, who has a strong background in general management and operations at companies like Pacific Bell and Telmax, will step in as an acting CEO or chief operating officer while an executive search is completed. Although the venture partner model is hardly unique to Mohr Davidow, the firm has taken it as far as anyone else. "This is the way we get our leverage as a VC firm," says Feiber. "We wanted to construct a firm where we can apply resources as quickly as possible." That couldn't happen with just a "handful of general partners," he adds, because each person is spread too thin. With the venture partners, "we have all these different skill sets readily available."

Mohr Davidow's approach appears to be working. Although it's dwarfed in number of general partners and amount of publicity by

firms like Kleiner, Mohr Davidow consistently winds up with great deal
flow in its target areas of e-commerce, Internet services, and infrastructure. This is where a lower profile helps; unlike, say, Sequoia,
Mohr Davidow is able to syndicate deals with firms like Kleiner and
Benchmark rather than simply compete against them. For instance, it
cofounded ONI Systems with Kleiner and also scored with joint investments in companies like Critical Path (with Benchmark) and Brocade
(with Crosspoint). "We understand what it means to take a couple of
people with a set of slides and an idea and make a company," says
Schoendorf. "We've been doing this for almost two decades, and our
record shows that we get the best returns in any kind of market environment."

BREAKING THE MOLD

Although their emphasis on particular sectors may vary, all the firms
just cited share a similar philosophy of how to invest. They want to be
the first venture investor in promising early-stage companies and get
deeply involved in their companies. But not every successful VC firm
follows this model, and two of the most resolute mavericks are Softbank Venture Capital and Draper Fisher Jurvetson.

When Masayoshi Son decided to take his Softbank Corporation
into venture capital in 1995, setting up a formal fund the following
year, he was met with nearly universal skepticism by the VC industry.
Softbank was a holding company whose large umbrella sheltered
everything from the trade show Comdex to software distribution to
high-tech magazines (it has since spun off Comdex and sold the magazines). *Dumb money,* the VC industry's most damning pejorative, was
swiftly applied to Softbank's foray into the field. And at first the firm
seemed to live up to the appellation, pouring hefty amounts of money
into what looked like second-rate Internet deals. Most venture capitalists might put $20 million into a single deal, but Softbank was will-
ing to make $100 million bets. One of those, in 1996, was in a tiny
Internet directory company called Yahoo. Softbank still owns 23 percent of one of the few profitable Internet companies, a stake now
worth billions, and has been able to sell off small portions of its Yahoo
holdings to finance other ventures. "We had very little to do with Yahoo's success," admits Gary Rieschel, managing director of Softbank

Venture Capital. "It's just that anyone who had a big early position in the Internet has ended up looking like a genius."[5]

Fast-forward four years to mid-2000, and Softbank Venture Capital, a recent merger of Softbank's early- and late-stage funds in Boston and Silicon Valley, has just closed a $1.6 billion fund, one of the largest in VC history, to boost its total under management to $2.6 billion. It has been able to increase its carry to the 30 percent level and still turn away money from potential limited partners. Two of its principals, Rieschel and Heidi Roizen, landed on the *Forbes ASAP* list of top venture capitalists. You seldom hear the expression *dumb money* aimed at Softbank any more.

There are reflections of both Benchmark and Kleiner in Softbank's approach. "We're entrepreneur-friendly because we live or die by quality of the entrepreneur," says Roizen, an entrepreneur for 15 years who only became a venture capitalist in mid-1999. Outgoing, obviously enjoying her new career, Roizen is dressed in a sleeveless black blouse that sets off her medium-length blonde hair the day I interview her. It is a sultry June day when the temperature hits 108 degrees in Mountain View, California, where Softbank is headquartered in a commercial zone next to the railroad tracks. "We made the *Forbes ASAP* list because we work so hard with our companies," Roizen adds. "We take a big position [a large investment in exchange for a hefty share of the company], and we don't make investments that compete with our companies." Softbank is known for its Internet *netbatsu,* which, like Kleiner's *keiretsu,* allows its portfolio companies to exchange advice and work together. Roizen and the other partners are each assisted by two *netbatsu* development officers, the equivalent of associates at other firms, who do research and help in recruitment. Softbank also has on staff two full-time recruiters, an attorney, a PR person, two mergers and acquisitions specialists, and a full-time incubator manager. And it has a strategic relationship with executive search firm Korn-Ferry. Talk about a *netbatsu!* Unlike its peers in either Silicon Valley or Boston, Softbank is a global investment presence, with 250 professionals outside the United States, but, notes Roizen, "we [at Softbank Venture Capital] control more money than the rest of the group combined."

Competitors may look askance at Draper Fisher Jurvetson, but everybody is watching what it's doing. DFJ, as it's commonly known, has an investment philosophy referred to by peers as "spray and pray" or "sprinkle and sprout." It puts relatively small amounts of money into a large number of companies, and awaits results. In the booming era of the late 1990s, this approach worked after a fashion, producing such successes as Hotmail, a Web-based e-mail service launched in 1996, and, more recently, Homestead.com, a personal Web page service. DFJ is also attempting to clone itself in several other cities, rather than just staying put in Silicon Valley, and, in mid-2000, unveiled its most daring innovation yet: a public VC fund called meVC (see Chapter 14).

Founding partner Tim Draper is as well known for his libertarian politics as for his unconventional attitude about venture capital. In late 2000 he was spearheading a pet libertarian cause, a California initiative on school vouchers to enable any parents to send their children to private schools. Draper spent $23 million of his own money on the initiative, which lost. What he wants to be remembered for, Draper tells me, is school vouchers and *viral marketing*. The latter is the idea that new technologies can be adopted through word-of-mouth recommendation. Draper came up with the concept when two young entrepreneurs came to him with an idea for Internet e-mail. "I suggested, can't you just put something at the bottom of every Web page: 'Get your free e-mail at Hotmail,'" he says. Hotmail's customer base grew to 11 million users in 18 months, and in 1999 Microsoft bought it for $400 million.

Draper has deliberately headquartered his company in plebeian Redwood City, California, down the road from an industrial plant. "I started out at Sand Hill Road, but we felt that to be independent, we needed to be outside the groupthink environment. We didn't want to just be one of the crowd. We want to change the world." He has a formula for doing that. In each of the seven other cities where DFJ has formed a partnership, the firm encourages formation of a local publication that writes about entrepreneurs as cool and exciting. The model for this is *Upside* magazine, the doyen of technology business publications that Draper helped fund in the late 1980s. (By way of disclosure, I was previously *Upside*'s executive editor.) "You have to promote entrepreneurs as heroes," says Draper. "People need to see that they can go out and do it themselves." He follows this publication by setting up a club that encourages networking among entrepreneurs and investors, such as the Churchill Club in Silicon Valley and the Zone Club in Los Angeles. Finally, DFJ goes in with a local investment office ready to fan the flames of entrepreneurialism. "Our strategy is to be local in a whole bunch of different pockets where cool things are happening."

Adds Steve Jurvetson, Draper's energetic young convert and now partner, "Tim builds a culture where people can rise on their own." In a dig at more control-oriented firms like Kleiner and Sequoia, Jurvetson maintains that venture capitalists should stick to what they do best—dealmaking—and let entrepreneurs run the show. "Entrepreneurs leave big companies to get rid of that parental feeling. They don't need it from us." DFJ's hands-off attitude has produced good companies, such as Four11 and Hotmail, but not great ones. The difference: The great, enduring companies buy out the good ones, as Yahoo did with Four11 and Microsoft did with Hotmail.

CRASHING THE PARTY

Because reputation and track record are so paramount in the VC industry, one wonders how a new firm ever gets off the ground, particularly in today's noisy environment. Countering that, though, is the massive flow of new money attracted by venture capital's extraordinary returns of the last several years—until the industry hit a wall in late 2000. The top-tier partnerships cited in Chapter 4 and in this chapter have little need for new sources of capital. In fact, they turn money away, so newcomer investors who want to get into venture capital must turn to these recently formed VC partnerships. Following are three examples of how new VC partnerships get started.

Like Benchmark, its model, Redpoint was formed out of the wreckage of two older firms, Institutional Venture Partners (IVP) and Brentwood Venture Capital. The rainmakers and young turks split from the existing firms because of unequal compensation and the feeling that some of the other partners were no longer carrying their weight. In Redpoint's case, the parting was a little more amicable than that of its predecessor. IVP and Brentwood will finish off their existing funds, whereas Redpoint is ensconced in IVP's former chambers on Sand Hill Road, where new space is almost impossible to acquire. The juxtaposition of the old IVP decor, which features numerous models of antique steam engines, trains, and presses, with the go-go image that Internet-focused Redpoint seeks to project is ironic.

Redpoint's leading partner, Geoff Yang, is a fierce competitor who seldom turns off his engine. One of Yang's peers says he "hates to lose" and "will do whatever it takes to win." Yang openly acknowledges Redpoint's aspiration to be in the super tier. "We're trying to emulate Benchmark," he says. "We saw an opportunity to change the landscape, and we took it." Focused on Internet investments, Redpoint uses the New Economy culture as its inspiration. "We really believe in branding," says Yang, who is willing to do a lot of press interviews. "In a noisy environment, entrepreneurs have to differentiate themselves, and brand VC will help them do that." Yang considers himself a career venture capitalist, and, in another reflection of Benchmark, has built a team of all-male partners who are similar in age (thirties and forties). However, their backgrounds are diverse, ranging from law to executive search to operating experience in start-ups. Yang says he won't make the mistake of holding on too long. "My goal is to see us build a team of people where we, the older generation, can gradually fade into the sunset," he says. "I don't want to retire as a venture capitalist. I want to do something else, something very different."

The problem for Redpoint is that it came into the game when valuations were at their peak and a new firm had to spend a ton of money to buy into even second-tier entrepreneurial deals. Redpoint did manage to raise two VC funds less than a year apart, a remarkably quick pace: The first fund was $600 million, and the second $1.25 billion. By late 2000, however, the firm was left with a grab bag of somewhat unappealing Internet plays, combined with holdover investments from its predecessors, so its returns are unlikely to be sterling, and limited partners may be reluctant to come in to a third fund any time soon.

Redpoint's most promising deal was with Old Economy stalwart Procter & Gamble (P&G): a site called Reflect.com that creates customized beauty products. "P&G didn't need our money or technical expertise in cosmetics," says Tim Haley, the Redpoint partner who pushed the deal and sits on Reflect.com's board. "They needed to understand how to build an Internet company." As Accel did with Walmart.com, Redpoint insisted that Reflect.com had to be a separate company far away from P&G. Although P&G retains majority ownership, Reflect.com has an independent corporate structure on a path to an IPO. "The core team severed relationships with P&G, so there's no path back," says Haley. "They sold their homes and they moved" to the San Francisco Bay area, where Reflect.com is based.

Another way to launch a new VC firm is to find a deep-pocketed backer who will put up all the money. Such was the case with Flatiron Partners, cofounded in New York in 1996 by a journalist, Jerry Colonna, and a venture capitalist, Fred Wilson, formerly of Euclid Partners. Flatiron took its name from the Flatiron district of New York, in the heart of Silicon Alley, and has focused on Internet investments there. The only limited partner is Chase Capital Partners, which has put a total of $800 million into two Flatiron funds. Softbank and Chase Capital Partners together bankrolled Flatiron's first fund, but Softbank then pulled out as it started its own fund. "When Softbank left, we thought about another partner, but Chase wanted to be exclusive," says Colonna. "We were also approached by three pension funds who offered to give us $1 billion. That's for three partners, one principal, and two analysts."

Colonna attributes his firm's rapid emergence into the limelight to several factors. The first is that as a longtime journalist (he and I worked at the same company, CMP Media, for a number of years), Colonna knows how to work the press. When we met for breakfast at the Sheraton Palace in San Francisco, the bearded Colonna, dressed casually in an open-necked sports shirt and jeans, was very comfortable with being interviewed. "The only difference between venture capital and journalism is you have investment banks instead of PR flaks calling you," he tells me. "You still have to separate the bullshit from the real." Unlike most venture capitalists, who at the time eschewed PR, Colonna tapped an outside contractor, Renee Edelman, to coordinate press coverage of Flatiron's launch in late 1996. As one of the first funds to concentrate on Silicon Alley, Flatiron scored a big story in the *New York Times* business section. After that, "every reporter in the country starts calling us," says Colonna. "We were just two schmoes sitting in an office at Chase. It was all accidental press. We were hot because no one else was saying Internet, early stage, and New York focus back then."

Colonna, who had a brief stint as a venture capitalist at CMGI before going off on his own, also tapped a couple of more experienced VC partners who bring needed gravitas. Cofounder Fred Wilson met Colonna on one of the deals that CMGI turned down. And Bob Greene, a former partner at Chase who served on Flatiron's investment committee, came over to the firm full-time in 1999. Then too, Flatiron's early deals have performed well. As of mid-2000, "we've invested about $355 million and have about $4.5 billion worth of gain," says Colonna. "We've had 13 companies either go public or get sold," including GeoCities, bought by Yahoo for $3.6 billion, and StarMedia Network, a Latin American portal that went public in 1999. Of course, Flatiron accomplished this during the golden era, when it was tough to do poorly, so its mettle in tough times is untested.

Likewise, Vector Capital got its start thanks to the largesse of a wealthy family. Located in San Francisco's downtown financial district, Vector was founded in 1997 by two young expatriates from existing firms, Alex Slusky of NEA and Val Vaden of Benchmark. At NEA, Slusky was the associate who was supposed to follow Jim Clark around in an effort to get the firm into his next deal. That next deal, Netscape, wound up with Kleiner, although contrary to published reports, NEA didn't dump Slusky because of that failure, he says. "Dick [Kramlich] isn't a spiteful guy. Anyone who understands venture partnerships knows a 26-year-old guy doesn't get the blame." In fact, Slusky says he turned down an offer from Clark to join Netscape as vice president of business development. Now in his early thirties, the earnest-looking Slusky, dressed formally in a white shirt and dark pants for our interview, informs me that he could have made general partner at NEA but chose to start his own firm. "Dick told me that I could stay at NEA and become a general partner, but I'd never be a founding partner. I wanted to look back and say, 'This is a firm that I helped build'".

From 1995 to 1998, Slusky was managing VC investments for the Ziff family, founders of the computer publishing powerhouse Ziff-Davis, with whom he had developed a relationship at NEA. "They said, 'Do this for us, and we'll let you build your own firm.'" After Ziff family members got out of publishing by selling their holdings to Softbank, they decided to handle their own investing. The $40 million that Slusky was overseeing became Vector's first fund, and he looked around for a partner. The Ziffs had been investors in the newly formed Benchmark, where Vaden was chafing a bit because the firm had decided to concentrate on early-stage investments rather than on his interests—special situations and revitalizations. "Val and I talked, and there was this complete mind meld," says Slusky. In early 1998, "we put a show together and started raising Fund II." Among the investors in that $175 million fund were Ziff, Perot Investments (Ross Perot), Vulcan Ventures (Paul Allen), MIT, and General Electric. "Having Ziff up front as an investor really helped us bring in the top names," says Slusky.

Vector has differentiated itself by focusing not on the raw start-ups favored by most VC firms, but on existing companies going through some rough spots. These include companies running out of capital because they were "bootstrapped," or self-financed by founders; spin-outs from larger corporations; consolidations; and turnarounds. Vector does not do more than three or four deals a year in order to allow the two partners to concentrate on the firms it has. "I don't believe in drive-by VC," says Slusky. Like Colonna, he can come up with some good sound bites.

By picking areas out of favor, Vector is able to find good deals even without a brand name. "We don't wait for things to walk into our door," Slusky says. "We define an area of interest, and then spend time and resources on identifying five companies that could do the best and try to back them." One example is Savi Technology, a former division of Raytheon that focused on supply chain management and logistics. "It was an orphan within Raytheon," says Slusky. He met with the head of the division, who wanted to make it a stand-alone enterprise. In May 1999 Vector bought 35 percent of the company for $6.5 million, a very cheap valuation for the time. Vector's partners spent the better part of a year strategizing with Savi on its business plan and building the team. "We turned a company focused on supply chain logistics for defense into a supply chain management company for commercial companies, moving it from systems integration into a transaction-based business." Nine months later, in early 2000, Savi raised a $50 million round from Accel, Mohr Davidow, and corporate investor Oracle at eight times the valuation Vector paid.

Although their long-term success remains to be proven in an era when public markets are declining, Redpoint, Flatiron, and Vector share at least one characteristic required to have any shot at making it: They raised money from quality backers. Chapter 6 introduces the money behind the kingmakers—the all-important limited partners who have committed to risk-based investing through up and down cycles.

CHAPTER SIX

The Buck Starts Here

T he limited partners who put up the money for venture capital
(VC) investments have played a vital, though largely unseen
role in the industry's development. If entrepreneurial endeavors, as we
know them today, wouldn't have existed without venture capital, then
venture capital wouldn't have existed without limited partners. These
partners, including university endowments, foundations, pension
funds, insurance companies, investment banks, and mutual funds, invest in each fund raised by individual VC firms. Typically, existing limited partners will "re-up" when a new fund is raised in order to keep
their place with a firm, but there is some churn as newcomers, such as
Benchmark and Redpoint, are formed, while old firms cease to exist.

Venture capitalists would seem to have a pretty good gig: They
take big risks with someone else's money, and only have to pay out
when one of the risks actually works. On the other hand, every limited
partner whom I interviewed agreed that venture capitalism has been
the best-performing asset class among their portfolios. The risks, by
and large, pay off over time. Limited partners also invest in public equities, other private equity (such as buyout funds), real estate, and
commercial endeavors, but an increasingly larger chunk of their
money is devoted to venture capital. In part this is because the 100 per-

cent–plus returns of the past few years have swollen the amount in that asset class.

The success of the late 1990s distorted the traditional relationship between venture capitalists and limited partners. With money easy to come by—from a variety of sources such as global investors, corporations, investment banks, and individuals—venture capitalists pick and choose among available limited partners and set more conditions for investing. The limited partners tell me that they're paying for the high returns of recent years by putting up with the increasing arrogance of venture capitalists. This reverses the situation of the dry period of the late 1980s and early 1990s, when money was tough to raise and having loyal limited partners was like having a claim on a known mother lode. Irwin Federman, who turned U.S. Venture Partners (USVP) around during that period, remembers trying to raise money when his firm was just barely making money. "We were asking them to buy the story [of our turnaround]," he says. "I had to depend a lot on good will." Ultimately, nearly all the limited partners USVP approached in that period invested. "We developed strong bonds that last to this day," says a grateful Federman. "We got to know them and they were embarrassed to say no."

Today, they'd be afraid to say no, at least to a top-tier VC firm, because they'd lose their places in the firm's funds and probably never get them back. At this point, some of the venture capitalists and their firms are wealthy enough to invest only their own money, but having limited partners spreads the risk and strengthens the network. Just as with a VC firm, money is no longer the primary draw with a limited partner. Rather, it is the prestige, experience, and contribution that a limited partner can bring to the VC network.

TAKE MY MONEY, PLEASE!

You wouldn't think a behemoth like CalPERS, which stands for the California Public Employees Retirement System, would have any trouble finding places to invest its money. CalPERS, based in Sacramento, California, is one of the largest pension funds in the world, with $170 billion under management. One could combine nearly all of the top university endowments and still not match CalPERS. When it decided to move into VC investing in the late 1990s, however, there was unexpected turbulence. "CalPERS was very arrogant and tried to dictate terms," says Dixon Doll, a longtime venture capitalist who runs Doll Capital Management in San Francisco. "VCs don't want to deal with someone who looks like they'll be an asshole." Besides, with money plentiful, the pension funds were no longer favored as limited partners because they were too big, too conservative, and too removed from the entrepreneurial world to add much value. The VC firms prefer limited partners such as major universities, which are not only knowledgeable about venture capital but also have ties to start-ups, which are often founded by students.

Clinton P. Harris, managing partner with Grove Street Advisors, the Wellesley, Massachusetts–based investment firm that is CalPERS' VC adviser, admits that the huge pension fund had to learn some humility. Accustomed to throwing its weight around with public companies, CalPERS tried the same tactics with VC firms and failed miserably. One problem was that it was so big that it had to use gatekeepers, or investment advisers like Grove Street, to handle its investment. "There's a cultural hatred of gatekeepers in the VC industry," says Harris, because historically these advisers had a very risk-averse approach to investing. "Venture capitalists didn't respect the gatekeepers and found them very insensitive and inefficient. So VCs simply refused to work with gatekeepers."

Grove Street, which won the right to manage CalPERS' VC investment in late 1998 through a competitive process, is trying to change that image. Because venture capital is now 25 percent to 30 percent of all private equity, and growing rapidly, "you want to be represented there," Harris says. "VC has done better than buyouts." And since CalPERS was an important, politically influential entity in California, "not to be welcome in the California venture industry was embarrassing." With $350 million from CalPERS in November 1998, Grove has managed to invest the money in about 35 different firms, including such newcomers as Idealab Capital Partners (see Chapter 13). But it hasn't been able to get into any of the super tier—Kleiner Perkins, Sequoia, or Benchmark. "They get offered three or four times the amount of money they need from existing investors," Harris says. However, CalPERS has invested in funds of some highly regarded firms, including New Enterprise Associates, Highland Capital, Austin Ventures, Morgan Stanley's VC arm, and Weiss Peck & Greer, recently renamed Lightspeed Venture Partners.

CalPERS' situation is hardly unique, according to Gary Bridge, managing director of Horsley Bridge Partners in San Francisco. Horsley Bridge is known as a *fund of funds*, which means that it aggregates monies from limited partners such as universities and corporations and chooses which VC firms to invest the pool in. He's a gatekeeper, too, but an expert one with a long track record of proven commitment. When I interviewed Bridge, who is low-key and rather media-shy, with metallic-gray hair and glasses, he had just finished raising $2.5 billion and was getting ready to pour it into 35 to 40 VC firms. Even Bridge, who is a well-respected power in the behind-the-scenes world of limited partners, now gets turned down occasionally by VC firms, however. "They used to come to us," he says. "Now we go to the VC office to present to them. The balance of power has shifted." Still, he adds, because of Horsley Bridge's quality reputation, "we're the ones saying no 10 out of 11 times."

Predictably, the top-tier VC firms are the most high-handed. "All the terms and conditions of the partnership agreements are take it or leave it," says Harry A. Turner, a managing director who spent 11 years at Stanford Management Company overseeing the university's $1.8 billion worth of investments in private equity. About 75 percent of that goes into venture funds, the other quarter into buyout and other types of investments. Venture capitalists have an "insufferable self-confidence," he adds. "It's hard to make a distinction between a deserved self-assurance and an inflated one. Arrogance has become endemic in the industry." (Turner left Stanford in late 2000 to join a philanthropic VC firm, Legacy Venture Capital.)

Even long-term VC partners such as Stanford and the Massachusetts Institute of Technology, which kick-started professional venture capitalism way back in the 1940s when it invested in the fund run by General Doriot, are becoming less of a concern to VC firms. As the size of a new VC fund pushes past $1 billion, the existing limited partners aren't always able to keep up their percentage share, either because they can't afford to or because the VC firm is so eager to bring in new money that it restricts the old. And the VC firms have also accelerated their fund-raising schedules. Where they once raised a new fund every three years, in recent years they've been coming back in about half that time. The upshot of all this is a shrinkage in terms of the market share that a limited partner will have in any one fund, as well as a corresponding decrease in clout.

For example, Turner says Stanford would like to be a 10 percent player in every fund in which it invests, but when you're talking about a $1 billion fund, that becomes too expensive. In a $100 million fund, Stanford could invest $10 million and stay at its 10 percent target. If it commits that same dollar amount to a $1 billion fund, it is merely a 1 percent piece of the pie. Allan Bufferd, the treasurer who oversees investments for MIT's $6.5 billion endowment, says that its largest investment in a single VC fund was $60 million, or just about 1 percent of its endowment, "That's the outer boundary for us," he says. Consequently, as VC funds swell, "we are getting ratcheted down," says Bufferd. "It's a seller's market on the VC side." The VC firms are in a position to dictate how much each investor is allowed to put in. Bill Spitz, the vice chancellor for investments with the Vanderbilt University endowment of $2.3 billion, says some VC firms are holding it to the same dollar amount even as their funds double in size: "You can beg and plead, but it doesn't get you much."

On the other hand, prestigious limited partners like Stanford and MIT are avidly sought by new VC firms and those aspiring to move up into the top tier. Like the best venture capitalists themselves, high-quality limited partners bring many intangible values. Says MIT's Bufferd, "We have the characteristics of a preferred investor. We're not fair-weather friends. We are supportive investors." Adds Stanford's Turner, "We have a lot of benefit because of the stature of our name and the professionalization of the staff." There's also Stanford's long-standing commitment to venture capital. "We're not fickle," he says, "and we give venture firms identification with the higher education cause."

WHY INVEST?

If VC firms have become so arrogant and dictatorial, why do the limited partners stay with them? Because so far, the returns have been worth it (see Figures 6.1, 6.2, 6.3, and 6.4). "Venture capital has done extraordinarily well over a long period of time," says Vanderbilt's Spitz. As with other endowments, he could boast of 100 percent–plus annual returns over the past couple of years with VC investments. Even before that, VC returns were in the high twenties and thirties. "The reason we invest in this stuff is to beat publicly traded stocks," he

FIGURE 6.1   HOME RUNS VERSUS FLOPS

	NUMBER OF INVESTMENTS	COST ($MILLIONS)	VALUE ($MILLIONS)	COST (PERCENT)	VALUE (PERCENT)	VALUE/COST
Write-offs	278	674	95	11	0	0.1x
Below cost	330	1,021	317	17	1	0.3x
At cost	69	243	243	4	0	1.0x
1–5x	685	2,613	6,524	44	11	2.5x
5–10x	178	627	4,471	10	7	7.1x
10–25x	136	481	7,997	8	13	16.6x
Over 25x	89	326	41,581	5	68	127.7x
Total	1,765	5,985	61,228	100	100	10.2x

Source: Horsley Bridge Partners.
Note: Analysis of 61 VC funds in which Horsley Bridge Partners invested between 1985 and 1996.

FIGURE 6.2 HOME RUNS VERSUS FLOPS (GRAPHED)

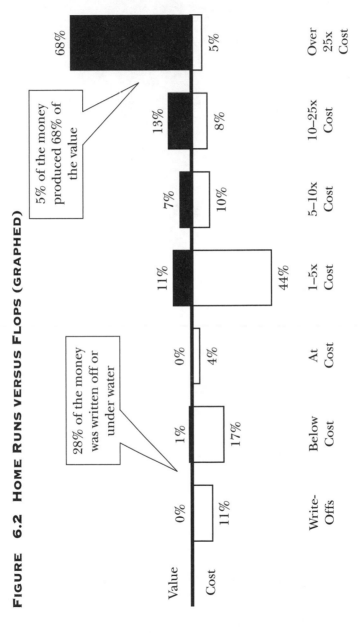

Source: Horsley Bridge Partners.

FIGURE 6.3   INVESTMENT RESULTS BY GOING-IN STAGE

	NUMBER OF INVESTMENTS	COST ($MILLIONS)	VALUE ($MILLIONS)	COST (PERCENT)	VALUE (PERCENT)	VALUE/COST
Seed	480	1,641	27,387	27	45	16.7x
Early	805	2,560	22,243	43	36	8.7x
Mid	257	881	8,465	15	14	9.6x
Late	220	899	3,120	15	5	3.5x
Other	3	4	14	0	0	3.8x
Total	1,765	5,985	61,228	100	100	10.2x

Source: Horsley Bridge Partners
Note: Seed produced the greatest amount of value.

FIGURE 6.4   ANNUAL RATES OF RETURN

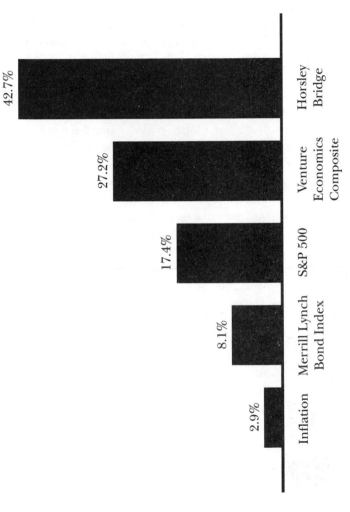

Sources: Bloomberg, Venture Economics, Horsley Bridge Partners.
Note: Data are for the 10 years ending March 31, 2000.

says candidly. "We want to earn the stock market return plus a 5 percent premium as a payment for the illiquidity." Since the long-term return on public stocks is around 11 percent, a VC return in the high teens "will make us happy."

The University of North Carolina, which has a $1 billion endowment fund, has gone from 1 percent to 14 percent invested in private equity, which includes both venture capital and buyouts. "We've had incredible success with venture investing," says chief investment officer Mark Yusko. "Venture capital makes a good investment for an endowment because we have a perpetual time horizon and don't have to worry about short-term volatility." In fact, a university endowment's enemy is not volatility, but inflation. "Your sole goal as an endowment is to provide a continually increasing real stream of payments," which means that universities need the diversification of private equity and its higher rate of return. Besides, Yusko adds, "there's a natural link between educational institutions and venture capital. So many of the entrepreneurial ideas come out of universities."

Even conservative investors, such as insurance companies, are finding venture capital too tempting to ignore. Phoenix Investment Partners, based in Hartford, Connecticut, manages about $500 million from Phoenix Home Life Mutual Insurance Company that goes into private equity. Insurance companies, which got burned by junk bond investments in the late 1980s, have been cautious about venture capital. "It's only a small percentage of Phoenix Home Life's investment assets," says Paul Chute, investment manager for private equity—around 4 percent of the total. On all private equity, which includes some buyout funds, Phoenix's return for pre-1990 investments was 18.5 percent, whereas from 1993 (when Phoenix got back into private equity) through December 1999, it was more than 50 percent. "Our hurdle has been 15 percent annual returns," Chute says. Because of the success of the 1990s, "we're debating whether to raise our allocation. In general, we're very happy with the asset class [of venture capital]."

Another factor that makes VC investing attractive is the ease with which one can distinguish a top-flight player from the rest. The division between the performance of top-tier venture firms and that of firms in the lower three quartiles is distinct in good times and bad. Says Vanderbilt's Spitz: "It's very different from the public arena," where money-management performance cycles up and down unpredictably. In venture capital, "the great firms are able to maintain their leadership over long periods of time." In a down period like the late 1980s, when the average firm earned a 5 percent to 7 percent return, top VC firms might be in the high teens, Spitz recalls. For venture funds raised in 1996, the top-quartile performers were turning 80 percent through early 2000, and the bottom quartile was in the single digits. "You consistently see very large spreads between winners and losers," he says. That kind of predictable staying power is a winner for long-term investors, for whom dependability is the highest virtue.

DUE DILIGENCE IN REVERSE

Because of the persistent differentiation between top-tier VC firms and everyone else, and also because each VC fund represents a long-term commitment of 10 years, limited partners do a considerable amount of due diligence before investing in a firm. It's very analogous to the research that venture capitalists conduct into the prospects of entrepreneurial companies, only this time the light is shining directly on the VC partnerships. The limited partners look at the talents of the individual venture capitalists, along with how they work together as a group. They check on succession issues—for example, how dominant is one generation in the partnership, and is any attempt being made to bring in new blood? Is one person the rainmaker, and could his or her departure or retirement completely undermine the firm? They pay close attention to the contentious issue of how the VC partners split up the carry—for example, is the division roughly equal, or do senior partners take the lion's share, leaving the younger ones to fume? And, of course, is this firm consistently a top performer in terms of returns to its limited partners?

Generally, the limited partners cited intangible factors as the basis for investing in a VC firm, although they all pointed out that those intangible factors should add up to good returns. "There's a lot more art than science in figuring out which VC you're going to commit to," says Jon King, associate vice president for investments at Dartmouth College. "You can do all the analysis in the world and figure out which partner has generated the best returns." The problem is that that doesn't tell you how the firm itself performs. It's like attempting to predict how a family will interact by checking out only the father or mother. For example, "Is Sequoia going to be the same when Don Valentine steps aside?" King wonders. "The firm has continued in his footsteps, but who takes his place going forward?"

Due diligence, sums up Stanford's Turner, "is a continuous process." Stanford, which has been doing VC investing since 1978, sizes up the investment fit between a VC firm's expertise and the opportunities available in the market. Lately, that has meant emphasizing information technology at the expense of biotech and retail. "The second thing we do is to confirm that the partnership can execute on its strategy," he says. The partners must trust and respect each other and have equitable financial incentives in place—in general, that means an equal share of the carry. Even with established firms like Sequoia, Kleiner Perkins, or Greylock, he likes to see "three distinct generations of investing partners" to make sure that a handoff will occur.

Gary Bridge, of Horsley Bridge, has a selection formula: People plus process equals performance. First, he says, you analyze the people in a VC partnership, including the continuity of the group, how long they've been together, their individual skill sets and contributions, their ability to help their portfolio companies, and any baggage left over from previous funds, such as struggling or failing companies that will consume time and attention. "You have to take into account if it's one partner who's generating all the good deals. If that partner gets hit by a truck, you're in trouble," Bridge notes. Finally, "I ask, 'Do the partners still have that fire in the belly?'" even if they've been investing for 20 years and are multimillionaires in their own rights.

Then Bridge focuses on process: Do the partners have a clear investment strategy; are they able to adjust to market changes; is the portfolio mix a good one (i.e., not too many overlapping companies, but adequate synergy so that they can work together strategically); are there enough experienced partners to properly invest and manage a $1 billion fund; and what sets the partnership apart from its peers? Bridge and his five U.S. partners will do reference checks, meet with the VC firm, talk to the chief executives of their portfolio companies, and then take a majority vote on whether or not to invest with the firm. It's a mirror image of the VC partnership meetings in which participants go thumbs up or thumbs down on a deal.

FLAG Venture of Stamford, Connecticut, has paralleled what Horsley Bridge did for institutional clients by aggregating money from wealthy individuals and families, and investing it in private equity, mostly venture capital. "We're not looking for one-hit wonders," says managing partner Diana Frazier. She searches for firms that were definably instrumental in the success of their portfolio companies. "There are a whole bunch of people who just got lucky and made money in this market," she says. "We want the ones who made a difference and can do it again." To that end, she seeks out "sustainable, long-term franchises" by identifying firms that take the trouble to mentor their junior partners and pay them fairly.

As an investment manager in the actuarial-based insurance industry, it's not surprising that Chute prizes results above all else. "The number one factor for us is track record," he says. "A lot of people can tell a good story, but we like to see realized results, not just unrealized appreciation." He does serious networking to find out about a firm's results, calling competitors, entrepreneurs, and other limited partners. (Though they seldom talk to the press, limited partners definitely swap opinions and stories about VC firms among themselves.) "We work to get an unbiased view of capabilities," says Chute. Integrity is another very important consideration because "as a limited partner, once you commit your money to the general partner [VC firm], you have almost no rights. You better believe the GP is going to do what they say."

MIT's Bufferd is another who stresses investment returns, but only those tested by time. He prefers a 10-year track record. "If there is survivorship for at least 10 years, you're probably dealing with the better firms to begin with," he says. He also likes long-term relationships because "one of the most difficult parts of the investment process is reviewing and assessing new people." Working with people for years "lets you know their behavior patterns, how they react to stress. You see them in weak times and strong times." MIT is still investing with the first two venture firms with which it started in 1977. Even though the two firms, which he declined to name, have gone through a number of transitions with their partners, "the continuity has always been there."

OUT WITH THE OLD, IN WITH THE NEW

Despite the continuity factor, there is turnover in the VC industry, and limited partners must cope with that. They must decide fairly soon after a new firm is formed whether or not to invest with it, because waiting can be fatal. For a hot newcomer like Benchmark, getting in on that very first fund meant not only obtaining an ongoing commitment from the partnership, but also participating in one of the best-returning funds of all times. "Benchmark's first fund, which had eBay, may have been the best venture fund of all time," notes Yusko. Of course, no one knew that going in. Balancing the decision to invest in a new fund is the fact that someone else might have to be cut, because many limited partners are now beyond their allocation targets on venture capital and don't have the capital to add anyone else. Once a limited partner declines to re-up in a VC firm's most recent fund, however, it's probably out for the count. Then, too, most limited partners have small, overtaxed staffs that do the investment analysis. "There are 250 firms trying to raise money today, including the buyout funds," says Spitz. "Every day two or three offering memoranda cross my desk. It's overwhelming." The decision to switch from one VC firm to another taxes resources and time incredibly, and is thus not made lightly.

"A few years back we were more likely to look at a new firm, someone who had a good reputation or track record," says Dartmouth's King. Today, with no room to increase the VC allocation, "it comes down to deciding whether to commit more to Sequoia or Accel or look at Redpoint." In the case of Sequoia and Accel, "they've delivered the goods." With new firms, even those like Redpoint, whose partners have respected track records, "there's always the organizational risk. They've paired up with new people, so you never know what the personal dynamic is going to be." On the positive side, "the guys who form new firms are very hungry, not content to rest on past performance. They want to prove to the world that they're the best."

At Phoenix Investment Partners, Chute has been steadily re-upping with the 25 VC firms he already partners with, leaving little room to add newcomers. In the past couple of years, Phoenix has added only three new firms. One of those was Mission Ventures, based in San Diego. "They were sponsored by local entrepreneurs because there was a dearth of local venture capital," says Chute. Not only did the partners have good track records, but the opportunities in San Diego and the relative lack of VC competition "made it a compelling story" as well.

FLAG Venture's Frazier says that new firms like Benchmark and

Redpoint are different from their predecessors because they come out of the gate with a specific brand. Benchmark, for example, publicized the fact that all the partners were receiving an equal carry. "It was a conscious decision to market themselves," she says. Redpoint is trading on the reputation of Geoff Yang and the distinguished history of its predecessors. But Frazier is cautious about getting into new firms immediately, no matter how well respected their partners. "We see hundreds of new funds, and none of them come to us with people that aren't smart. Smart is necessary but not sufficient."

Stanford's Turner adds that when a firm like Redpoint is formed out of two preexisting entities, "I have quantitative data and reputational track records of the partners from [predecessor firms] IVP [Institutional Venture Partners] and Brentwood. The reputation of those guys and what they had accomplished was very compelling." Stanford, currently invested with about 25 firms, is willing to go above its VC allocation for such compelling opportunities, says Turner. As for pruning, it is rare. In the last 10 years he has only dropped three firms. "Dropping someone has to do with investment performance. They're missing strategic opportunities and investing in the wrong places."

MIT is currently investing with about 30 VC firms, of whom seven or eight are new relationships, Bufferd says, although that doesn't necessarily mean that the firm itself is new. "Maybe we were wrong the first time in turning someone down," he says. "We try to be aware of what's happening in the industry. Most of the new firms are outgrowths from some previous activity." For MIT, deciding to terminate a firm relies on a number of factors, including a decline in performance, some change in organizational dynamics, or an "anticipation of something being awry," he says. "There is no hard-and-fast rule. We probably make as many mistakes in those decisions as one of the new firms. It's a soft science." In either case, "you make the decision cautiously, going in or going out, because you're investing considerable staff resources and time."

Among limited partners, the same tiering that exists in the VC world can be seen. Experienced limited partners who can add value, such as the best universities or savvy investors like Horsley Bridge, are investors in the top VC firms, even though their share of the individual funds may be decreasing. The wave of new money trying to get in—investors who have no history in the VC world—goes to newcomers or to second- and third-tier firms.

CARRYING ON

Between 70 percent and 80 percent of the profits derived from venture investing are returned to the limited partners who put up the
money. That sounds like a good deal until you recall what the VC firms
get for basically using the money the way they see fit for 10 years. The
firms charge an annual 2.5 percent management fee for making the
investments and take 20 percent to 30 percent of the profits as their
carry, which is divided primarily among the general partners—10 or
fewer people at most firms. The 30 percent carry level includes
Kleiner, Sequoia, Benchmark, Redpoint, Accel, Matrix, Mayfield, and
Softbank.[1] The management fee and the rising carry have become
sore points with limited partners, especially as fund sizes have surged
past $1 billion and as fund-raising has accelerated. But there's not
much that limited partners can do about it except pull out, and then
they may regret it. Says Bridge, "Obviously, we'd prefer that these
firms not to go from 25 to 30 percent or from 20 to 25 percent, but
we're not in the driver's seat. We don't want to lose our position."

Here's one story of how you can lose your position. A limited
partner who asked not to be identified had the opportunity to re-up
its investment in a new Kleiner fund back in the early 1980s, when
Kleiner had not yet become the star it is today. It had, however, just
boosted its carry to 30 percent. "Kleiner was one of the early ones to
go to 30 percent, and there were people here who didn't think it was
reasonable, so we left," says the limited partner. And it has never been
able to get back in. "It clearly falls under the heading of sometimes you
get what you pay for. Kleiner has turned out to be worth every penny."

The VC firms argue that to grow their partnerships and add new
people, they require more carry, in addition to the management fee.
But that argument doesn't hold a lot of water with the limited partners, who point out that not one partnership has increased its payroll
anywhere near the proportion by which profits have gone up. The
management fee is irksome because it is collected on every fund in direct relation to the size, although sometimes it will go down as the
fund runs its course. What this means is that instead of collecting 2.5
percent every three years on a $100 million fund, which was a typical
pattern up until the late 1990s, VC firms are now collecting 2.5 percent, or $25 million annually, on a $1 billion fund, and they're raising
a new fund of that amount every 18 months or two years. Because the

funds are active for years, the VC firms are collecting that 2.5 percent on five or six different accounts, which means that income from management fees alone can exceed what the carry was five years ago. "When they were raising $50 million funds, 2.5 percent was reasonable," says Spitz. "With billion-dollar funds it's not reasonable." And then there's the carry. Take a $1 billion payoff, such as Kleiner and Mohr Davidow each reaped on ONI Systems, "work out what 20 to 30 percent of that is, and look at the carry attributable to each partner," says Turner. "You'll see very big numbers. Even mediocre performance can be richly rewarded."

Longtime Silicon Valley venture capitalist Dixon Doll agrees that the cash compensation to partners and others "has become astounding." Entrepreneurs-in-residence at top firms get $500,000 a year "just to hang out at firms and look for a company," he says. Big-name VC partners pull down $1 million–plus salaries. Coupled with their take of the carry, nine-figure cash compensation figures aren't unheard of. The structure was designed to provide the general partners at a VC firm with pay for performance, and they have certainly delivered. As returns inevitably go down, however, an outcry over fees and carries might follow.

Bridge shared Horsley Bridge's returns with me on every fund it has raised and invested with VC firms since 1985. The first one was a $200 million fund, which returned 15.5 percent annually to investors, or about 2.7 times the original investment. Since then, here's what his aggregate funds have done: Horsley Bridge (HB) 2, 1988, $227.5 million, 31 percent, 4x; HB 3, 1992, $225 million, 75 percent, 12x; HB 4, 1995, $300 million, 101 percent so far; HB 5, 1997, $500 million, 223 percent so far; HB 6, 1999, $1.055 billion, N.A.; HB 7, 2000, $2.5 billion, N.A. But the current returns aren't sustainable, he says. "We've told our clients we can deliver an 18 to 22 percent net IRR [internal rate of return] over the long term."

At the University of North Carolina, the 12-month trailing return for venture capital through March 31, 2000, was 212 percent, according to Yusko. The five-year compounded return was 44 percent annually. By contrast, the institution's target rate of return on private equity is 5 percentage points above that of public stocks. "All this other stuff is gravy," Yusko says, and won't continue. "IRRs will go down. It's like playing poker. At the end of the game, the cards speak." And you can't really calculate IRR until the fund finishes its 10-year cycle and all the profits have been distributed. "At the end of the 10 years, you know how much got," he says. "Our expectation is that we'll get 2.5 to 3 times our investment over a 10-year life."

At FLAG Venture, Frazier doesn't even like sharing her returns with the wealthy individuals who invest in her aggregate fund, because they're so high that they'll create unfulfillable expectations. "We promised them 25 percent, and the returns have been triple-digit," she says. "We didn't want to dazzle them with those numbers." Like her peers, she cautions investors that a more difficult market "will separate the men from the boys," and everyone's returns will decline.

The goal of all these limited partners isn't to achieve a particular IRR, but to stay with the top-tier VC firms and achieve a long-term net return that's demonstrably greater than that from other asset classes. Stanford is typical. Over the long term, Turner expects an annual IRR of 20 percent and a net of three times invested capital over the life of the fund. Since the beginning of its venture program in 1978, Stanford's IRR through the end of 1999 was 28.2 percent. From 1995 through 1999, it was 100.3 percent. "Everybody in the industry agrees that returns over the last five years are unsustainable," sums up Turner. "I'll stick by my 20 percent expectation for the next 10 years. That's still the highest among asset classes."

MONEY CHANGING

Another sticky subject for VC firms and their limited partners is *distribution*—the process by which profits are delivered to the partners, after the entrepreneurial companies in which venture capitalists invested have gone public or been acquired. Usually, the VC firms turn over stock in the newly public entity or the acquirer. It sounds simple, but it's not. The stock can't be liquidated all at once because that could impact the market, so VC firms dole out distributions in pieces, or *tranches*. And because the carry is calculated at distribution, the VC firm wants the value of the stock to be at its highest point, so it will try to time the public market. This irritates limited partners, who would prefer to be entrusted with the stock as soon as possible. Says Turner, "Venture capitalists have always insisted on distributing at their discretion. They don't recognize that they have sophisticated LPs [limited partners] who know how to manage public stocks." Stanford, for example, has a portfolio of unsold stocks from distributions worth several hundred millions of dollars. Venture capitalists "are the *private* equity experts, and stock management is not one of their skills. Their arrogance leads them to think that it is," he says.

To find out about the shadowy world of distribution, I turned to Paul A. Reese, senior managing director of Shott Capital LLC, based in Boston and San Francisco. Shott was formed in 1991 as the first registered investment adviser for distribution management—it acts as a middleman between the VC firm and its limited partners in handling distribution. In mid-2000 Shott was managing about $2.5 billion worth of distributed securities for its 52 clients, which included endowments, foundations, and corporate funds.

About 70 percent of VC distributions are in stock, and the rest in cash, if the exit event has been for cash, such as a buyout or acquisition. Reese says that VC firms used to sell the stock after an initial public offering and distribute cash, but that practice became less popular after Sequoia's December 1991 distribution related to Cisco Systems. At the time its limited partners got $122 million in cash, representing a 67x return or a 186.9 percent annualized return. Sounds great until you calculate that if the distribution had been in stock and all the shares had been held, they would have been worth $3.7 billion five years later, and $28.7 billion on September 30, 2000! (Both figures include Sequoia's then–20 percent carry.) Sequoia, which was a hero when it distributed, in retrospect looks like a sharpster. Of course, no one could have forecast Cisco's overwhelming market surge, yet the limited partners lament, "If only Sequoia had distributed the shares." "The general partners [venture capitalists] realized it's a no-win situation," says Reese. "If you sell the shares and distribute cash and the shares go down [in value], no one will remember. If they go up, people will say we wanted the stock. So they give them the stock."

While some VC firms are considerate of their limited partners and hand over clean, liquid stock, meaning that it's free of restrictions regarding when and how it can be sold, others "distribute stock with no concern as to whether a company is liquid or the stock is restricted," Reese says. Restrictions are related to how long a company was privately held before going public—the Securities and Exchange Commission requires at least two years before the stock can be distributed unrestricted. VC firms also must await conclusion of the so-called lockup period (set by the investment bank that takes a company public, and typically 180 days) before distribution. "Other times they don't distribute for a more controversial reason," says Reese, "because they don't like the stock price." For instance, during the lockup period, the share price plummets to $9 after opening at $20. If the VC firm believes the price will recover, "they will defer distribution because the story isn't over until they distribute and take their carry."

To avoid roiling the market value of the stock too much, distributions take place in pieces. "You can't take a young company where only 30 percent of the stock is in the hands of the public and distribute in one day another 30 percent of the company," notes Reese. "You've doubled the float, and the stock will tank." Instead, the venture capitalists might split the stock into four tranches and distribute one per quarter. But it's obvious that they are timing the market. "When there's a big down move in the market, we receive far fewer distribution notices [from the venture capitalists] for a while," he says. With an upturn, distribution picks up.

The distribution process sums up the relationship between VC firms and their limited partners: The venture capitalists distribute in a way that boosts their own profits, but the rewards for the limiteds have been so good that they don't dare complain too much. As Spitz notes, "It's very hard for us to realize [our gains] at the distribution price because typically the price goes down. Investors are getting big slugs of stock, and they sell." A VC firm may distribute at a $120 share price and, the next morning it's down to $114. The best the limited partner can do is reap the $114. "They get you going and coming," he says of the VC firms, "but if you paid 10 cents a share, you can't cry too much." He gives this example: Vanderbilt's share of Sequoia Capital's investment in Yahoo was initially valued at $29,000. "We netted $54 million after it was distributed by Sequoia," says Spitz. "When it works like that, it's great."

What makes it work like that is the quality of the entrepreneurs in whom the VC firm invests. Paralleling the separation of VC firms into various tiers, entrepreneurial companies can be ranked, subjectively, in the same way. In a self-fulfilling prophecy that perpetuates and enhances the best VC firms, the most promising start-ups seek them out first. Chapters 7 and 8 describe how venture capitalists invest the money they raise from limited partners, and the interaction that is at the heart of venture capital: dealing with entrepreneurs.

CHAPTER SEVEN

The Pitch

Venture capitalists would not exist without entrepreneurs willing to take their money in exchange for a piece of the dream. The venture capital (VC) industry depends on the willingness of select individuals to take risks: small groups of people within an existing company who decide that now is the time to break off and form their own venture; engineering students who develop a cool technology, such as a browser or a way to download music, that could form the basis for an entirely new market; or the inveterate inventor tinkering in a garage who comes up with something like a home computer. These are the raw materials out of which venture capitalists shape the Netscapes and the Apple Computers of the future. That's why the first thing that Tim Draper does when he sets up an offshoot of Draper Fisher Jurvetson in a new city is to start a publication or a network that fans the flames of entrepreneurialism. For in areas where people won't take the risk of starting a new company—and possibly failing—venture capital has no field of dreams to reap.

In the United States today, it has become fairly easy—some would say too easy—to start a new venture. Notes Kleiner Perkins' Vinod Khosla, "The entrepreneur is the new American hero. Everybody wants to go start a company." The hard part is what comes after: turning a start-up composed of just a few people with a business plan into a "real company." That's where the best venture capitalists recognize the epitome of their value: in applying their strategic knowledge and their instincts to that process. For a time at least, the venture capitalist "marries" the entrepreneur, promising to be there in good times and bad, in sickness and in health, until an initial public offering (IPO) or a merger parts them. Says Greylock's Henry McCance, "Most marriages require a period of courtship to develop mutual trust and mutual respect. If you haven't built that foundation, divorce in this business is painful."

This chapter and the next look at how venture capitalists and entrepreneurs build that foundation, starting with "the pitch," the initial plea for funding that entrepreneurs make. In its most pared-down form, called the two-minute elevator pitch, the entrepreneur must define in a sentence or two the great idea that engages the imagination of the venture capitalist, like Cisco's Sandy Lerner did with Sequoia: "We network networks." Venture capitalists are hounded with pitches everywhere they go, via e-mail and phone calls, when they dine out, when they ski or play golf. Typically, in order for an entrepreneurial team to make a full-fledged pitch—about a half-hour presentation with PowerPoint slides followed by questions from the venture capitalists—they must have a recommendation from someone the venture capitalist respects. At that point, the team pitches to a single partner, who will either become the champion for the idea with the rest of the partnership or steer the group elsewhere. The next step is a presentation to the entire partnership; one thumb down from any partner is usually enough to send the entrepreneurs on to another VC firm.

ONE-ON-ONE WITH TRUSTIX

Sand Hill Road has become a mecca for entrepreneurs from all over the world, which hits home when I attend a presentation by the two founders of Trustix, based in Trondheim, Norway. In March 2000 they meet with Stu Phillips of U.S. Venture Partners (USVP). Before the meeting, Phillips tells me that the Trustix team has been referred by another entrepreneur, Krish Panu, whose company USVP funded. Getting a referral is the first hurdle that an aspiring entrepreneur must jump. "Last year we did 32 new investments," says Phillips, who is

slight, dark-haired, and soft-spoken. "More than 80 percent were re-
ferrals from people we knew. It's the first-order filter. We get 8,000
business plans a year and pick 32." From a preliminary phone call, he
has determined that the Trustix people "believe in what they're doing.
I haven't seen anything that said they were bored one night and decided to start a company." That feeling, coupled with the recommendation from Panu, buys Trustix a precious half hour of Phillips' time.

The four of us sit around the large table in USVP's conference
room. Trustix CEO Havard Wollan and chief technology officer Orjan
Berg-Johansen, who are probably in their mid-thirties, both wear suits
(dark in Wollan's case, an ill-advised olive green in Berg-Johansen's)
but no ties. Evidently they've been told about Silicon Valley's informal
dress code. They talk about their dream in Norwegian-accented English, and Phillips asks occasional questions underscored by his lyrical
Welsh accent. All from the Old World, these three have been sucked
into the epicenter of the New Economy.

Wollan describes Trustix's founding two years ago as a Linux
company. In early 2000 Linux is hot because it's a shareware operating system available free to anyone who wants to download it, in contrast to Microsoft's, Apple's, or Sun's proprietary systems. That makes
Linux politically correct, and freely exploitable by companies like
Trustix. The company has just launched its first product—a Linux-
based firewall—and plans two more in the information technology
administration space. IBM's European division has expressed interest.
Another option is for Trustix to provide outsourcing for companies
that use Linux and want to improve security.

To get its start, Trustix was "bootstrapped," self-funded by the
founders and a small government grant. From friends and individual investors known as *angels*, it then raised a round of $1 million to develop
its existing three products, and now is seeking a second round of $10
million. The 20-person company "is short of everything," says Wollan.
"We need to hire 20 to 30 more engineers." The $10 million will also be
used to ramp up marketing and sales in the United States, possibly move
into the wireless space, and open an office in Silicon Valley, although
engineering and research and development will stay in Norway.

Phillips cuts to the bottom line: "How will you make money? How
big is the market opportunity?" Wollan maintains that the Linux firewall market alone could reach $1.5 billion. Phillips questions how
much Trustix can charge for its product. "A large number of cus-

tomers where software costs nothing is a zero-dollar market," he points out. "The technology that you've created is impressive, but the question is, How big a business can you build, and what will it take to get you there? You need to find a big meaty target." He then takes the two through some market-size calculations indicating that the business demand for Linux firewalls and administration will be much smaller than Wollan has projected. "To build a meaningful company, you'd have to have a huge share of this market," Phillips concludes. Wollan tells him that in five years he wants Trustix to achieve $500 million in sales. "If you want to build that kind of a company, you need 30 percent of a $1.5 billion market," says Phillips. "The challenge of building a pure brand in that kind of market is very expensive. You'd be better off finding somebody who already owns the channel and making a deal with them."

By this time it's apparent that USVP will not be funding Trustix. The market size just doesn't jibe with what Phillips and his peers want. But the meeting has still been helpful to the Trustix founders. They have learned that they must refine their business plan and find a market niche that demonstrates the potential for much greater growth. Phillips says that he will e-mail the Linux company that USVP funded and ask its principals to meet with Trustix. He has given the two their allotted time and a bit more. We all shake hands, and Wollan and Berg-Johansen take their quest somewhere else.

A GYM ON WHEELS

Not every pitch for venture capital concerns high technology (see "Wild Pitches"). Dan McClure and Tom Nelson want to offer wellness services to overstressed Silicon Valley workers by bringing the gym to them. They've won a half hour of Tim Draper's time by bidding on it at an auction that raised money for a local school. Draper, apparently bemused with the whole thing, lets me sit in on the pitch. McClure and Nelson, who look to be in their late twenties, are a refreshing contrast to the pasty, indoors-looking engineers who usually make entrepreneurial pitches. Wearing T-shirts with "GymVan" emblazoned on them, they are lean, trim, and tan. The tall, dark-haired McClure works for a local health club, and the lighter-haired, more compact Nelson manages an on-site facility for a large Silicon Valley corporation. In Draper Fisher Jurvetson's rather gloomy interior conference room, McClure confesses that the whole notion was his wife's idea. "She told me, 'You're going to make a billion dollars with GymVan. It's like Webvan, but GymVan.' At first I thought, that's stupid. Then I thought, it might work."

He apologizes because his computer blew up, so he doesn't have any PowerPoint slides. He does, however, have a written version, to which he supplies his own sound effects: "It's total fitness to the rescue . . . We're going to bring total wellness to small and medium companies. We'll drive the gym through their front door." (He makes sounds like a television announcer and a van driving.) Draper interrupts the show with a practical question: "If they work out in your van, how about a shower?" McClure, thankfully dropping the sound effects, replies that the van will provide a dry/wet towel service if the company doesn't have a shower.

The entrepreneurial pair hands Tim a drawing of a huge bus and informs him that the vehicles costs about $115,000 fully loaded with equipment they'll need for their service. They plan to have several of these buses, and a fitness Website has already agreed to provide the equipment free in exchange for advertising. Nelson lays out the financial strategy: Companies would pay GymVan $100 an hour with a three-hour minimum per day. That works out to about $6,000 a month, and customers are obligated for at least six months. Draper wants to know the usual: How big is the market? McClure says that GymVan can lease the trucks for $40,000 a year and handle three customers per truck. "By our second year we're making $4.5 million with 25 vans per area." He waxes enthusiastic about all the services they can offer, from straight workouts to ergonomics to massage therapy.

Draper acknowledges that it's a cheaper way for a company to offer fitness services than building a club. But what about the social aspect of a club? Says McClure, "We're going to help you keep employees because we're providing a fantastic service. You can pump iron or kickbox with your coworkers." Draper, who has been smiling slightly throughout the presentation, suggests an alternative funding source, such as a bank loan. McClure replies that GymVan wants to hit the market with a rush. Says Draper, "Then you should talk to the Benchmark guys because they did Webvan. Give Bob Kagle a call and use my name." He also tells McClure to work on his numbers before he approaches Kagle. "$4.5 million doesn't do much for us."

WILD PITCHES

Ask a venture capitalist, "What was the craziest idea anyone ever pitched to you?" and you either get a blank look because there were so many, or something immediately comes to mind. Here are the responses that came to mind:

There's the chicken-shit deal. Chicken farms have a big problem disposing of chicken waste because it's toxic. Chicken farms feed the chickens soy protein, which is expensive. Chickens are enormously poor digesters, so the waste is mostly undigested proteins. This guy came out with a way to recycle the proteins. He would take chicken waste and use jet engine blasts to heat and vaporize it. Detox it and they eat it again.

Tony Sun, Venrock Associates

One guy had a device that took the fat out of hamburger. He brought us up all these fast-food hamburgers. He took one and stuck it in the machine. Then he took out this tube full of greasy fluid that came out of that one hamburger. It was disgusting. We didn't invest because we didn't think it had a commercial prospect, but we got a free lunch. Since then, about eight years ago, I've probably not had more than a half dozen hamburgers. I keep seeing that tube of fat. Maybe it wasn't such a wacky deal.

Irwin Federman, U.S. Venture Partners

We had one for robot sex booths in bars. . . . We had another proposal for a portable nuclear reactor. You just drove it up and plugged it in. . . . We had one for a company that would make a kit to convert your toilet into a bidet. . . . I had a guy with a Formula One driving license who wanted to be subsidized for two years in car races. He was an Arab, and he promised he'd be the greatest sports figure in the Arab world. The promotional opportunities would be huge. He called me two weeks later and said he'd given up racing and now had a medical device company.

Seth Neiman, Crosspoint Venture Partners

Three guys walked in who looked like Berkeley burn-outs from the sixties. One guy said he'd developed a way to control computers with brain waves. I said, "Can you hook these electrodes up to my head and let me open Microsoft Word?" He said, "We haven't perfected it that much, but you can see some flickering." I told the other two guys don't quit your day jobs.

Mark Gorenberg, Hummer Winblad Venture Partners

We had the guy with a flying saucer. . . . We had another guy with an idea for edible pants. . . . And another who wanted to capture methane from farting cows.

Tim Draper, Draper Fisher Jurvetson

This guy wanted to bring icebergs from Alaska to Southern California for drinking water. We couldn't figure out the economics.

Arthur Rock, Arthur Rock & Company

I had a company pitch me on putting up little compartments to store groceries from Webvan-like operations when people aren't home. They were going to pay neighborhood kids to watch the compartments. It was easy for us to say no.

Peter Dumanian, Red Rock Ventures

PITCHING TO A CROWD: SHADOWPACK

For start-up teams who manage to win over one VC partner, the next hurdle is higher: convincing the entire partnership that an idea is worth a million-dollar bet or more. Swaying a group of sharp-eyed cynics who've gone through thousands of pitches takes a heap of showmanship, something like auditioning for MGM. In contrast to the earlier one-on-one meetings with a lone partner, this time the setting is formal, and the slides outlining strategy and defining potential customers and partners are a must.

In April 2000 I join a group of 10 partners and associates at Mohr Davidow Ventures on Sand Hill Road to hear a pitch from the three founders of Shadowpack. The Dublin, Ohio–based company intends to offer enhanced services for wireless devices, which has piqued the interest of partner Michael Solomon, who is sponsoring the group. The wireless arena intrigues the VC pack at the moment because many believe it will be the next paradigm shift as we move toward universal, 24/7 connectivity. Before the Shadowpack team comes into the Mohr Davidow conference room, Solomon gives a brief preview: "This is the first wireless Web deal I think is compelling." He has a couple of connections to Shadowpack: He started a company 20 years ago with one of the board members. "Also, the CEO's second wife's son-in-law is a business partner in a Columbus gym with my wife's sister's husband." Everyone laughs as they try to grasp this tortuous relationship.

Shadowpack is represented by Lance Schneier, president and chairman; Chuck Maynard, chief technology officer; and, just recruited out of Palm, which makes wireless devices, Nick Berner, the vice president of business development, who will set up an office in San Francisco. The team is not the fabled group of twenty-something engineers most people picture when they think of entrepreneurs. They are older, more experienced. For instance, Schneier is a lawyer whose first start-up was in the natural gas industry in 1982. After he sold the company to Enron, he ran its internal VC effort. Now he's got the itch to do his own start-up. "We're going to create a new wireless experience, enable a higher level of relationships," he says. "We'll be accessible from virtually any mobile access device, like Palm, smart phone, PDA, pagers, linking to the Internet or an intranet."

Maynard passes out several Palms to do a demo of the Shadowpack interface and services, which include the ability to find customized news, weather, sports, and entertainment sites. You can also order services, such as a movie ticket, and pay for them, because Shadowpack prepares a profile that includes your credit card information as well as personal and business interests. The anticipated revenue streams include advertising, subscription fees, commissions on e-commerce transactions, and customer acquisition bounties. Shadowpack has agreements with several hardware vendors (including Palm) who have a total of 650,000 customers, of which they expect to nab 165,000. Schneier got Shadowpack started with $400,000 of his own money, plus $800,000 from friends and family. "We're looking for $20 million with possibly a follow-on rather quickly after that," he says, trying to appear casual, but it's obvious that Shadowpack is rapidly run-

ning out of money. The $20 million would be used for marketing, con-
tinued application development, and customer acquisition, estimated
at $50 to $100 for each one.

After the Shadowpack team leaves, the Mohr Davidow partners
discuss whether to offer a term sheet. The group concludes that there
will be a single big winner in wireless content. Says Solomon, "The
only advantage here is who gets it done first and right." Jon Feiber
adds, "I think it's a winner-take-all game. There are 100 companies
chasing this. You need to build an aggressive team and spend for the
marketing." He wonders whether Shadowpack is the one that "can win
an end-user land grab." Partner Nancy Schoendorf agrees with him:
"It's a very interesting business, but it will take a ton of capital because
they'll have to create a brand. Are these the guys who can do it?" Veteran Bill Davidow points out that building a consumer brand is expensive and, given the current state of Nasdaq, doubts whether the
company can go public within a year and raise the $100 million it will
need. One alternative, Feiber replies, is a corporate round, getting the
hardware vendors to participate. Growls Davidow, "This sounds like a
bunch of day traders sitting around talking about a new $4 trillion
market. You've got to convince yourself these are real applications
people will pay real money for."

Solomon realizes that there's not enough conviction that this
team can be the big winner in wireless, and he says that he will do more
research into the market. A few weeks later I get an e-mail from him:
"We decided not to invest. . . . It is a highly competitive market with
many different players all trying to solve the same problem." Shadowpack does manage to get funding from a Midwest VC firm, Capital
Technology Group in Columbus, Ohio, and in July 2000 launches its
first product into a crowded space.

CUSTOMER MANAGEMENT: ALERT1ST

Highland Capital Partners has dual headquarters in Boston and San
Francisco, where its newest partner, Keith Benjamin, is based. Benjamin was a highly regarded Internet analyst at Robertson Stephens &
Company before Highland recruited him. Now Benjamin is trying to
prove himself on this new turf by generating deal flow, bringing in entrepreneurial companies that Highland wants to fund. On April 25,

2000, several other Highland partners have flown out from Boston to join Benjamin in San Francisco to assess one possibility: Alert1st, a San Jose–based start-up in the customer relationship management (CRM) space popularized by heavy hitters like Siebel Systems and Oracle.

Highland is represented by Benjamin, along with Boston partners Sean Dalton, Josaphat "Jo" Tango, and Wycliffe "Wyc" Grousbeck. Alert1st's team is headed by CEO and former Apple product manager Phil Beisel, who, knowing that I'll be attending, has come prepared with a 1993 issue of *Forbes ASAP* (the magazine I work for) that has a photo of him swigging down beer after Apple's Newton team finished that project. He and Alert1st's cofounder and chief technology officer Greg Seitz both came out of Apple and then did another start-up, Wayfarer Communications, which was sold to CRM player Vantive in 1998 for $22 million. So they have a reasonable track record that has earned them a place at this table today.

Beisel, who is pudgy, with blond-brown hair, does most of the talking. The bearded Seitz, wearing a flower-print shirt that does nothing to belie an engineer's reputation for kooky dress, and round-faced, bespectacled Jim Chapman, the vice president of product management, chip in with occasional comments. Beisel explains that Alert1st offers Internet-based software that allows companies to improve the customer experience by targeting its best customers and solving their problems proactively. Alert1st's software automatically warns Website operators when customers are having problems such as poor performance, inability to navigate the site, or shopping cart difficulties that short out a potential transaction. "We're looking at identified customers, noticing their problems, and supporting them," says Chapman. "Our product is sold to people who care about what goes on in customer support."

During questioning from the partners, Grousbeck, in particular, is skeptical, because Alert1st is focusing on a narrow niche that demands serious selling to corporate customers, and the company has not yet recruited a sales and marketing executive. "The problem here is selling, not inventing the technology," he says. Beisel tells him that Alert1st has seven potential customers for its test software, mostly in the business-to-business (B2B) area. Grousbeck notes that the existing CRM players will simply promise that they can incorporate Alert1st-like services into their own technology. "I don't mean to be abrupt," he adds unapologetically. "I'm just telling you my concerns. If I didn't,

Keith [Benjamin] would wonder why I just nodded all the way through this meeting."

Beisel, struggling to salvage the meeting, says that Alert1st is selling two products with a projected average price of $40,000 to $50,000, so revenue per account will be $80,000. Customers also will pay a licensing fee based on the number of their customers who use the technology. "We're not here to tell you about hit-and-run e-commerce," he says. "We're talking about customers who have ongoing relationships with their high-value customers." Alert1st has raised $300,000 in seed financing from its three founders as well as individual investors. With seven people on the team, the company now seeks a $5 million first round of venture capital to enable it to fill out the team and finish the product launch. That will be followed by a $13 million round that would pay for a sales force and brand marketing. "We see the opportunity of becoming a one-stop shop for customers to buy a dynamic infrastructure to service people," Beisel sums up. "We can help companies identify their most valuable customers and give them a better quality of service."

A couple of weeks later, I have a lunch meeting with Beisel, who tells me that he's not very confident of getting funding from Highland. "People either see your vision, or they don't," he says. While Benjamin has supported Alert1st, Grousbeck "has taken some arrows in the [CRM] space" on a previous investment that didn't do well. Beisel agrees there's a problem: "The good news is that our sector is hot; the bad news is that it's noisy"—that is, overcrowded. He respects Grousbeck's tough questioning. "If you don't get the money out of these guys, at least it makes you think really hard about your business." What venture capitalists want, he concedes, is unbridled opportunity, a product that fills a gaping hole—not a nice-to-have niche product like Alert1st's.

By the end of that week, Beisel hasn't gotten a formal rejection from Highland, but he's decided that the deal isn't going to happen. Benjamin has told him that the partnership is stuck because Alert1st doesn't have a "killer VP of sales." It's a catch-22 because without funding from a top-tier venture firm, Alert1st can't attract a killer sales executive. Meanwhile, a half dozen other VC firms have turned him down, and Beisel is scrambling to fill the funding gap. One venture capitalist who said no, Crosspoint's Seth Neiman, told Beisel that the team and the business plan were pretty good, "but if I don't see you as a $2 billion market cap, I can't do the deal. I can't expend the time on it." At least, sighs Beisel, "he told me what he really thought."

Benjamin tells me that Alert1st just had to cut through too much clutter with a business model that wasn't that compelling. The concept of selecting premium customers and treating them differently makes sense, he maintains, possibly as an add-on to an existing CRM vendor. By August, Alert1st had raised another $1 million with private investors but had yet to land a VC investor. Beisel planned either to grow the customer base and then try again for venture capital or to sell the company. "Either way, we win," he says.

DIALING FOR DOLLARS

Considering the ration of deals seen to deals funded at top-tier VC firms, it's not surprising that none of the pitches I watched got approved. But I interviewed a number of entrepreneurs whose start-ups did obtain the all-important imprimatur of dollars from a good venture capitalist. They did it by coming up with an idea that had the potential to be big, and then impressing the venture capitalists with their energy and determination to carry out the idea.

One of these was Autodaq, a B2B automotive company in San Mateo, California, that was only a few months old when I visited the founders in January 2000. The company aimed to provide an Internet-based marketplace serving dealerships and other businesses that buy and sell used vehicles, replacing or at least augmenting the fragmented series of physical auctions used today. The two founders, CEO Adam Boyden and vice president of market development Andrew Iorgulescu, are young, in their late twenties. Boyden is stocky and blunt, with a clipped British accent; Iorgulescu is taller, leaner, and more polished. Both have some previous experience: Boyden with an international consulting company, and Iorgulescu with Internet companies Infoseek and Autobytel.com.

"I decided that VC was essential in starting a company today," says Boyden. "The brand name of the VC firm was less important than the quality of the individual who would sit on our board. Our mantra: You choose your VC first, then the firm, and then the deal. A lot of people make the mistake of choosing the deal first." Autodaq's team, which also included another consultant and an attorney, talked to about a dozen VC firms and got eight term sheets. They picked veteran Dave Marquardt, who had helped fund both Sun Microsystems and Microsoft in the early 1980s and is now with August Capital. Boyden and Iorgulescu signed a term sheet giving up one third of the company for $5 million, including $4 million from August Capital and $1 million from several angel investors.

"Dave was the only person who played it straight," says Boyden. "He liked our model because it was one of the few he'd seen that could make money." Too many of the other venture capitalists were obviously just interested in doing a deal. "You learn to look through the mists of bullshit," says Boyden. "At our second meeting Dave looked me in the eye and said, 'You're going to have to get some adult supervision to run the company.' He thought we were four punks. Other VCs would look us in the eye and say, 'We think you're wonderful.' You knew very well they'd ring up a headhunter [to find a new CEO] the moment they signed a check."

In a separate interview, Marquardt confides that he did think the Autodaq guys were pretty crazy. None of the four really had any serious business experience, "and yet they were going to change the auto industry in the U.S." Still, it was a big idea and one that attracted contrarian Marquardt. He nods in agreement when his partner, Andy Rappaport, chimes in. "The best deals are always the craziest," he says. "Sun was a bunch of university hackers with no proprietary technology." Rappaport is quicker with the sound bites than the slower-speaking, deep-voiced Marquardt. "If you want to go where the big wins are, be a little bit crazy," Rappaport adds enthusiastically. "Conventional wisdom leads to conventional returns. If you're afraid of being fantastically wrong, you'll never be fantastically right."

By August 2000, Autodaq had grown to 70 employees, moved into new offices in Menlo Park, California, had customers in three segments (rental cars, finance companies, and manufacturers), and was closing on a $50 million second round of financing. Not yet the big win that Rappaport was talking about, but hopefully on its way.

UNDER THE RADAR SCREEN: FIREDROP

Another raw start-up that got an almost immediate response from eager venture capitalists was FireDrop, whose technology called Zaplet improves e-mail communication and collaboration. (In late 2000 Fire-Drop took the name Zaplet.) Headquartered in Redwood Shores, California, FireDrop was so hot when it was founded in late 1999 that its VC backer, Kleiner Perkins, kept it in stealth mode (no press releases or mentions) for about 10 months before the product was launched. The stealth mode no doubt came naturally to cofounder and president David Roberts, who had the most unusual background of any entrepreneur I interviewed: He was a former spy, or, rather, an officer and executive manager in the U.S. Central Intelligence Agency.

The two of us meet in May 2000, after FireDrop has moved into its headquarters in a vast stretch of new buildings just past Oracle's Emerald City–like complex. During the previous stealth mode, the street was not yet visible on maps, and the phone number was unlisted. The brand-new buildings, abutting treeless courtyards, overlook wetlands that are fast disappearing amid the onslaught of dot-com invaders. Roberts's corner office has long banks of windows on two sides, through which you can hear the wind howling off the marsh. It is decorated, probably by someone else, all in beige. On this day Fire-Drop has brought in Chinese food for the employees, so Roberts, the public relations specialist sitting in on the interview, and I fill up our plates and bring them back to his office. Roberts tells us that when FireDrop moved in only a few weeks ago, the building was wide open; now all the space is taken and they're looking for more.

Not surprisingly, Roberts won't talk much about what he was doing for the CIA or where he was stationed. He is probably in his mid-thirties, tall and slender, with dark, close-cropped curly hair and olive skin. He could pass for many nationalities, I think—a useful trait in his previous career. "I was a career officer in the CIA, which is actually very entrepreneurial," he tells me. As anyone who has seen a spy movie knows, agents perform other jobs during the day for "cover." Because many of the entities the CIA seeks to infiltrate are run as big businesses, such as drug cartels, "the agency [he really does call it "the agency"] needs people who understand business. For example, you may want to understand very carefully how to make an illegal drug cartel fail."

Roberts has a few somewhat more conventional skills deemed useful in a technology start-up: He has an MBA from Harvard and a BS in computer science, engineering, and artificial intelligence from MIT. He also was involved in technology transfer for the electronics system division of the U.S. Air Force. "I understand how to manage and protect a large complex system," he says. "The great majority of satellite systems are built by the nation's national defense contractors. We oversee those businesses with the intent of assuring America's global information superiority."

Despite his CIA career, or maybe because of it, Roberts is quite comfortable chatting one on one. "This is my real job," he assures me, although he remains a reservist in the military. However, he's obviously relieved when he can talk about FireDrop instead of the agency. "The applications we're developing have new capabilities that people want within e-mail," he says. Zaplets can be programmed to self-destruct so that the message doesn't pop up later at an inopportune time. Information can be shared and interacted with by multiple participants. And FireDrop's technology can create self-routing messages that go through a series of people in a specified order.

FireDrop got started when Roberts met Brian Axe, the other co-founder, on a houseboat trip arranged by mutual friends. They discovered that both of them were trying to solve a similar problem: how to coordinate something as simple as a weekend trip via e-mail. You want everybody to see the message and pick days when they can go. It wasn't possible to do that with e-mail as it existed in mid-1999. Axe had a typical entrepreneurial background: stints in marketing and operations at Hewlett-Packard and IBM, followed by an executive position at start-up Sportsline/Golfweb. When he and Roberts started talking, Axe was the entrepreneur-in-residence at a Silicon Valley incubator, Reactivity, which would briefly house the FireDrop team. The two put together a working prototype and a business plan, then started pitching to a handful of select VC firms, leaving the one they really wanted, Kleiner Perkins, for last.

At first, the two entrepreneurs were only looking for $1 million, but in the fevered atmosphere of late 1999, "we started realizing you need to ask for large amounts of money," says Roberts, so they boosted it to $5 million. Through a friend of one of the partners at Reactivity, he managed to land a one-on-one session on July 27, 1999, with Kleiner partner and Sun Microsystems' founder Vinod Khosla. It was a fateful meeting. "We knew we needed a swing-for-the-fences VC, and that Vinod could be it," says Axe. "We expected him to chew us alive." Instead, Khosla told them right away that he wanted to do the deal. "I thought there's no way anyone could make up their mind that quickly," says Roberts, "but Vinod keeps a mental checklist in his head: Is it viral marketing? Is it patentable? Does it fill a real need?" Evidently, all the answers were yes.

The following Monday Khosla brought the pair in front of Kleiner Perkins' weekly partnership meeting. This time, at Khosla's behest, Roberts and Axe had boosted their estimate of the kind of business they could do by a thousandfold. With Khosla behind the deal, the Kleiner partners (sans John Doerr, who was away) paid rapt attention. "It was a totally different thing they hadn't seen before," says Roberts. "At the end they said they didn't want us to talk to anyone else for 48 hours and they'd make something happen. I agreed to 24 hours." That night Kleiner sent over a term sheet, offering $5 million in exchange for a portion of the company that Roberts would not disclose. Presumably, it's somewhere in the 25 percent to 35 percent range that Kleiner prefers. "They were asking for more than we wanted to do, so we had some reservation," he says. "But then we figured that if we go with them, the likelihood of being successful is much higher. We thought about that for 20 minutes; then the next day we signed it and it was done."

AT ARM'S LENGTH

Not every entrepreneur seeks out venture capital. After all, you have to give up a big piece of your company and cede a considerable amount of control to some outsider who may or may not share your vision. If you can afford to self-fund your company, or it's generating enough cash flow to be an ongoing entity, why bother with venture capital? Homestead.com's Justin Kitch thought that way for several years. Tall, dark-haired, in his late twenties, and very thoughtful and deliberate about what he wants with his company, Kitch founded in 1994 a consulting company, KartoffelSoft, focused on educational software. It was based on a thesis he'd written while getting his BS degree from Stanford. "At the time, I couldn't imagine taking in VC and having someone else tell me how to run the company," he says.

Kitch, whose unexpected claim to fame is that he is the Guinness World Record holder for leapfrogging, had a brief, unhappy experience at Microsoft that drove him into the entrepreneurial arena. "I started a company because I didn't want to go into the corporate world," he says. At Microsoft in the summer of 1994, he worked on children's software, but to the eager Stanford graduate, the project lacked vision. "I sent an e-mail to Bill Gates and said I'm disappointed with the kind of software coming out of the kids group. We should be doing more aggressive and creative stuff. This is just a market ploy." Gates fired back a two-page e-mail defending the software and the process. "It was clear to me," says Kitch, "that what he was about was dominating the software world, and for that they had to have an educational entry. I was about changing the world."

In three years, KartoffelSoft had grown to about 30 employees and, as a consultant for children's software, brought in respectable revenues of $4 million annually. In late 1997 Kitch thought about applying some of the same principles to the Internet and spun out Homestead.com to help individuals create their own Websites. "We took the KartoffelSoft philosophy of empowering people with software but changed the application to building a Website," says Kitch. Homestead customers get elements for creating their Websites free. "We make money because we have a massive number of customers, so we're a distributor channel for advertisers." Homestead also collects a fee for transactions done through its site.

With the consulting business now profitable, Kitch didn't need venture capital to fund Homestead, but he realized that he did need the expertise and the recruiting help that venture capitalists bring. "My attitude about VCs changed as we became more focused on specific products and the Net," he says. After Homestead won an award at the 1998 Internet Showcase, a trade show featuring new Web-based products and services, "we got a lot of attention from venture capitalists," he says, including a letter from Kleiner Perkins expressing interest. But Kitch was reluctant to sign on with a VC firm that would take control. "We weren't looking to be somebody else's definition, which is what we would get with Kleiner or Sequoia," he says. "You can learn a lot about VC firms sitting in their lobby listening to the receptionist. Some of them are very partner-focused, and others are very company-focused." At many of the firms, "you get the feeling that this is our vision and here's how you can fit."

He raised a first round of venture capital in March 1998, taking $3.7 million from Draper Fisher Jurvetson (DFJ), plus another $800,000 from Intel as a corporate investor. "I picked the VC firm based on the personalities of the people there," he says. "DFJ would let us run the company but still be there when we needed them, helping us with contacts, industry buzz, and recruiting. I felt it was the right balance. Some of the other firms think it's their business and you're the agent for them." Homestead raised two more VC rounds, $18.5 million in April 1999 and $35 million in January 2000, before going public later in the year. Other investors included Institutional Venture Partners and Global Retail Partners. By August 2000 Homestead had 150 employees.

Through all the financing rounds, Kitch managed to retain voting control of his company. "The key with VCs is to have leverage, or they'll eat you up," he says. "I was able to retain control because I was profitable going in. I never do business when I don't have leverage." Kitch is savvy about the importance of leverage in dealing with venture capitalists. They are powerful personalities who put themselves into a position where they can take over the reins of an entrepreneurial venture when it isn't hitting the targets set in the business plan.

The VC-entrepreneur marriage opens with the all-important pitch process, an elaborate courtship that sets the stage for how the two parties will continue to relate. The entrepreneur's initial presentation of the idea is the prelude to asking for funding. The venture capitalist has several possible responses, including rejecting the idea outright, engaging in negotiation and refinement, and locking up the deal right away. The entrepreneur typically forges his or her closest relationship with the lead venture capitalist but must also be able to reach out to additional investors, including other venture capitalists as well as corporations. Raising money is a never-ending task for an entrepreneurial venture, even as it struggles to launch a product and meet its goals. Chapter 8 charts the rollercoaster-like ups and downs of several entrepreneurial companies as they cope with competition, market changes, and the demands of their VC investors.

CHAPTER EIGHT

Working Hard for the Money

As one entrepreneur told me, once you sign the check, the venture capitalist owns you. Indeed, in the original model, money was the predominant value added of the generalist venture capitalists who invested across the board in varying kinds of companies. Today the value added, especially for early-stage venture capitalists, lies in the expertise they supply to the company. The venture capital (VC) business has become one of specialists who bring "deep domain knowledge" to their companies. Former entrepreneurs are recruited into venture capital not only for their marquee value but also because they've been there, done that. A series of operating roles, rather than a purely financial background, is the preferred résumé at most early-stage VC firms. In this chapter, we'll see why.

Early-stage venture capitalists who trade money for a one-quarter to one-half chunk of a company are not content to be passive investors. Nor would any self-respecting entrepreneur give away so much of the company without something more than money added to the equation. A VC partner, usually the one who championed the entrepreneurial company in the first place, takes a seat on the board of the firm's new investment, becoming heavily involved in guiding the company's strategy and tactics as it grows. In the speeded-up business model of the Internet era, moving as fast as possible is critical, so the brand name and connections of the venture capitalist become an important tool in recruiting key team members and attracting partners and customers.

Venture capitalists are able to keep their hands in after they sign the first check because the company will need additional capital to fuel its growth. It must meet certain benchmarks—such as filling out the team, landing a certain number of customers, and launching a product—to earn each new round of funding at, hopefully, a stepped-up valuation. During the dot-com fallout of late 2000, many companies closed their doors when they were unable to generate follow-on VC rounds. As noted, early-stage venture capitalists prefer to invest alone in the first round; but in subsequent, larger rounds, they are eager to gain the stamp of approval of being able to attract other investors, including additional VC firms and highly regarded corporate participants such as Intel, Cisco, or Oracle. The early-stage VC firm will maintain its position by increasing its investment in later rounds, but will not do so by itself. The company's continued existence depends, then, on achieving the goals that not only keep its original VC firm on board but make it palatable to new investors as well.

Still, there is not one right way of growing a successful entrepreneurial company. The venture capitalist's level of involvement ranges from becoming virtual CEO of the company to showing up for occasional board meetings, and includes all stages in between. In fact, the venture capitalist's participation is driven by the experience of the entrepreneurial team. As you'd expect, greener teams demand more from their venture capitalists. But it's also true that many venture capitalists are would-be entrepreneurs at heart who get off on the thrill of building a company from scratch. They tend to gravitate toward situations where an inexperienced founder might not have the muscle or the will to fend off a heavy-handed venture capitalist.

FANNING THE FLAMES AT FIREDROP

The strategy and even the organizational look and feel of Fire-Drop/Zaplet, the enhanced e-mail company introduced in Chapter 7, were heavily influenced by lead VC investor Vinod Khosla of Kleiner Perkins. There are worse people to be influenced by; Khosla has hit more home runs recently than any other venture capitalist, including the more lauded John Doerr. But when Khosla is your investor and board member, you tend to follow his script. David Roberts puts it delicately: "Many VCs invest in a lot of companies knowing that one success will pay for dozens of losers. I don't think Kleiner has that strategy. Vinod is careful about how he spends his time. He can have very high participation levels."

At first, cofounders Roberts and Brian Axe were just excited to get such a highly regarded venture capitalist. "I wasn't concerned about [Kleiner's] cookie-cutter reputation because I didn't know about it," says Roberts. "What I was thinking about was how they had been able to create companies like Amazon. I had no idea how involved they would become." But 10 months later, by mid-2000, he had ceased regarding Kleiner as an *investor.* An associate at the firm corrected him when he used the term. "We're partners," the associate told him. Khosla became even more than that. During this period of the company's existence, Roberts speaks to Khosla every day, and "95 percent of the time he is calling me," the entrepreneur reports. After every conversation, "I'll have so many action items I'm worried. He will remember every one and two days later he's calling me to ask about them." Roberts has learned not to expect positive feedback. "If I send Vinod an e-mail with 20 things that I've done, his message back is what happened to this one that I didn't do." Khosla also spends about a half a day every week with the staff, having one-on-one conversations with people in the company as well as with other entrepreneurs and experts outside it. "It astounds me that he has any other company besides this one," says Roberts.

His eyes were opened when, at his public relation firm's behest, he flew out to New York to join the venture capitalist at an analysts' meeting. It turned out that the meeting was actually about optical networks, where they were going and why they were important. It was a topic that Roberts knew nothing about. "I was wondering what I was doing there," he says. Khosla gave a well-reasoned presentation on optical networks (Kleiner's investments in the sector include ONI Systems, Cerent, and Corvis) and then segued smoothly into FireDrop: "What FireDrop is doing will raise the need for bandwidth for the entire world." Roberts was awed by Khosla's ability to integrate two very different worlds: "I remember once seeing my father sit down at the piano and play Bach. I didn't even know he played. I had that same exact feeling with Vinod—how expert he was in this other field."

Neither Roberts nor Axe ever took the title of chief executive officer, because the company had already launched its search for a veteran manager. Until the position was filled, which took nine months, Khosla was the virtual CEO. "He is the architect of our strategy," says Roberts. "He usually tells me what he wants to do because we're in a hurry and there's so much ground to cover." One example was Khosla's insistence that FireDrop change from a functional organization to separate business units for each market area it was targeting. "Vinod wanted the business units to function independently," says Roberts, each with its own engineering team and its own sales and marketing staffs. This was opposed by most of the management team, so Roberts initially resisted the change. At his request, Khosla came in to explain his reasoning, which was that FireDrop had a wide-open application development environment that could be applied to many different fields. In a functional organization the managers would be tripping over each other trying to figure out which customers to service. Khosla's structure would force each unit to focus on a particular customer, including consumer, e-business, small and medium business, e-commerce, and dot-coms. And that's what FireDrop did.

"In a way we're both leading the company but standing on different hills with different views," says Roberts of himself and Khosla. "The combination is synergistic." But after too often finding himself in the middle between Khosla, who wanted to go one way, and the staff, who wanted to go another, Roberts told the senior staff to deal directly with Khosla. Then the two of them talk. Roberts uses a Star Wars analogy to describe Khosla's ability to get people to follow him. "He has the force with him," says Roberts. "Remember in Star Wars the heroes had a mind trick. They would tell the guards, 'These aren't the droids you're looking for.' The guards would then reply, 'These aren't the droids we're looking for.' Vinod tells the staff, 'You guys need to do this deal.' The staff comes back to me and says, 'We need to do this deal'."

Through almost a year of working closely with Khosla, Roberts has learned when he can push back and when he can't. "The difficulty with Vinod is sensing when something is very important to him and when it isn't. He tends to have the same level of passion and determination in communicating when he likes it a lot or a little." The best way to find out what's key to Khosla is through inaction, he has found. "If it's not important to him it will die. If it is he'll keep asking." For instance, Khosla wanted to bring in a manager whom he thought would be good for the company, but some of the staff didn't think the candidate was a good cultural fit. Roberts put off hiring the guy until he was picked up by another company, and Khosla finally backed off.

Another historic Kleiner strength is recruitment, and Khosla has been active in that role as well. He directly helped to recruit two people to the senior staff, "and all of them were attracted by Vinod's and Kleiner's reputation," says Roberts. Kleiner sets high standards. When the founders wanted to bring in a vice president of business development who had previously run sales at a $1 billion public company, "Kleiner didn't feel he was good enough. They wanted me to hire him at a lower title, but he wouldn't come for that." However, thanks to Kleiner's reputation, FireDrop's adviser/investor list is unequalled and includes Bill Joy and Andy Bectolsheim, two of the original founders of Sun Microsystems; Art Kern, a board member from Yahoo; and industry pundit Esther Dyson.

In July 2000 Khosla used his connections and his persistence to land a high-profile CEO for FireDrop, Alan Baratz, who had formerly run Sun Microsystems' Java software business and then left to become managing director at investment firm Warburg Pincus. He had spent only a few months at Warburg when Khosla came knocking at his door. "Vinod was very tenacious with Alan," says Roberts. "He first spoke to him in November, and Alan said he was happy at Warburg." But Khosla kept calling, urging Baratz to at least look at FireDrop as an investment, and at last Baratz agreed to meet with the management team and see the technology. "Vinod got him in the door, and he found what we were doing very exciting," says Roberts. In fact, what FireDrop is attempting to do with its e-mail Zaplets—establish a platform that others will build on—is the same thing that Baratz was doing with Sun's Java technology.

Opting for someone with a technology rather than a marketing background, FireDrop whittled down a list of 150 CEO candidates to arrive at Baratz. "When you hand over your whole company to one person, you really want to be sure," says Roberts. "What is wonderful about Baratz is that he has been through a platform play with Java. He's articulate and incredibly smart, especially in terms of being able to look at complex situations and focus in on what we need to do." Roberts, who now has the title Chief Zaplet, says he will do whatever the company needs him to do. Axe has also stayed on board, helping to lead strategic initiatives. Once Baratz came in as CEO, Khosla became much less active, which is as it should be. Says Roberts, "Alan has to be able to come in without previous conceptions, take a new fresh look at everything, and come up with his own areas of focus."

Roberts described his relationship with Khosla as that of an athlete with a passionately involved coach. "Vinod has unquestionably changed the company for the better," he says. As of late 2000, Fire-Drop's head count was just over 200 people, and the company was on the fast track to an initial public offering (IPO). In October it changed its name to Zaplet and repositioned itself to focus on delivering its technology to large companies, with plans to launch a new software package in 2001. FireDrop/Zaplet also closed a $90 million funding round that brought in such investors as Integral Capital, Amerindo Investment Advisors, and the partners of Credit Suisse First Boston and Robertson Stephens. On the corporate side, Cisco, Novell, Oracle, Research in Motion, and Andersen Consulting's VC arm have come in.

"I've learned to trust Vinod's experience even though what he suggests is not necessarily what I would have done," Roberts says. "He's been right in so many cases," such as in his insistence that FireDrop could do a thousand times the business that Roberts and Axe originally projected. "We've already done the thousandfold. Vinod is the master." With hindsight, says Roberts, this kind of VC/founder relationship works "as long as the founders are comfortable with the idea that the investors become part of their team. Kleiner becomes part of a new kind of management structure which may be unique to them. They participate very directly in running the company."

PLUMBING THE HEIGHTS WITH PLUMTREE

San Francisco–based Plumtree Software wants to be the Yahoo of corporate Websites, so it's only fitting that the company was funded by the same VC firm that backed Yahoo: Sequoia Capital. Plumtree (the name is a reference from James Joyce's *Ulysses*) has a typical pedigree: It was founded in February 1997 by a group that departed from database giant Informix when it decided not to pursue the group's project. "We wanted to build a Web desktop for corporate users that would show them everything important to them," says Glenn Kelman, founder and vice president of marketing. "Informix wasn't interested, so we left." Kelman, nearing 30, is not the hotshot engineer you usually find breaking away to start a company. With a BA in English from the University of California at Berkeley (he came up with the literary name of his company), Kelman tells me that he really wanted to be a writer and got into entrepreneurial ventures literally by accident. Destitute as a writer, he was working as a bicycle messenger when he crashed and broke all the fingers of his right hand. That's when he wound up working in technology.

Although Plumtree is in San Francisco's financial district rather than Silicon Valley, it has all the trappings of a Valley start-up—from the cubicles where everyone is bent over his or her computer to the cardboard cutout of Superman on the second floor to the blond male receptionist with a nose ring. In the tiny kitchen the vending machines dispense free candy, snacks, and sodas.

Like FireDrop/Zaplet, Plumtree is a creation of both its founders and the venture capitalist who, for a time, took the helm of the company: Sequoia's Pierre Lamond. The hawk-faced Frenchman's roots go back to the very genesis of Silicon Valley: Fairchild Semiconductor. Then Lamond, who's just about old enough to be Kelman's grandfather, had a series of executive positions in the semiconductor industry before joining Sequoia in 1981. Sequoia had funded Kelman's original company, Stanford Technology Group, which was acquired by Informix, so it was natural for Plumtree to return to the VC firm. "Sequoia has a weakness for ideas and markets," says Kelman. "Other investors wouldn't have had the confidence to invest in our idea. They would have felt the management team wasn't complete, but Sequoia has a peculiar arrogance that management is interchangeable." He adds, "I never had the vanity to think they liked me personally. Or if I did it was dispelled quickly."

Plumtree had little problem obtaining its initial financing. Lamond, who had championed the company, told the founders that Sequoia was committed before they even made the presentation to the whole partnership. "I went into the presentation at Sequoia, and no one was paying attention to us," says Kelman. "Don [Valentine] was writing a note to someone who had sent flowers. . . . They called us later and said the check's in the mail." Sequoia put in $550,000 in a seed round, followed by another $1 million on completion of a prototype product. Says Lamond, "With Plumtree, we invested in a concept. We all suffer from information explosion. How to organize the information you get and how you limit the input to the truly useful was the premise of the company. It was only an idea. The team put meat on it."

But first there were a few bumps along the way, notably when the original chief executive of Plumtree, one of the founders, decided to leave the company in mid-1998 at a critical juncture. Plumtree was trying to raise $4 million in follow-on financing, and its CEO was departing. Not a good thing. Kelman, who was a close friend of the CEO, acknowledges that "it was apparent he wasn't the one to do it. He starts things but he doesn't finish." On the night before the presentation to Sequoia for the new financing, Kelman knew that his friend was on his way out. "I had just told Pierre that everything was solid, and I was miserable," he says, concerned that he would be misrepresenting the company if he didn't talk about the CEO's departure but afraid to betray a friend's confidence. He telephoned his friend and said he had to tell Lamond the truth. "I called Pierre and said, 'We have a problem, and I assume you won't fund the company.'" Kelman was already picturing how he would have to drive to nearby college campuses and tell his new recruits that he wouldn't be hiring them after all. But Lamond reassured him, "Don't worry about it. We'll still fund the company." At the presentation, though, tough-talking Sequoia partner Doug Leone was openly skeptical: "My ears are falling off, sitting there on the floor, because I don't see where your fucking revenues are coming from," he told Kelman.

For this round Lamond wanted to bring in other investors, and not every VC firm is as sanguine about the interchangeability of leadership as Sequoia is. In the spring and summer of 1998 Lamond and Kelman drove around Sand Hill Road trying to raise the rest of the money. "It was just Pierre and this 27-year-old kid." Lamond drove his own car, a 1997 BMW 540, since the alternative was Kelman's beat-up Honda Civic, which the latter had purchased to spruce up his image. Until then, Kelman had lived the carefree "Berkeley granola life" with few possessions. "I didn't want to ride my bicycle over to Sequoia," recalls Kelman, "but Pierre liked to drive his own car." Even with the improvement in transportation, Plumtree wasn't an easy sell. The demo kept crashing; the potential investors kept squirming. Lamond would calmly say, "I think you should invest in this company." At that moment, Kelman realized, "This guy has the right stuff." He asked Lamond why he didn't pull out of the deal. Lamond replied, "Because you were so fanatical that this would work."

During the push for the financing round, Kelman felt like he was bluffing without any cards. Nonetheless, he knew better than to show weakness or doubt around Lamond, because that might have convinced him to dump the company, or at least the founder. "If you ever waver with Sequoia, it's not as though they're going to pat you on the back and send you on your way. You have to have strong convictions," says Kelman. Every once in a while, Lamond would ask him, "Do you still believe in this? If not I'm going to walk out the door." To Kelman, it was obvious that Sequoia was determined not to let Plumtree fail solely because it was a Sequoia company. "They weren't going to watch us sink like a whale turd to the bottom of the sea and have people say that was a Sequoia company."

Kelman remembers Lamond's unusual method of motivating him to stick with it. During the dog days, while he was waiting for a meeting with the venture capitalist, Kelman overheard Lamond chewing out another CEO on the telephone. "He made a point of keeping me in the room while he talked to this CEO, who had been about where we were with his company. I thought we were this unhappy family with this unique problem. Then I hear this guy vacillating about the same kind of thing. After Pierre finished chewing this guy out, he hangs up and says to me, 'Another one I pulled from the ashes, just like you.'"

In large part because of Sequoia's reputation, Plumtree did manage to raise its $4 million in mid-1988. Sequoia, which put in $2.5 million, was joined by two other investors, investment bank Hambrecht & Quist's venture arm and a new firm, Red Rock Ventures. "If we didn't have Pierre, we couldn't have done it," says Kelman. Meanwhile, Lamond had launched a major CEO search and was in effect the acting chief executive for about eight months. "I kept the company alive and put it on the right track," he says with no pretense of modesty. "It takes a lot of time and effort to run a company. One might argue that the return on investment is not warranted. I like it, but I don't want to do it full-time."

He didn't have to, because by August 1998 Lamond had convinced John Kunze, a longtime veteran of Adobe Systems who had risen to become vice president of its Internet products division, to join Plumtree as CEO. Kunze, in his mid-thirties, is rather laid-back, a calming contrast to Kelman's intensity. He acknowledges that Sequoia's rep was what induced him to take the headhunter's call. "When Pierre invites you, you take the meeting." Kunze had been with

Adobe since 1985, when it was only 30 people, and was now searching for another start-up. "I was looking for a company in a marketplace I could be passionate about. I wanted one backed by A+ VCs, but also with a chemistry and culture where I had a good fit."

Plumtree seemed to have all of that. "I was happier joining a company that was already started," says Kunze. "I like to build teams and guide the process." Once he was on board, Lamond disengaged himself from the day-to-day operations. "He wanted to give me some room to work," says Kunze. "He promised me, 'It will be your company, not mine.'" Kunze's task was formidable, but it's one that any entrepreneurial CEO is charged with: Help the company get traction, and move from zero to meaningful revenues. When it didn't happen soon enough for Lamond, he told the Plumtree team at the beginning of one board meeting, "I left the Uzi in the trunk, or I would have lined you up and shot you all."

As of late 2000 Plumtree had 147 licensed customers, including Kmart, BP Amoco, and Pharmacia, and 180 employees. It posted $3.8 million in revenue in the first quarter, $4.9 million in the second quarter, and $8.7 million in the third, above its announced expectation of 20 percent quarter-over-quarter growth, and was en route to an IPO in early 2001. Once traction happened and Plumtree's IPO was imminent, the intensity picked up noticeably. "There's now this frenzy of excitement at the board meetings," with everyone anticipating the public offering, says Kunze. He acknowledges, "The strength of Sequoia has helped make this company what it is today."

FINDING THE BALANCE: WORKS.COM

The Kleiner and Sequoia model of deep involvement with their companies is not the only way to go. In fact, when Bo Holland started his company, Works.com, an Internet business purchasing service based in Austin, Texas, he was determined to avoid the hands-on VC approach. As a senior manager at struggling Citrix Systems, he had watched Kleiner's John Doerr take over. "Citrix was in deep trouble," Holland acknowledges. "We ran out of money several times. John Doerr helped us find a business model that worked. The company had completely lost control, and all the decisions were made by the venture capitalists."

Although he admits that Citrix wouldn't have made it without Doerr asserting his leadership, Holland wanted to run his own show. When he founded Works.com in 1997, "we saw the opportunity to take big technologies and deliver them to small companies by building Internet-based services." The idea of making software a shared resource delivered via the Internet, rather than a costly in-house purchase, was a fairly new one in 1997, although it has since mushroomed into the ubiquitous application service provider (ASP). But Works.com was a pioneer that developed a new architecture for software delivery and now runs a purchasing service with 4,000 customers, delivering a new application capability every six weeks.

Works.com got $750,000 in seed funding from an individual investor, then visited California to look for a VC firm. Holland and his team wound up presenting to Hummer Winblad Venture Partners, with whom former investment bank analyst Bill Gurley had recently signed. "We met with a lot of VCs who turned their noses up at our service model and didn't get it," says Holland. "Bill got it." Several weeks later Hummer Winblad became the lead investor in a $3.5 million first round that also included a local Austin firm, Trellis Partners. Because Gurley had come from the public market side, "he had great intuition about what's going to be significant and how we could prepare to become a public company," recalls Holland. But probably to the entrepreneur's relief, Gurley didn't have any operating experience and thus showed little inclination to become involved in running the company.

"Bill prefers the suggestion mode to the ordering mode, although there are levels of suggestion stronger than others," says Holland. For instance, the venture capitalist came up with the idea of charging a simple transaction fee, rather than some fixed monthly rate, for Works.com's service. "This becomes our customers' purchasing mechanism for everything they want to buy. We just add our fee," says Holland.

Then Gurley, in a surprise move, left Hummer Winblad in March 1999 to go to Benchmark Capital, which had a competing investment to Works.com with Ariba. Gurley called Holland to tell him of the change and assure him that he wanted to keep the relationship with Works.com intact. "It was a bizarre situation," says Holland. "I felt like the child of a divorce." But Hummer's John Hummer and Benchmark's Bob Kagle worked out a deal that allowed Gurley to continue representing Hummer's investment and sit on Works.com's board. Although Kagle is on the board of Ariba, he and Gurley "have a Chinese wall; they don't talk about what Works.com and Ariba are doing," says Holland. "I couldn't be more impressed with the integrity."

He feels like the VC firms played their proper role at Works.com, unlike what they did at Citrix. "The VC world is about sifting through tons of information and new ideas," Holland says. "It's very difficult for them to map back to the daily operations of a company. You've just barely begun executing on the ideas from last time when they come up with a new one, so you end up doing a lot more tacking than you should." Ideally, he believes, "you want a strong management team to balance out a strong VC. You need the separation of church and state so you're not just tracking the ideas instead of executing. If one side or the other is weak, it doesn't work." Even as a board member, the venture capitalist should stick to looking for new ideas, while the management should run the company, he says. And that balance has been maintained at Works.com, which in mid-2000 completed a large purchasing agreement with Dell Computer and a partial merger with W. W. Grainger, a provider of business maintenance and repair services, that left it in good shape for a planned IPO.

TAKING A SMOOTHER ROAD

Another company that seems to have achieved the right balance with its venture capital investors is @Road, a Fremont, California–based company that provides wireless services to fleets of mobile vehicles. Although lead investor Stu Phillips, of U.S. Venture Partners (USVP), never had to step in to run the company, he helped initiate a critical repositioning that thrust @Road into a large and underserved market.

In August 1998 Taiwan entrepreneur Rod Fan approached Phillips with an idea to bring global positioning system (GPS) technology to the fleet business. By bouncing signals off satellites orbiting the Earth, GPS can pinpoint the location of a vehicle or anything else carrying the right equipment. Fan, whose background was in semiconductors, had been involved with a company building GPS chip sets, but the price for that technology had dropped sharply to commodity levels. Fan wanted to start a new business selling GPS to companies with large, mobile fleets.

Phillips did some due diligence and discovered that even though there seemed to be a huge need for technology that would tell a moving company or a postal delivery service where all its trucks were, the landscape was littered with the bones of dead companies that had tried to do just that. Wireless giant Qualcomm did have a $700 million line of business called Omnitrak, providing a location-messaging service to about 300,000 long-haul vehicles. But with 43 million commercial vehicles in the United States, Qualcomm's 300,000 "was a drop in the bucket," says Phillips. He called customers of one failed company and was told that they had bought from a succession of now-bankrupt entities and were still in the market for a solution. "If there's such a strong need, it's clear there's a big market," says Phillips. Why, then, had no one been successful? It turned out that the failed companies had tried to build out their own infrastructure, in effect a cellular business parallel to the wireless carriers.

Phillips and Fan seized upon a simple but apparently so-far unused solution: They would partner with the wireless carriers and reposition @Road as a service provider. This accomplished two things: @Road would avoid the tremendous build-out costs of the failed companies, and instead of a onetime sale, it could collect a continuing revenue stream from monthly licensing fees. "@Road would have no infrastructure requirements," says Phillips. "They could use the government's GPS system, the U.S. cellular network, and the Internet. They get to leverage infrastructure somebody else has paid for. And once you sell this service, you own your customer."

There were three pieces to the business: equipment for each vehicle, a massive database to keep track of everything, and a series of applications such as two-way messaging and maintenance reports. @Road develops and maintains the database and partners with other firms on the equipment and the applications. With a lower cost structure, @Road could also target mid-sized fleets that had not been well served by previous GPS vendors. With that business plan in place, USVP invested $3 million and was joined by Institutional Venture Partners (IVP), which also put in $3 million. Each VC firm took 20 percent of the company and one board seat. "We all shared a broad vision of what we could accomplish," says Phillips. "The total market worldwide is 300 million vehicles."

One thing that remained to be settled was who would lead @Road. Like many technology visionaries, Fan was better at being a chief technology officer than a CEO. Unlike many of them, he knew it. "Rod told me, 'I'm not the guy to run this company,'" Phillips recalls. "We started off with a clear agreement: hire a CEO." @Road launched a CEO search and found a candidate, Krish Panu, who had experience in both the chip and wireless industries. The IVP venture capitalist on @Road's board, Pete Thomas, had also been on the board of Atmel, where Panu was a vice president and general manager. "I had multiple choices about where to go," says Panu. What drew him to @Road was the promise made by Thomas and Phillips that "this will be your own show; you run the company."

The stolid, round-faced Panu has more than 20 years of technology experience, although his dark hair shows only a trace of gray. In mid-2000, when I interview him at a complex that @Road will soon be leaving for larger quarters, he's readying his PowerPoint presentation for the IPO road show and is eager to try it out on me. (The IPO would be delayed by public market conditions until later in the year.) Unfortunately, his laptop computer won't project onto the big screen, so I sit beside him to look at the slides. @Road is positioning itself smartly as an Internet services company. "The next phase of the Internet is distribution," says Panu, which demands location-specific information of the type that @Road's data center provides. At this time, @Road has grown to 260 people, nearly all of them hired in the past year, and has raised a total of $63 million in four funding rounds. It also has strategic marketing agreements with such major wireless carriers and equipment makers as AT&T, Ameritech, Bell Atlantic, GTE (now Verizon), and Ericsson. Leading chip maker Intel is both a partner and an investor.

Panu believes that @Road, which has patented its technology for connecting GPS to the Internet, has tremendous opportunities. Potential customers include everyone from school bus operators to limo fleets to any business that has cars, vans, or trucks that move. @Road is also moving toward the rollout of personal location services, partnering with automakers to provide consumers with a smart vehicle hub that always lets them know where they are. Panu is satisfied with his low-key but high-performance venture investors. "A good business model doesn't require a rock star," he says. "You have to build a strong technology base, deliver revenues, show consistency. I'm very happy with the people we have. They're trying to build the company, not hype it. The flash doesn't last. You have to build a solid foundation for a multibillion-dollar company."

@Road managed to go public in September 2000, selling 7 million shares for $9 apiece and raising $63 million in a deal led by Credit Suisse First Boston. Buffeted by tough conditions in the stock market, @Road finished the first day of trading at $7.19 and, by December, had dropped below $2 a share. Such were the travails of a newly public high-tech company after the sea change in public attitude during the second half of 2000.

VENTURE CAPITALISTS AS THE ENEMY

Venture capitalists make good friends, but bad enemies. As we've seen in the preceding examples, they can be harsh, manipulative, self-serving, and tyrannical. And that's when they're on your side! One of the worst things an entrepreneur can do is to run afoul of his or her venture capitalist, because that is usually a prelude to getting black-listed—not only dumped from your present company but possibly barred from future opportunities. As Zaplet's Dave Roberts saw it, you take your career in your hands when you cross someone like Vinod Khosla. Most of the entrepreneurs I interviewed, although they might complain of too much interference from venture capitalists, universally agreed that they could not have made it without them. And to have any shot at another entrepreneurial gig, they needed the venture capitalist's recommendation. Young and heady entrepreneurs like to take the bit in their teeth and run the company entirely their way, but the older guys know better.

Take Hugh Martin, the CEO of ONI Systems whose successful IPO was described in Chapter 1. Before coming to ONI, Martin had more than 20 years of experience with entrepreneurial companies, starting in 1980 with a now-forgotten minicomputer company called Ridge Computers. Ridge had impeccable credentials: it was funded by the legendary Arthur Rock and Bill Hambrecht, who was a power in both venture capital and investment banking. Martin, who was 24 years old when Ridge started, wound up in charge of research and development. During Ridge's eight tempestuous years before it closed its doors, he learned a lot about dealing with venture capitalists. "The management at Ridge made a mistake in coming to view Art and Bill as adversaries," says Martin. "The only time the VCs exert control is when they think their investments are at risk." Maybe listening to the venture capitalists would have made a difference; maybe not in Ridge's case. Minicomputer companies were a dime a dozen in the 1980s. The industry acronym for all the start-ups was JAWS, or just another workstation (company).

Despite the turmoil, however, Martin did not burn his bridges. He came out of Ridge with lasting connections that would land him a position at his next company, Apple, where Rock was on the board and where he would wind up meeting with Kleiner Perkins. That led him eventually to ONI. "The biggest mistake young entrepreneurs make is to see the venture capitalist as an antagonist," says Martin. "The value of venture capital partners is their advice and connections. If you're completely adversarial, you can't take advantage of either one."

The companies described in this chapter were readying themselves for the all-important IPO. Next, we'll see how these liquidity events actually come about as the VC investors let their portfolio companies fly off on their own and reap big bucks when they do. We'll also get a glimpse into the important role that investment bankers play in handling this transition from private to public company and discover why a viable public market is essential to entrepreneurial success.

CHAPTER NINE

A Partnership Made in Liquidity

Like the limited partners on one side of the venture capital (VC) money spectrum, the investment bankers on the other side have a symbiotic relationship with venture capitalists. For venture capital to succeed, it must have a way of reaping the investments that it sows in entrepreneurial companies. First, that requires a public market that will embrace new companies—notably the Nasdaq, which has become the leading global marketplace for technology ventures, although regional exchanges exist in London, Hong Kong, Tokyo, and elsewhere. Second, it requires investment bankers, or underwriters, who manage the intense, complex process of turning a private company into a public one. As we saw in Chapter 1 with ONI Systems' emergence, that process is exhausting, fraught with regulatory conditions, and uncertain. Once the entrepreneurial venture is "out" in the public market, investors' whims drive the share price and the company's prospects.

Investment bankers and VC firms may need each other, but that doesn't mean they always like each other. Some venture capitalists view the investment bankers as johnny-come-latelies who swoop in to collect their 7 percent fee on the IPO proceeds after the heavy lifting has been done. "I would rather see a dentist or a proctologist than an investment banker," snarls Sequoia's Don Valentine, who's very open in proclaiming his disdain for the banking industry. "Investment bankers have invented rape and pillage. The entrepreneur works 12 hours a day for years to build the company. The investment bankers come in and charge us 7 percent. It's a monopoly pricing structure." Most of Valentine's peers would not put it quite so bluntly. "Clearly, investment banks have a vital function," says the more diplomatic Mark Gorenberg, of Hummer Winblad Venture Partners. Not only do the banks take companies public, but they manage follow-on offerings (mergers and acquisitions) and help in strategic positioning. Perhaps most importantly, once a company is public, the investment banks are home to the research analysts, such as Morgan Stanley's Mary Meeker or Merrill Lynch's Henry Blodgett, whose opinions can literally make or break a company.

Besides, today the same shift that occurred with the limited partners has occurred with the investment bankers: Both groups admit that the balance of power right now rests with the venture capitalists, especially the top tier, and their start-ups. Companies with investors like Kleiner Perkins or Sequoia can compel the investment banks to compete in staged beauty contests or bake-offs for the right to take these hot deals public. On the other hand, landing a gold-standard investment bank as the lead underwriter, as opposed to a more obscure second-tier bank, helps brand the initial public offering (IPO) and goose the share price.

Turnover in the VC industry has been mild compared to what's happening in investment banking, where consolidation has driven all of the investment bank pioneers in technology into the embrace of larger entities, with varying degrees of success. "There's a greater gap today between the haves and have nots of the investment banking world," says Cristina Morgan, codirector of investment banking at Chase H&Q (renamed JP Morgan H&Q at the end of 2000). "You have boutique businesses on one side, and on the other, you have the behemoths. It's very painful to be in the middle. You're too big to be small and too small to be big." There is now a growing separation between the large, full-service, global banks, and the smaller, boutique players that once did the bulk of technology deals.

THE BAKE-OFF

To get a sense of the investment bank selection process, let's return to Plumtree Software, introduced in Chapter 8. The San Francisco–based company provides corporate portal software, which lets companies create customized desktops for employees and customers. For a while Plumtree had struggled to get financing, but once it hired a permanent chief executive and began to land important customers, revenues ramped up, and it was hot. You know you're hot in the Bay Area when outsiders sense you're nearing an IPO and want to get in on the deal. Says CEO John Kunze, "As we moved along in our funding, my garbage man asked me for [stock] warrants. Our landlord wanted warrants to expand our lease."

In June 2000 Plumtree had raised $23 million in mezzanine funding, traditionally the last financing round before an IPO. Kunze says that solid growth in the previous three quarters helped turn once-reluctant investors into enthusiastic competitors to get into the round. "Our model is to plan for 20 percent compounded quarterly growth and plan expenses accordingly," he says. Mezzanine investors included Ford, Procter & Gamble, and Credit Suisse First Boston (CSFB), along with previous funders Sequoia Capital and Granite Ventures, which is affiliated with the JP Morgan H&Q investment bank. But there was one more impediment before Plumtree could start the IPO countdown: It needed a world-class chief financial officer. As we saw with ONI Systems, that position is critical to the IPO process. And none of the three gold-standard technology underwriters that Plumtree wanted as its lead bank—Morgan Stanley Dean Witter, Goldman Sachs, or CSFB—would get serious without that position filled.

Plumtree launched a five-month search, using top headhunter Ramsay Beirne along with Sequoia's in-house recruiter, and snagged Eric Borrmann, who was the number two financial guy at Network Associates, a company in the same enterprise software arena as Plumtree. Borrmann also had experience running a European operation. He accepted the offer in June and joined Plumtree the next month. In August Plumtree picked its lineup of bankers: CSFB as the lead, with Robertson Stephens and Dean Rauscher Wessels as the co-managers. An important deal will have three or four banks on its prospectus, with the lead bank on the left.

"It's absolutely critical to have a gold-standard bank as the lead," says Kunze. "Their competitors will all say they can give you an equally high-quality deal and have as good a distribution, but there's not the same brand appeal." Any company hot enough to be courted by the Big Three in technology is more than likely going to pick one of them. Another vital consideration for a company is assuring itself of top analyst coverage after the IPO, when it can get lost in the noise of all the newly public entities. That's why companies prefer three to four underwriters on a deal, because those banks' analysts will follow them when they're public. CSFB's analyst Brent Thill, who covers Internet and infrastructure companies, pitched hard for the Plumtree deal. "He met with us seven or eight times to make sure he understood what we were doing," says Kunze. "You have to have a high-quality analyst who's willing to back you, who's credible with investors, and who can stand up and present your vision, your plan, and your company as well as you could."

Among the top three, "you assume you have parity in distribution and brand," says Kunze. That is, all three can attract a broad range of high-quality institutional investors who will buy in at the initial offering. What tips the scale is the analyst's interest and the bank's ability to commit to the company. For example, he notes, if the bank has too many other IPOs in the pipeline, it might not be able to give Plumtree its full attention. "You want them to bring you out on the schedule you want." Among the five or six banks competing for the lead position on Plumtree, CSFB had the inside track because it had already handled the company's mezzanine financing round and knew the business. Still, it was not a slam dunk, as can be seen by analyst Thill's efforts to make sure his bank got the deal. The venture capitalists also play a role in the selection process, although the ultimate decision is the company's. Kunze singled out Sequoia's Pierre Lamond and Granite's Ruepen Dolasia as being especially helpful in evaluating the prospective lead bankers.

Founder Glenn Kelman adds that Lamond was very patient during Plumtree's growing pains. The company had originally intended to do its IPO in the first half of 2000, but Nasdaq's plunge derailed that. While many venture capitalists were panicking and pulling out of companies that couldn't go public, Sequoia stuck by Plumtree. "Pierre [Lamond] used to say the [market] pendulum swings back and forth," says Kelman. "He'd tell me, 'If you hire responsibly and stay lean, it's always easier to get fatter than to go on a diet.'" However, notes John Hogan, Plumtree's vice president of engineering, it was also evident that Sequoia wouldn't hesitate to dump the company if it misstepped during the IPO delay. "It's easy to get lulled into the feeling that the VCs are this altruistic group here to help you," he says. "They will be out of the back door if things go south. They're in business to make money."

During the IPO countdown, the CEO, not the venture capitalists or the rest of the executive team, emerges as the key figure for the company. "The IPO is a kingmaking process for the CEO," says Kelman. "When we were selecting our investment bank there were 70 people in the room, but only one person was talking: the CEO, who gets watched very closely." Whereas a private company is more of a team endeavor, "the lines of power are clarified in a public company. The CEO has to be the only spokesperson," he says. Of necessity, that meant that Kunze removed himself from much of the day-to-day operations and took on more of a publicly visible role.

Assuming that technology stocks on Nasdaq did not continue their free fall, Plumtree was planning an IPO in 2001. On August 24, 2000, it had the "org meeting," the formal triggering event of the IPO countdown. At that meeting, says Kunze, "the banks come, the auditors come, and the lawyers come." The group reviews all the logistics, and Kunze stages an early version of the road-show presentation. Once the organizational meeting has occurred, Plumtree and its lawyers, auditors, and bankers will have two drafting sessions per week on the prospectus until it's complete. Then the road show will occur, and the lead banker, CSFB, will set a target price, followed immediately by the IPO.

Says Kelman, "You learn to be very sensitive to any delays by the investment bank. If you're a hot deal, they'll murder, rape, and steal to drive it through." In a bleak period for IPOs, Plumtree's deal was hot because "we're an only child," he says. Nonetheless, "up until the day you price, you never stop selling your banks [on your prospects]. You want them to keep telling their salespeople that this is the hottest stock offering going. CS First Boston would walk today if this was a turkey and we were going to make them look bad." The IPO process is an emotional buildup designed to draw in the investment bank salespeople, who will in turn convince the institutional investors.

Expecting he'd be heading a public company by 2001, Kunze was cautious about making any "forward-looking statements," which are proscribed by the Securities and Exchange Commission, on the company's prospects. "We've been counseled by the banks that we've got to be profitable within four to six quarters of the offering, and we're following that counsel," he says. "No longer are investors interested in investing in an idea with the hope and prayer that management can turn it into a business plan."

THE GOLD STANDARD

You'll seldom see any of the top three banks on the right of the prospectus, that is, taking a nonlead position. Goldman Sachs, Morgan Stanley, and CSFB all told me they were somewhere north of 80 percent in taking the lead role, which encompasses organizing the road show and handling the pricing. The lead banker does get a financial payoff, although that's not the only reason to jockey for the position. Remember, the underwriters together take 7 percent of the proceeds from the offering at the announced price. For instance, ONI Systems had an initial price of $25 per share and was raising a total of $200 million, of which its four banks took $14 million. Generally, the lead banker gets 45 percent to 60 percent on a deal with three underwriters, and 40 percent to 50 percent on a four-handed deal. It's customary for the share of the proceeds to decline slightly as you read from left to right on the prospectus. Thus, a typical split might be 50–30–20 on an IPO with three underwriters, or 40–30–20–10 on a four-handed deal.

As in the VC world, the investment bankers zealously guard their reputation and vie furiously to lead the best deals, for the IPOs are branding events not only for the companies, but for the banks as well. Being the lead on an IPO positions the bank to handle the company's follow-on financings, mergers and acquisitions, and other financially rewarding transactions (see Figures 9.1 and 9.2). The Big Three investment banks got there in much the same way that the top-tier VC firms did: through consistency and sustainability. Morgan Stanley, Goldman Sachs, and CSFB were not the first to see the value of the new economy companies; that honor belongs to the boutique San Francisco investment banks, notably Hambrecht & Quist (H&Q), Montgomery Securities, and Robertson Stephens, which grew up alongside the technology industry. (From the East Coast, Alex Brown, which opened an office in San Francisco, was also an early player in technology.) But the white-shoe New York–based banks came on with a rush into Silicon Valley, establishing offices on Sand Hill Road or in nearby Palo Alto. And they could offer a breadth of services—such as debt financing, retail trading capability, and global presence—that the expanding technology industry increasingly required.

Through the early 1980s, technology was an esoteric niche for the major investment banks, says Brad Koenig, managing director of investment banking at Goldman Sachs' bustling Sand Hill Road office. Over the next decade, with the emergence of such companies as Microsoft, Intel, Apple, and Sun Microsystems, the New York banks began to take notice, although they were still laggards in going after the business. Then the Internet exploded on the scene in the mid-1990s, triggering an outpouring of new companies and new IPOs. According to Koenig's figures, there were 100 Internet IPOs between 1994 and 1998, 250 in 1999 alone, and another 50 in the first quarter of 2000, with 150 companies in registration to go public. "That's 600-plus public companies with a market cap in excess of $1 trillion," he says. "Technology has gone from a niche business to become the most strategic, most rapidly growing, and, soon, the largest industry sector within investment banking." And one that the New York banks could no longer relegate to a niche practice.

With much greater resources at their disposal than the smaller boutique banks in San Francisco have, the New York banks spruced up their technology practices, grooming or luring away top analysts and bankers. All three set up large offices in Silicon Valley: Goldman Sachs and Morgan Stanley right next to each other on Sand Hill Road across the street from Sequoia and Kleiner; CSFB a couple of freeway exits away in Palo Alto. Says Koenig, "You can't be a leading global investment bank today and not have a strong technology practice." He believes that as the Internet transforms every facet of business, "our entire investment banking business is going to be driven by technology." That means that technology investment banking is no longer a business driven by personality, as it was in the early days, but has become an institutional presence. And the Big Three "are focused and capable and credible in high tech," says Koenig. "When the H&Qs started, they had the successful analysts and bankers in high tech. Now we have the best analysts, the most expert bankers, the distribu-

FIGURE 9.1   INITIAL PUBLIC OFFERINGS IN THE U.S. MARKET

MANAGERS	PROCEEDS ($MILLIONS) 1999	RANK	MARKET SHARE	NO. OF ISSUES
Goldman Sachs & Co.	14,547.0	1	21.2	54
Morgan Stanley Dean Witter	13,967.5	2	20.3	49
Credit Suisse First Boston	9,805.1	3	14.3	98
Merrill Lynch & Co. Inc.	7,569.1	4	11.0	41
Lehman Brothers	2,905.5	5	4.2	32
J.P. Morgan & Co. Inc.	2,785.5	6	4.1	10
FleetBoston Financial Corp.	2,683.8	7	3.9	45
Salomon Smith Barney	2,530.8	8	3.7	22
Deutsche Bank AG	2,118.7	9	3.1	28
Bear Stearns & Co. Inc.	2,086.5	10	3.0	26
UBS Warburg	1,277.2	11	1.9	9
Chase Manhattan Corp.	1,277.1	12	1.9	23
Mediobanca	611.5	13	0.9	2
Banc of America Securities LLC	518.5	14	0.8	8
Prudential Securities Inc.	356.5	15	0.5	9
CIBC World Markets	352.6	16	0.5	8
U.S. Bancorp	326.9	17	0.5	8
Thomas Weisel Partners LLC	264.2	18	0.4	6
Dain Rauscher Corp.	244.0	19	0.4	4
Société Générale	228.3	20	0.3	3
Top 20 totals	66,456.3		96.8	485
Industry totals	68,663.2		100.0	543

2000

Goldman Sachs & Co.	18,291.3	1	22.7	62
Morgan Stanley Dean Witter	13,247.8	2	16.5	50
Credit Suisse First Boston	11,351.7	3	14.1	83
Merrill Lynch & Co. Inc.	10,347.6	4	12.9	39
Salomon Smith Barney	8,948.2	5	11.1	33
Deutsche Bank AG	3,327.9	6	4.1	27
Lehman Brothers	2,671.5	7	3.3	31
FleetBoston Financial Corp.	2,104.3	8	2.6	29
Chase Manhattan Corp.	1,616.5	9	2.0	28
China International Capital Co.	1,319.4	10	1.6	3
UBS Warburg	1,300.2	11	1.6	15
J.P. Morgan & Co. Inc.	952.1	12	1.2	8
Bear Stearns & Co. Inc.	863.0	13	1.1	9
CIBC World Markets	685.2	14	0.9	8
Banc of America Securities LLC	672.7	15	0.8	7
Société Générale	432.8	16	0.5	6
U.S. Bancorp	321.5	17	0.4	5
ING Barings	317.4	18	0.4	3
Prudential Securities Inc.	256.0	19	0.3	3
Thomas Weisel Partners LLC	203.8	20	0.3	3
Top 20 totals	79,230.7		98.4	452
Industry totals	80,507.2		100.0	450

Source: Thomson Financial Securities Data.
Note: Data exclude closed-end funds. Data for 2000 are through December 19.

FIGURE 9.2 ANNOUNCED U.S. MERGERS AND ACQUISITIONS

ADVISER	RANK VALUE ($MILLIONS) 1999	RANK	MARKET SHARE	NO. OF DEALS
Goldman Sachs & Co.	672,455.8	1	42.7	246
Morgan Stanley Dean Witter	518,397.7	2	32.9	234
Merrill Lynch & Co. Inc.	467,989.0	3	29.7	177
Credit Suisse First Boston	428,920.5	4	27.3	383
Salomon Smith Barney	246,665.7	5	15.7	212
Lehman Brothers	193,844.4	6	12.3	126
Lazard	178,725.4	7	11.4	64
Bear Stearns & Co. Inc.	169,048.5	8	10.7	76
Chase Manhattan Corp.	166,478.7	9	10.6	138
J.P. Morgan & Co. Inc.	117,545.2	10	7.5	81
UBS Warburg	72,621.8	11	4.6	125
Deutsche Bank AG	71,860.4	12	4.6	103
Wasserstein Perella Group Inc.	60,750.4	13	3.9	59
Allen & Co. Inc.	59,621.4	14	3.8	7
Evercore Group	40,882.2	15	2.6	1
Houlihan Lokey Howard & Zukin	39,846.0	16	2.5	87
Greenhill & Co. LLC	37,437.6	17	2.4	15
FleetBoston Financial Corp.	31,923.1	18	2.0	62
CIBC World Markets	30,417.8	19	1.9	84
Enskilda Securities	26,909.0	20	1.7	1
Deals with adviser	1,455,406.2		92.5	2,632
Deals without adviser	118,936.1		7.6	8,525
Industry totals	1,573,790.0		100.0	11,153

2000

Goldman Sachs & Co.	748,806.3	1	42.6	231
Morgan Stanley Dean Witter	575,632.3	2	32.8	187
Credit Suisse First Boston	553,478.0	3	31.5	393
Merrill Lynch & Co. Inc.	502,788.8	4	28.6	162
Salomon Smith Barney	417,668.8	5	23.8	193
Wasserstein Perella Group Inc.	266,750.1	6	15.2	36
Chase Manhattan Corp.	218,336.4	7	12.4	124
J.P. Morgan & Co. Inc.	198,717.9	8	11.3	100
Lehman Brothers	161,764.7	9	9.2	126
UBS Warburg	131,778.6	10	7.5	80
Bear Stearns & Co. Inc.	111,760.4	11	6.4	63
ING Barings	103,651.2	12	5.9	58
Bank of America Securities LLC	89,470.7	13	5.1	70
Thomas Weisel Partners LLC	72,577.9	14	4.1	33
Dresdner Kleinwort Benson	62,052.7	15	3.5	8
Deutsche Bank AG	57,685.8	16	3.3	86
Lazard	53,629.1	17	3.1	48
CIBC World Markets	49,328.3	18	2.8	38
Houlihan Lokey Howard & Zukin	27,582.9	19	1.6	86
Broadview	23,687.1	20	1.4	72
Deals with adviser	1,630,229.1		92.8	2,204
Deals without adviser	126,768.4		7.2	8,088
Industry totals	1,756,990.3		100.0	10,291

Source: Thomson Financial Securities Data.
Note: Data for 2000 are through December 19.

tion network, the M&A expertise. We're taking increasing market share."

The histories of CSFB and Morgan Stanley are indelibly intertwined through the name of one legendary banker, Frank Quattrone, who worked at both of them. Bill Brady, managing director of CSFB's technology group in Palo Alto, lived the history. He and Quattrone were both on Morgan Stanley's investment banking team for a decade or more, witnessing the explosive growth of technology through the late 1980s and early 1990s. In 1987 technology was one of the smallest industry groups within Morgan Stanley, Brady recalls; by 1995 it was the largest. But he and Quattrone were concerned because the bank was not hiring to keep pace with technology's growth, even though it was the first of the Big Three to open a Silicon Valley office in 1994. After Morgan Stanley took Netscape public in 1995, "we had an early view of how the Internet would change the world," says Brady. He and Quattrone wanted Morgan Stanley to boost its Silicon Valley staff massively, but the bank brass were reluctant. "They talked about being fair to the forest products and auto groups," he says. "We told them if we don't staff up, we're going to leave. We're doing more revenue than anyone in the firm." But the brass still balked, and in April 1996 Quattrone and Brady left, taking about a dozen other key people with them.

After a stint with Deutsche Bank, the team wound up in early 1998 at CSFB, which was a full-service investment bank without much of a technology practice. "CS First Boston said they would take the whole team and give us the same independence we were used to," says Brady. Today, CSFB has 320 people in its technology group, including 175 in the Bay Area, and can compete on an equal footing with Goldman Sachs and Morgan Stanley. "Morgan Stanley was truly dominant in technology," says Brady. "Now it's one of the Big Three, but it's no longer dominant. The fact that CSFB can go in and beat them would never have happened in 1995."

Paul Chamberlain, managing director of Morgan Stanley, remembers it from the other side. "I came out here [to California] to put fingers in the dike after Frank Quattrone left in April 1996," he says. He had been sitting pretty in New York, having just wrapped up the huge deal in which Lucent Technologies was spun out of AT&T as a public company. "It was going into the Easter weekend, and we were celebrating the Lucent IPO," he says. Then came a three-line news item saying Quattrone had left along with 15 key people. "The popular lore was that Brad Koenig [of Goldman Sachs] was popping champagne corks," Chamberlain says. At Morgan Stanley the champagne was corked for a while. "We understand that our franchise is firmly connected to the New Economy companies," he says. "Quattrone's departure made us redouble our effort." Since 1996 Morgan Stanley has seen a fourfold increase in its Silicon Valley business, according to Chamberlain, while its market share in terms of fees generated from technology has increased from the high teens to the mid-twenties.

"In investment banking there are three firms that really matter," he says. "Boutique firms like H&Q were the pioneers. We didn't start a dedicated practice until 1983." Morgan Stanley got into the Apple Computer IPO because Bill Hambrecht "brought us in." Today, however, all the major investment banks are building up their Silicon Valley practices. "This is now the auto-row approach to investment banking," says Chamberlain. Goldman Sachs' Koenig adds that the competition for the lead position among investment banks is even keener than that of venture capitalists going after their deals. "Unlike in the venture business where you might get several firms participating in a financing, it's a zero-sum game for us," he says. Getting in as the lead banker means winning the lion's share of the lucrative IPO fees. Through early December 2000, Goldman Sachs had collected $908.4 million in IPO underwriting fees for the year, CSFB $706.5 million, and Morgan Stanley $667.4 million—that compared to a combined $1,894 million for everyone else.[1] But there's even more money to be made in forging a continuing relationship with fast-growing entrepreneurial companies. "From that [IPO] point on, we'll be the leading investment bank for that company over its life cycle," notes Koenig. Picture, for instance, getting in early with Cisco Systems and being the lead banker on its nonstop merger express.

TRIAGE IN THE INDUSTRY

What's happened to the other guys? In the late 1990s, the three pioneering San Francisco technology investment banks were all acquired by larger commercial banks as part of a consolidation sweeping the financial industry. The commercial banks wanted to get into the sexy Internet sector with its wealth of IPOs and mergers, and the specialist banks needed to broaden the expertise that they could offer their increasingly sophisticated clients. Montgomery Securities wound up in the arms of Bank of America, becoming Bank of America Securities; Robertson Stephens joined with FleetBoston Financial, but retained its name; and H&Q was bought by Chase Manhattan in December 1999 and became Chase H&Q (then JP Morgan H&Q). Following closely on the heels of that deal, Prudential Securities bought another San Francisco–based technology bank, Volpe Brown Whelan. (Two East Coast firms that had been important technology players also got scooped up: Alex Brown by Deutsche Bank and Cowen & Company by Société Générale.) All this left only a handful of independent investment banks based in San Francisco. The two primary independents were both started by expatriates from the pioneers. Thom Weisel departed Montgomery to found Thomas Weisel Partners, while Bill Hambrecht left Hambrecht & Quist before it was acquired and started W. R. Hambrecht & Company.

Cristina Morgan, who joined JP Morgan H&Q's predecessor in 1982 as a research analyst and moved into investment banking in 1984, has a long-term perspective on how the field has changed. "What's led to consolidation is the compaction of cycles in the technology industry," she says. By that she means that entrepreneurial companies previously had little use for debt products or other traditional banking services until they had matured for a number of years. Now the growth cycle has accelerated so much that newly public entities pursue transactions that they prefer to finance with debt instead of with their volatile stock. "The ability and desire to go into the next layer of the capital structure, which is debt, occurs much sooner [after an IPO]," says Morgan. "Financial instruments are nothing but weapons in a business strategy," which means that banks must be prepared to offer an array of weapons, not just mezzanine financing and IPO expertise. Another incentive for the publicly traded investment banks to merge was to allow their shareholders to reap the benefit of a higher valuation. Although investment banks had fostered the Internet IPOs, their own valuations hadn't always shown a corresponding boost.

In late 2000 the consensus among the insiders I talked to was that of the consolidated investment banks in San Francisco, Robertson Stephens had been the early success but was fading as it lost its key players; Montgomery (Bank of America) and Prudential Volpe were foundering; and it was too soon to tell with Chase H&Q. Indeed, in

September 2000 Chase Manhattan announced that it would acquire J. P. Morgan, a massive deal that would entail the integration of Chase H&Q with J. P. Morgan's investment banking business. In January 2001, Chase H&Q became JP Morgan H&Q. Thus, it's hard to pronounce any of the merged entities a resounding triumph.

Jim Feuille (pronounced *Foy*) has been a participant in the San Francisco investment banking scene since the early 1980s, having worked at both Robertson Stephens, where he was managing director of technology investment banking, and at Volpe, where he was chief operating officer. He left the latter in early 2000 after it was taken over by Prudential. When I interviewed him, he was trying to figure out where to go next, perhaps into venture capital. In his mid-forties, with receding brown hair and a high forehead, the mild-mannered Feuille was visibly tired of the machinations in San Francisco's technology banking business. "These acquisitions all take place because the [commercial banks] want to buy their way into investment banking and, on the sellers' side, the major shareholders want to cash out." But if there's no strategic fit, the combinations can be disastrous. For instance, Montgomery's acquirer, Bank of America, was determined to turn a very successful boutique firm into a competitor of Morgan Stanley. "It tried to change the culture really quickly," says Feuille, by doing such things as more than doubling the number of research sectors. "People were unhappy and started pouring out." By contrast, Robertson Stephens prospered initially because it landed with a partner, FleetBoston, "who left it completely alone." Ironically, both Montgomery and Robertson Stephens had once faced a similar fate, when NationsBank merged with Bank of America and wound up with both investment banks in the process. It chose to divest Robertson.

Most of the commercial banks and investment firms involved in these deals have the philosophy that they will run investment banking because they're the larger, acquiring entity. But that's a big mistake, say insiders, because these acquirers don't have the requisite knowledge or relationships with entrepreneurial companies and venture capitalists. For example, says Feuille, who witnessed the painful Prudential-Volpe restructuring firsthand, Prudential's integration strategy "infuriated [the Volpe] people." Instead of sharing the pain of layoffs among both entities, Prudential eliminated the Volpe trading floor and then walked in to the bankers and analysts extolling the virtues of the merger. "What they forgot is that a small investment bank is like a family; we all know each other," says Feuille. "They threw money at people to keep them, but who wants to work for them? They don't know what they're doing."

Tom Volpe, who stayed on as chairman of Prudential Volpe at least at first, says that the acquisition was necessary because the old Volpe Brown Whelan couldn't have continued to be competitive alone. "All our competitors had been bought, and we looked small," he says. He acknowledges that with Prudential "we've had significant turnover." However, he defends the termination of the Volpe trading floor because it duplicated what Prudential already had. And, notes Volpe, one of the new investment banks, W. R. Hambrecht, "hired those people." To employees who complain that "it's not like the good old days," Volpe says that they've got selective recall. The "good old days" had their bad spells as well.

Thom Weisel was also disappointed in the acquisition of his bank, Montgomery Securities. "They [the acquirer] told us we would be totally autonomous," he says, but it didn't happen, and he bailed. Echoing Feuille, he believes that the commercial banks especially are heading for a fall as they impose their management style on investment banks and take a strictly balance-sheet approach to appraising entrepreneurial companies. "The [commercial] bank mentality is not suited to companies with no earnings and brand-new revenue. They're just totally ill-equipped," he says. "They don't have the quality of people to build relationships with entrepreneurial companies. There's a huge battle brewing between investment and commercial banks in who wins the war for the [entrepreneurial] client."

Cristina Morgan and David Golden, who are codirectors of investment banking at JP Morgan H&Q, believe that the combination will ultimately be successful because there's little overlap between the businesses of the new parent and the former Hambrecht & Quist, although the announced JP Morgan integration could change that. Also, unlike some of the other acquirers, Chase took a largely hands-off attitude toward H&Q. "When we built out the merger model, we had synergy goals for the first 12 months," says Golden. "We thought we could get $100 million of incremental revenue on top of our $650 million and Chase at $2 billion." At the end of February 2000, Chase H&Q had already achieved $93 million in incremental revenue in a merger that occurred only two months before. "We tried to get the businesses at Chase and H&Q integrated early," says Golden. "Hopefully, two or three years from now we won't be saying who's Chase and who's H&Q." Morgan told the story of accompanying two Chase employees on a pitch to an entrepreneurial company preparing to go public. While Chase could not have handled the IPO, the old H&Q did not have the global reach nor the analysts' line-up the company wanted. "Now we have the financial muscle and global reach of Chase combined with the domain name of H&Q," she says. "This [IPO] company needs both."

Of course, while the San Francisco banks attempt to get accustomed to their new owners, the Big Three competitors are rubbing their hands. Says Goldman Sachs' Koenig, "The consolidation deals have been largely unsuccessful because it's difficult to take a business completely based on people and put it within a large bureaucratic organization." What it's really about is stodgy, institutional commercial banks acquiring fast-moving entrepreneurial entities. "It's a different template," he says.

SERIAL INVESTMENT BANKERS

The San Francisco investment banking firms were as entrepreneurial as the companies they served, and when the inevitable consolidation with bigger firms began to occur, many of the pioneering founders opted out. Just like serial entrepreneurs, you now find Thom Weisel and Bill Hambrecht heading their own eponymous investment banks. Weisel's approach is more conventional; he's re-creating the old merchant bank model stressing a combination of investment and market making. Hambrecht, however, embraced a vision of revolutionizing the IPO process by offering an alternate pricing method called the *Dutch auction* through W. R. Hambrecht & Company. Early results have been mixed, at best.

Thomas Weisel Partners is housed on the top (37th) floor of the Pacific Telesis building, in the opulent executive suite that used to belong to PacTel's executives before the Baby Bell was taken over. The lobby has oriental rugs on a white marble floor and is adorned with modern paintings and sculptures. Weisel's own office features photos of the Tour de France bicycle race, which he helped sponsor at Montgomery and continues to do so at his new firm. In middle age, Weisel is a frank, gray-haired man who still moves with the lithe quickness of an athlete. He was a five-time national speed-skating champion in the 1950s and a national masters cycling champion in the early 1990s.

Weisel describes his firm as a merchant bank rather than a full-service investment bank, meaning that it concentrates on technology financing and private equity investments. "We have a major interest in partnering with venture capitalists and entrepreneurial companies who don't just view the IPO as an isolated incident," he says. However, venture capitalists told me that merchant banks like Weisel's often compete with them. Thom Weisel's continuum of services, in fact, includes venture capital, private placements, and, of course, the IPO and follow-on services such as research analysis. It's apparent that Thomas Weisel Partners in part is a return to the old days, when there was a place for specialist firms. "There could be a number of upstarts like ourselves that are able to attract talented people and build a new platform," Weisel says. "We're proving there's a future for focused firms. The venture capitalists love us because we're 100 percent aimed in this area [of technology]."

Weisel, like most of the other investment bankers I interviewed, dismisses W. R. Hambrecht's auction model. "We will incorporate the new technologies and delivery systems that the Internet has to offer when it's appropriate," he says, "but the Dutch auction is a failed concept." Rather then having the investment bank set an IPO offering price with the hope that it will then pop, or rise dramatically in the first day of trading, a Dutch auction determines a market-clearing price by having investors submit bids via the Internet indicating how much they're willing to pay for shares. The price is then set at the lowest level at which the company could sell all of the shares being offered. The idea is to allow individual investors more parity with large institutional buyers in reaping the benefits of a hot IPO. But the problems have been manifold. For one thing, as Weisel points out, the Dutch auction is not very compatible with traditional IPO underwriting, which means that Hambrecht has been the sole manager on some of his offerings. That limits how much analyst coverage the company will get in the aftermarket. Second, because the IPO, as discussed in Chapter 1, is very much a branding event for a new company, having the share price barely budge in the first day of trading is a letdown.

In the face of almost universal skepticism about his model, I was curious to find out Bill Hambrecht's motivation. Making a deliberate statement, he has located W. R. Hambrecht & Company in a gritty area of San Francisco's south of Market district, just a few blocks from the Hall of Justice and the jail. Surrounded by auto shops and bars, the bank is in a converted brick warehouse with exposed ducts and a metal spiral staircase leading to the trading floor. By contrast, Weisel and the other San Francisco–based banks are in the more elegant financial district north of Market Street. Hambrecht himself is something of a surprise. With thinning, reddish-brown hair, he has a raw-boned face sporting, on the day I meet him, a prominently cut lip. He looks more like an aging boxer than an investment banker.

He knows what I've come for and immediately launches into a description of his vision. "When we started H&Q in 1968, we thought there was enough activity in Silicon Valley that it would be a decent way to make a living. We turned out to have a tiger by the tail." He's hoping for a repeat in W. R. Hambrecht. "I share the entrepreneurial virus," he says. "I had backed away from H&Q but wasn't ready to move into a ceremonial job." In the mid-1990s, as he was withdrawing from H&Q, he talked to colleagues about how to harness the Internet in investment banking. "The answer I heard was, 'We're doing real well; don't rock the boat.'" He had his epiphany when H&Q, along with Goldman Sachs, handled the public offering of one of the first boutique beer breweries, Sam Adams. The company president, who wanted to offer shares to all his customers, put an IPO ad as a neck hanger on beer bottles. "In about a month we had 120,000 checks totaling $50 million," Hambrecht recalls. And three years later more than 50 percent of the original buyers still held the stock.

The Dutch auction was born out of his determination to allow *affinity groups,* made up of individuals with an interest in the company, to participate in the IPO, rather than have to wait until big institutions flip the stocks in the aftermarket at a tremendous profit. Hambrecht now acknowledges that in the hypermarket of 1999 and 2000, the Dutch auction did not offer enough pop to be attractive to the vast majority of companies. By late 2000 Hambrecht had underwritten four Dutch auction deals, none of them major, and had a fifth in registration. His company had comanaged a total of about two dozen mostly conventional IPOs. But Hambrecht wasn't giving up on the Dutch auction, which he felt would be "an easier sale" with Nasdaq trending down. He was also working to build up a traditional investment banking infrastructure with traders and research analysts. "What we found is that the auction won't work without us doing everything an investment bank does: Sell to institutions, trade the stocks, and follow them," he says. "We'd like to be the eBay of the financial services community."

Ultimately, investment banks must change their ways because on-line trading is a "disruptive technology," says Hambrecht, echoing the Clayton Christensen nomenclature that has swept through Silicon Valley. (Christensen has joined W. R. Hambrecht's board.) He sees banks like JP Morgan H&Q and Robertson Stephens competing with the Big Three by broadening their offerings and adding to their costs. "My theory is, use disruptive technology to deliver the product at significantly lower cost."

SYMBIOSIS WITH VENTURE CAPITAL

Don Valentine's comments notwithstanding, most investment bankers and venture capitalists realize that they have a pretty good thing going and that each needs the other to keep it going. Indeed, while I was interviewing him, Valentine took a call from Thom Weisel and promised to do him a favor. As technology grew from a specialized niche into the powerhouse it is today, venture capitalists and investment bankers in the field developed longstanding relationships and learned who can be trusted. Says Weisel, "The venture guys we know tell us the truth. They don't bullshit. If Don Valentine says something, I listen." JP Morgan H&Q's Cristina Morgan notes that the venture capitalists and investment bankers who have been around for a while have seen good times and bad. "We've invested together, made money together, lost money together. As a result of that, there's mutual respect on both sides."

Then, too, these two groups of entrepreneurial financiers wind up living in the same neighborhoods and running into each other at social functions and local restaurants. This is especially noticeable in the concentrated technology milieu of Silicon Valley. The investment bankers and venture capitalists of Sand Hill Road play together in golf tournaments and ski events, take their children to the same soccer practices, and donate to the same United Way. It's those relationships that are endangered by, on the one hand, consolidation within investment banking, and, on the other, the newcomers who are flooding into venture capital (see Chapters 12 and 13). It's no wonder that the

Big Three investment bankers—Morgan Stanley, Goldman Sachs, and CSFB—and their counterparts among the top-tier VC firms move generally in lockstep. That is, a Kleiner company expects from the start to be taken public by one of the gold standard firms, while Morgan Stanley and its peers anticipate that Kleiner will come to it for lead banking services.

While there are no exclusive agreements, certain investment banks tend to pair off more frequently with certain VC firms. For example, Morgan Stanley has an especially close relationship with Kleiner because it helped the VC firm raise its first fund more than a quarter century ago. Morgan Stanley has also taken public a number of Kleiner's biggest hits, including Netscape, and was a cofounder of Kleiner affiliate Integral Capital in 1991. When the investment bank decided to open a branch in Silicon Valley, it used Kleiner's offices until its own office across the street was finished. "We also look at Benchmark, Crosspoint, Accel, and Sequoia as high-pedigree companies," says Morgan Stanley's Chamberlain. "There is a validation of knowing that the company has a board member from a Sequoia or Crosspoint." But Morgan Stanley focuses on another two dozen high-quality VC firms as well because "to be bringing to market the best companies, you have to cast your net pretty wide." Bill Brady, of CSFB, says it too works closely with Kleiner. "We also do a lot of deals with Accel, New Enterprise Associates, and Sequoia."

Goldman Sachs often pairs up with Benchmark; partner Bruce Dunlevie worked at Goldman Sachs before he went into venture capital with Benchmark predecessor Merrill Pickard. "We're the lead investor on 60 to 70 percent of Benchmark's deals," Brad Koenig says. "We also go after Kleiner, Sequoia, Accel, and others." He evaluates all the top venture capitalists and proactively attempts to forge relationships with them. It's a virtuous cycle for the top investment bankers and venture capitalists to work together. "We both have the network of investments, track record, insight, and experience," says Koenig. "Once you're perceived to be adding value, you see all the best deals, which enhances the value of the network." However, like his peers, he says the balance of power has definitely swung toward venture capitalists and entrepreneurs. "If we get a call from John Doerr or David Beirne, we drop whatever we're doing to go visit the company they recommend and understand its market position."

Though primarily known for their role as underwriters, investment banks are also keen participants in VC investing. Typically, the investment banks' internal funds invest in late-stage funding rounds and don't take board seats or an active advisory role except in the IPO process itself. But there are exceptions. In particular, Hambrecht & Quist, now JP Morgan H&Q, has combined active VC investing with banking services since its inception. "That's one way we differentiated ourselves," says Nancy Pfund, the managing director of Access Technology Partners, one of JP Morgan H&Q's venture funds. A former research analyst, Pfund believes there's natural synergy between VC and investment banking services. "We wanted to link our private equity expertise with the technology-analytical skills of our research department," she says. "They're a great source of deal flow and recruitment. We give the bankers and researchers incentives to identify promising new deals." As one of a number of VC investors, JP Morgan H&Q can't insist that the companies in which it invests use it as the IPO underwriter. "You don't want to be seen as imposing a decision on a company that may not be in its own best interest," says Pfund. "All we can say is we'd like a chance to tell you our story. Many times we do end up being involved in the IPO."

Volpe predicts that venture capital and investment banking will become even more intertwined in the future. "The venture industry is structurally evolving the same way investment banking did 10 years ago," he says. Like investment banking in the 1980s, venture capital has moved from a peripheral to a central player, and it has generated huge rewards for participants. "Venture capital has become an important, high-paying institution, and turnover is starting to appear," he says. "That's being driven by greed. Anybody who has been near this business has done way better than they should."

Chapters 10 and 11 will peel back the facade and look at what venture capitalists really think about the companies they invest in and how they respond when greed turns to fear. First we sit in on several partnership meetings and get a behind-the-scenes peak at the freewheeling strategizing sessions in which VC partners engage. Then we look at the "dark side" of risk investing.

CHAPTER TEN

Behind the Curtain

A staple of every venture capital (VC) firm is the weekly part-nership meeting, which typically takes up most, if not all, of Monday. I soon learned not to try to reach venture capitalists on the first day of the work week, because they would be tied up in that meeting. I realized that in order to get the authentic VC experience, I needed to attend a few of these meetings. Not an easy task. Venture capital has remained a private industry for a reason: Its participants like it that way. And they're not eager to open up their internal processes to a prying outsider who wants to expose them to the world. It took some negotiation, but I managed to persuade three firms to let me sit in on their partnership meetings: Highland Capital Partners of Boston, Hummer Winblad Venture Partners of San Francisco, and Redpoint Ventures of Sand Hill Road. (In addition, Highland, Draper Fisher Jurvetson, Mohr Davidow Ventures, and U.S. Venture Partners were all kind enough to allow me to attend the entrepreneur pitches presented in Chapter 7. Those pitches can be contained within the partnership meeting or done separately.)

Before presenting an in-depth description and bits of the dia-logue that occur at these meetings, a little background is in order. All of the partnership meetings I attended occurred during the second quarter of 2000, when the euphoria of the golden era was beginning to subside. The Nasdaq public market, home to virtually all the initial public offerings (IPOs) of new technology companies, had taken a nasty tumble in April. Public dot-coms were trading far below their initial offering price, and private companies were forced to postpone their IPOs, and some were closing down because they couldn't raise any more funding. Consequently, the mood among venture capitalists, as we see reflected in these meetings, had become more somber. There was still a keen sense of competition not to miss out on the best deals, but it was tempered by a renewed discrimination aimed at choosing only the best.

On display at these meetings is the semidemocratic decision-making process of a VC partnership. The general partners within a firm are more or less equal participants, although certain partners tend to lead discussions and force issues to a conclusion. Also present at these meetings are other members of the VC firm, including entrepreneurs-in-residence, former founders who supply their expertise for a time but are usually searching for an interesting company to join; venture partners, such as lawyers, consultants, and headhunters, who trade specialized expertise for a piece of the carry and a place at the table; and associates, eager young MBA students or graduates who do a lot of the research in exchange for the experience and a very tiny piece of the carry. Associates are generally not on a career track to become a partner. Rather, the intention is to get them hooked on entrepreneurialism and then send them off to gain the now-preferred operating experience at start-up companies.

The meetings take place in large conference rooms where the participants sit around one big table. Often, one or two partners will be present via video- or teleconference. As prospective investments come up, the general partner who is championing the company leads the discussion, while the other partners make ad hoc comments. Associates are more likely to speak only when a specific question is directed at them, or when there's a general polling of everyone at the table.

OVER THE TOP AT HIGHLAND

Founded in 1988 by veteran investor Bob Higgins, now the managing general partner, Highland has revitalized itself in recent years with the addition of energetic new partners, notably Dan Nova, and by open-ing an office in San Francisco to give it a bicoastal presence. It has scored some big Internet successes, such as eToys, Ask Jeeves, and Ly-cos, although it's not yet spoken of with quite the same respect that Boston-based counterparts Greylock and Matrix Partners garner. Yet Highland is getting close. Another coup was luring Internet analyst Keith Benjamin to become its San Francisco–based general partner. Benjamin, who spent 17 years following public software and Internet companies, says he wanted a lifestyle change because sell-side analysts tend to burn out after 40. He and Nova generate a lot of the Internet deal flow for Highland.

Benjamin is the host of the partnership meeting that I attend, which is held in Highland's new office on the 31st floor of the Bank of America building, one of downtown San Francisco's most prestigious landmarks. (Next month, the Boston office will host the big meeting; in between will be more narrowly focused sessions in which selected partners meet.) The conference room, with huge banks of windows on both sides, overlooks the Transamerica Pyramid and has sweeping views of San Francisco Bay, where tugboats and ships reminiscent of an older era glide slowly by. Present at the meeting are Higgins and an-other veteran, Paul Maeder; Nova and Benjamin, both in their 40s; three younger partners, Sean Dalton, Josaphat "Jo" Tango, and Wy-cliffe "Wyc" Grousbeck; public relations specialist Michael Gaiss; and senior associate Cristy Barnes, the only woman in the room besides me. A couple more people from Boston participate via a conference call. Scheduled to start at 1 P.M., the meeting is grounded for more than an hour by delays in some of the flights bringing partners from the East Coast.

Higgins finally calls the meeting to order shortly after 2 P.M., as several partners continue to nibble on the sandwiches and salads brought in for the occasion. The agenda includes discussions of sev-eral approved investments that are awaiting funding, term sheets in process where Highland has made an offer to invest, current deals un-der negotiation, updates on portfolio companies, and some general information on Highland recruiting, press mentions, and planned events. (The agreement I made to attend these meetings was that I wouldn't name the entrepreneurial companies or give specific details on their funding.)

First up is a company that provides business-to-business (B2B) services for nonprofit entities such as school districts. Benjamin, who brought the deal in, reports that Andersen Consulting is willing to put in $35 million as a strategic partner. "Andersen will be the army to go after county, state, and some federal contracts," he says. For this significant follow-on financing, "we've asked the company to rebudget so the total dollars in this round could get them to breakeven if we have a nuclear winter," Benjamin reports. *Nuclear winter* is industry shorthand for the cycles when money dries up, the IPO window shuts, and companies must scrape by on their cash at hand to survive. Nova remarks that companies always resist when they're first asked to rebudget. It's only after they've gone through the dry period that they realize the rebudget was crucial. "I've been telling my companies that if you've got 12 months of cash, make it last 18," he says.

The partners then engage in brief discussions on several more deals that are awaiting investments from corporate partners. Corporate money is preferred right now because corporations invest for strategic reasons—that is, the start-up can provide them with needed services or access to a potential market—and aren't as likely as financial investors to be scared off by the downturn in the public markets.

From there the topic shifts to *incubators,* which are VC-like firms that incubate start-ups by providing office space, executive search, and other services (for more on incubators, see Chapter 13). Traditional venture capitalists like the Highland partners don't think much of this trend. Nova says disparagingly, "I read an article on the plane that says there are now over 800 incubator firms." No one seems to believe that so many can survive. Higgins cites an incubator building in Boston where everything that has gone in has failed. "I'm sure it's haunted," he jokes. Grousbeck suggests, perhaps not totally in jest, "What we need to do is invest in companies that service incubators, like investment banks and financial services." Nova summarizes the group's take: The incubator business model depends on taking huge ownership positions in relatively few companies. "The incubators get screwed no matter what," he says. "If the company is successful and goes up in value, they have to put so much in to keep their ownership stake. They also get screwed when it goes down."

Returning to the agenda, the group moves on to several companies that are seeking funding from Highland. Tango has one that would sell furniture via the Web, but he's skeptical. "It's something like all the pet food companies on the Web," he says. "It's hard to figure out how to make it work. There are no barriers to entry." Benjamin describes a start-up with niche technology that allows you to highlight any portion of an online article and then e-mail it. An Ask Jeeves executive is on the board of advisers and is urging Highland to invest. Says Benjamin, "I met with the CEO, who looks like he's 24 going on 14. He's also got this heavy facial hair thing going on." Benjamin liked the technology, but wondered about the potential market. "My first reaction was I didn't like the facial hair. My second was how big is the market."

In an update on Highland's portfolio companies—its existing investments—one has just gotten a new round of financing with a $75 million valuation. The company, in the now-out-of-favor business-to-consumer (B2C) space, has an average order size of $136 and is spending 10 cents to generate $1 in revenue. Quips Nova, "The headline is good, but underneath they're still B2C."

At this point, the meeting takes a startling turn for the East Coast partners, who are about to realize that they're not in Boston any more. Benjamin has arranged a birthday surprise for Dalton, which consists of a singing telegram delivered by a big, hairy man in drag. Gripping a handful of huge balloons by the string, this guy is adorned in a short green sparkling dress and fishnet pull-up stockings that do nothing to hide the fact that he doesn't shave his legs. He wears heavy lipstick and a wig of long, black, curly hair. When Dalton is pointed out, the man approaches him: "We know how you like to toot your horn. Here it is," he says to the red-faced young Bostonian, handing him a small noise-maker along with the balloons. Then he sings in a strained falsetto: "Come on to my house. I'm going to make you candy. I'm going to make you everything." He continues with a suggestive chorus asking, "Where did you sleep last night? Was she worth it?" To Dalton's evident relief, he finishes by leading the rest of the partners, who are laughing defensively, in a traditional round of "Happy Birthday." By this time the bewildered people on the conference phone have figured out that something weird is going on. "I must admit we're a bit confused," one comments. After the birthday performer leaves, the receptionist brings in plates with huge slices of chocolate cake, and we all dig in. Speaking as an unreformed chocoholic, the cake was well worth the performance.

After this, which could scarcely be topped, the meeting draws swiftly to a close. The partners talk briefly about how to spin the news

about a new hire, a former *Wall Street Journal* reporter who will specialize in European investments. This turns out to be Jon Auerbach,
who covered technology for both the *Journal* and the *Boston Globe* and
was also a foreign correspondent for the latter. Public relations specialist Gaiss describes several media interviews that the partners will be
doing, and cites a *Red Herring* article on top VC firms that included
Highland. Such branding is particularly important to a firm hovering
on the edge of the top tier. Highland is planning a conference in November that will feature its new San Francisco office and, hopefully,
further enhance its image as an exciting investment player in the Bay
Area. They talk about whom to invite, for example CEOs of portfolio
companies based here, and what activities to offer, perhaps a trip to
the nearby wine country. No one suggests inviting back the birthday
performer.

HUMMING ALONG AT HUMMER WINBLAD

Hummer Winblad Venture Partners may not be among the super tier
of VC firms, but it certainly gets just about as much publicity. That's
due largely to the high profile of founder and partner Ann Winblad,
who was one of the first women entrepreneurs in technology when she
cofounded an accounting software firm in 1976, and one of the first
women in venture capital when she cofounded Hummer Winblad in
1989. Winblad, who among other accomplishments once dated Bill
Gates (he's an investor in her firm), winds up on numerous lists of major players in the technology industry. *Upside* magazine called her one
of the 100 most influential people in the digital age; *Vanity Fair* named
her one of the top 50 leaders of the New Establishment; and *Business
Week* included her in its elite 25 power brokers in Silicon Valley. Her
partner John Hummer is no slouch either. A former pro basketball
player for six years, he got an MBA from Stanford and began his VC
career in 1983.

Hummer Winblad was one of the first VC firms to specialize: In
1989 it made a prescient choice to invest solely in software, now expanded to encompass Internet services and content. The San Francisco firm doesn't shy away from controversial investments. Portfolio
companies include both Napster, whose music-swapping program
earned the ire of big-name bands and a lawsuit by the Recording In-

dustry Association of America, and Pets.com, the pet supply site whose spendthrift ads featured a singing sock puppet. The proliferation of pet-related sites on the Internet is almost universally derided by competitors as an example of the sloppy investing of the B2C era. Winblad defends Pets.com, pointing out that as of mid-2000, it's the only pet food seller that was able to go public. At the time, she noted, Pets.com was less than 300 days from a three-person start-up. "We built a distribution channel from scratch. It's too soon to judge its success." (A few months after this interview, Pets.com, plagued by widening losses and a deteriorating share price, shut down after it couldn't find a merger partner. Napster, on the other hand, cut a stunning deal with Bertelsmann that could prove the basis of its salvation.)

On June 12, 2000, I show up for an all-day partners' meeting at Hummer Winblad, which takes place in the second-floor conference room of its headquarters in San Francisco's South Park, a trendy area of Internet start-ups jostling with old warehouses and car shops. And you can walk to the Giants' intimate new baseball stadium, Pacific Bell Park. Hummer Winblad's office retains the old industrial flavor of the area, with wood floors, brick walls, high unfinished ceilings, and dark interior spaces. The conference room, in which the large rectangular table barely fits, has a window on one end that looks down on a busy street. Sounds of urban life—sirens, car alarms, and honking—swirl up from below. Occasionally the meeting pauses because of the noise.

Among those at the meeting are cofounders Winblad and Hummer, who present a study in contrasts. She is petite, with blonde shoulder-length hair, while Hummer has gray hair and a former basketball player's towering height, with a deep, penetrating voice. Two other partners, Mark Gorenberg and Dan Beldy, also attend, along with Hummer Winblad's newest partner and chief operating officer, Chuck Robel, just hired from PricewaterhouseCoopers. One partner is missing: Hank Barry, a lawyer who's the acting CEO of beleaguered Napster. Other participants include entrepreneur-in-residence Brad Peters, two associates, and two summer associates. The Hummer Winblad group is far more diverse than that of any other VC firms that I saw. There are three women at the table, including one Hispanic and one African American, as well as an Asian man. And Hummer's big black dog, Chief, ambles in and out at will, occasionally depositing himself under the table for a snooze. The agenda includes progress updates from existing companies, presentations by new companies, and general discussion of market trends. A briefing from two Robertson Stephens analysts on the B2B market concludes the long day, which stretches from 9 A.M. until about 6 P.M. with a short lunch break.

First up is a Hummer Winblad portfolio company with technology for enhanced voice services over the Internet. The company has a critical meeting tomorrow with Microsoft, which wants to offer voice-activated content on MSN, and the two executives are running through their presentation to get feedback from the Hummer Winblad partners. The value proposition for Microsoft is that this technology can make MSN more useful and accessible for customers. The partners warn the executives to be careful when dealing with Microsoft. Winblad, for one, points out that company's reputation for fishing for technical information or customer names that it then uses for itself. Make sure you're dealing with people who can make something happen, she tells the two executives. Then she adds, "If you don't get the deal, go for the people." (Gorenberg tells me the next day that the meeting with Microsoft has gone well and will be followed by more negotiation.)

Then Hummer Winblad is pitched by a new company, which is offering online negotiation software for B2B market makers and corporations. In other words, companies that want to set up B2B marketplaces or utilize one can use this start-up's software to ease the process. The CEO makes the presentation, assisted by the director of finance, who keeps butting in unexpectedly. The start-up, incorporated in December 1999, has launched its product, is about to sign up its first customer, and expects to have 10 customers by year-end. It has 11 employees, mostly engineers, and has raised $800,000 in an early round. For this second round, it has already been offered $5 million from one investment firm at an $18 million premoney valuation, and it is seeking another $2 million from Hummer Winblad. That would take the company through year-end without any revenue. Winblad tells the two, "You've done a lot of impressive work with $800,000. Now we'll excuse you so we can talk about you."

It's clear during the ensuing discussion that the Hummer Winblad partners are not impressed with this company's team. "They're a bunch of engineers," says Hummer, "missing a good marketing pitch and person." Winblad dismisses the financial person as a "jack-of-all-trades and master of none—he likes to talk about everything. If somebody has an equivalent product with a sharp sales and marketing organization, they could do better." Gorenberg offers a lukewarm defense, acknowledging the need for more due diligence. "It's an interesting space and a credible company," he says, but it's "augmenting a process people do every day through personal contact. Is it improving a process or requiring a change in behavior?" Hummer suggests placing a call to the CEO's references to see if "this guy's flat-out brilliant or just a good engineer." (A few days later, Gorenberg tells me that the associates checked the references and looked at the competitive landscape: "We decided this company is too late to market and the team is missing too many pieces. We're going to tell them no.")

Next is a personal update by two executives from Hummer Winblad portfolio company Viquity, which allowed me to use its name. The Sunnyvale, California–based company offers contract manufacturers and distributors Internet-based systems that allow them to communicate with and respond to their customers. It has raised $10 million in venture funding, including $4 million from Hummer Winblad. CEO Chris Grejtak and chief technology officer and founder Sandeep Jain make the presentation. Viquity needs to build out its direct sales force and get more influential anchor customers. Grejtak says that Viquity will target small and medium companies, which he believes are underserved in the B2B market. The stumbling block is that product distributors, which have invested in their own supply chain software, are discouraging their customers from using Viquity. Says Grejtak, "I feel like the kid in the back of the room who never gets picked because there's 15 John Hummers in front of him. We don't have a big bully to force us in, like Cisco." Hummer Winblad promises to work with Viquity to line up strategic partners who will help market its technology. (Over the next few months, I get several press releases from Viquity announcing partnerships with other Internet commerce companies.)

After Viquity leaves, the partners go around the room and give timelines for when various portfolio companies will run out of money. At that point, Hummer Winblad must decide whether to keep investing, try to find a buyer for the company, or simply allow it to fade away. A couple of companies are trying to raise new rounds of financing at increased valuations, but, says Hummer, "All of these guys have to realize the world has changed. They're worth less than they were on the last round. That's the part no one's getting."

The conversation about one company, Gazoontite.com, which

sells dust-free products for allergy sufferers via a Website and retail stores, is especially enlightening. Hummer, who is on the board, says with frustration: "I've basically given up on the company. They did everything I told them not to. There's no CEO. They're going to run out of money, and I don't want to write another check. How do you attract a CEO with no money in the company?" The other board members, only one of whom is a venture capitalist, haven't been supportive, he adds. "It was a clever concept, but they've blown the opportunity. I've lost total confidence in the team." Beldy is sympathetic to Hummer's frustration: "They're still drinking their own Kool-Aid," he says of the company executives. Hummer would like to sell Gazoontite for $15 million, which essentially would get Hummer Winblad's money back. "When they come and ask us for money, we just say no," he concludes forcefully. Gorenberg replies, "John's already parachuted out of the plane," and draws chuckles from around the room. About a month later, I notice that Gazoontite's clever billboard on Highway 101 approaching San Francisco, which gave a daily pollen count, is gone. (Gazoontite does find a buyer and winds up filing for Chapter 11 bankruptcy protection in October 2000, which is why I can reveal its name. Although Gazoontite shuts down its online sites, it continues to operate its retail stores.)

Following a snack-like lunch consisting of caesar salad and a cup of soup, the partners start the afternoon by considering, and rejecting, several new deals. These include an exchange that would buy and sell semiconductors, a spinout that would set up Websites for senior citizen centers, an application service provider for chip design, and an online assessment service to match up job applicants with company needs. Of the first company, Hummer says that all the exchanges are becoming commodity businesses, driving prices to zero. "I'm not doing any more investments here." The spinout targeting seniors generates a lot of jokes about the need to design Websites with big letters, but no fervor for funding. The others meet a similar fate.

There is more interest in the final company that is seeking funding, Popular Power (its team let me use the name), which has three executives here in person. CEO Marc Hedlund, who is stocky and blunt, explains that the San Francisco–based company intends to tap into the excess computer power of all machines that sit idle for up to 14 hours a day in corporations and then sell that power via the Net. A leading investment bank that has 9,500 Pentium machines is interested in being a customer for derivatives analysis. Other potential clients include businesses with large-scale problems to solve, such as risk analysis, drug design, protein folding, neural networks, and genetic algorithms. "We think we could do 10 to 30 percent of the high-performance market," says Hedlund. Popular Power would pay a fee to computer owners, whereas customers would pay Popular Power based on computing time plus bandwidth usage. Newly hired marketing manager Debbie Pfeifer says Popular Power has already demonstrated its model in the nonprofit world, providing a computer model of a human immune system used to design a better flu vaccine.

Hedlund, who was previously at Lucasfilm, puts up a slide with the accomplishments (first product of its kind, viral word-of-mouth marketing) and risks (unproven market, long sales cycle, possible security breaches) of Popular Power. He's quite open about the fact that the management team is unproven, and he assures Hummer Winblad that he's willing to cede control to a veteran CEO. Popular Power has raised $460,000 from angel investors and is seeking a first venture round of $3 million to $5 million, which would allow it to add employees (it's currently only 10 people) and boost sales.

In the follow-up discussion, the Hummer Winblad partners are intrigued by this new approach but worry about the complications of building up a market. Posits Gorenberg, "Will somebody pay real money for an application if they don't know what environment it will be running on?" Winblad adds, "The risk is the market, not the team or the technology." Beldy feels that the deal, which is priced at a fairly low valuation, is worth doing. The company has generated considerable interest (600 inquiries) just from word-of-mouth marketing and no formal campaign, he notes. "My sense is that it's a very smart team, very upfront about what they have and don't have. You do need a killer vice president of business development to look at the opportunities. At this price I'd take a flyer on it." (But it turns out that, at least for the present, Hummer Winblad decides not to take a flyer, for lack of a near-term killer application for all the computing power that Popular Power would liberate. Gorenberg tells me that Hummer Winblad gave Popular Power a "soft no," and the company will pay another visit after it lands more customers. "Then we'll be forced to make a hard yes or no," he says.)

ON POINT WITH REDPOINT

Redpoint, as introduced in Chapter 5, is a VC newcomer but hardly a neophyte. The firm was formed in August 1999 by six partners who broke away from two existing firms, Institutional Venture Partners (IVP) and Brentwood Venture Capital. Its constituents openly proclaim that Redpoint aspires to the super tier of venture capitaldom: to be ranked with Kleiner Perkins, Sequoia, and Benchmark. The six founding partners are all men in their thirties and forties; the undisputed leader is Geoff Yang, who focuses on communications and the Internet. The other founding partners, all present at the May 15, 2000, meeting that I attend, include Tom Dyal, in his mid-thirties, the youngest of the six, specializing in data networking; Jeff Brody, a garrulous, energetic investor in consumer Internet companies; Tim Haley, in his mid-forties and the oldest, a former headhunter with 17 years of recruiting experience; John Walecka, the quietest of the bunch, focused on infrastructure; and, via a videoconference link, Brad Jones, a career venture capitalist with a law degree who heads Redpoint's Los Angeles office.

IVP, which will continue to manage the existing portfolio while Redpoint focuses on new investing in Internet technology, has bequeathed the new firm its valuable facility on Sand Hill Road. It's almost impossible to get new office space on Sand Hill these days, which is why new firms tend to locate in either San Francisco or Palo Alto. But the old IVP conference room is tight for the number of players that Redpoint brings to the table for the meeting. Seventeen people are ensconced in the black leather chairs surrounding the table, which fills the entire room. Among them are Redpoint's associates, venture partners, and entrepreneurs-in-residence, along with a few guests who have specialized expertise in something that's on the agenda today. The morning lineup includes companies that are undergoing active due diligence for possible investment (designed with a "P3" priority for tracking), hot deals that need an immediate decision ("P2"), and updates on companies with which Redpoint has already made a commitment ("P1"). Later, the group will discuss general items related to the partnership, including recruitment, raising a second fund, lining up strategic partners, and even "rumors and scuttlebutt." All of these topics are dutifully listed on the detailed agenda, which also rotates the chair of the meeting among the various partners. On this day Yang is the designated man in charge.

Each deal under consideration has a team of two to four people from Redpoint, including one or two partners plus associates, who have met with the company and conducted the due diligence into its prospects. This typically consists of talking to customers, partners, and competitors to assess the market space; polling references on the management team; and assessing the business plan's financial projections. The team then must defend the prospective investment in the free-wheeling discussion that involves the entire partnership. Redpoint, like its peers, limits the new deals it will undertake, so each one undergoes laborious consideration. In fact, Redpoint, with 35 to 50 deals a year, is probably on the high end of early-stage investors. As Dyal tells me prior to the meeting, the uncertain state of the public market has been a reality check on the deals that Redpoint looks at. Private money will probably have to keep start-ups going for two years or more. Consequently, "you're looking for defined business models with a clear execution strategy," he says. "Where you have a fuzzy business model or lack of execution, that's a deal-breaker."

First on the agenda are two start-ups in the same space: providing wireless services and remote access to the Web. Both companies have problems: one lacks a CEO and the other doesn't have any reference customers. "It's an execution horse race," is the way venture partner Peter Gotcher sees it. The first company to fill in its team and start signing up customers is going to win. Brody believes the wireless market is so huge that there's room for more than one winner. "There's three constituencies that everyone is going after: the [telephone] carriers, device guys, and content providers. The device guys want as many offerings as possible, so various companies are going to get traction." Yang sounds a note of caution: If wireless turns out to be just a tool rather than a brand-new market, it may not support any big winner. "If it's a small market and you can't handicap the winners, you stay out," he says. But Gotcher, who is on the wireless team that researched these companies, argues that people will eventually access more content on wireless than on PCs. However, he agrees with the group that it's difficult to pick either of the two companies they're considering because "there's not enough differentiation" between the business models. "Neither one is a slam dunk." He and the wireless team agree to do more research and report back at the next meeting.

Yang gets off a good line about the next company, a telecom start-up with a team of founders who just left their existing company the previous Friday. "If this is going to happen we've got to do it quickly," he says. "The next thing you know they'll be asking for the right to vote." This is in reference to the fact that the founding team is extremely young, in their early twenties. This is followed by a technical discussion of another telecom play, which would sell broadband equipment to the regional Bell operating companies (RBOCs). Venture partner Jim Mongiello sums up the pluses and minuses: While there's a real need for the product, the sales cycle will be lengthy because the RBOCs take their time. And start-ups have a tough time coping with all the environmental issues that the RBOCs must deal with, such as heat dissipation. Dyal chimes in, "This is a good market, but not a monster." Yang tells Dyal and Mongiello to talk to the team again and make the decision. "If you come back negative, we'll back off," he concludes.

The group quickly dispenses of several more companies seeking funding. One would service call centers with voice-activated services, but the partners decide it's a crowded, fragmented niche where the likely outcome is an acquisition. Not an interesting enough profile to draw in Redpoint. Another is an East Coast company that would aggregate content from branded Websites and distribute it via personalized daily e-mail. The dissuading factors for Redpoint are the company's location and a general feeling that only the first entrant in this market is likely to do well. The third company, which would reformat streaming media to offer it on demand (i.e., movies on the Web), is a little more intriguing. Entrepreneur-in-residence Michael Tanne, who's championing the company, will do more research on potential customers such as Microsoft's Web TV unit.

The partners, who have not manifested much enthusiasm for anything, perk up at the possibility of investing in a company that will offer a national broadcast data network utilizing the HDTV spectrum. Notes Yang, "The Internet right now is a request transaction network. What if it was a set of applications for publish and subscribe?" That is, this company could facilitate the creation of specialized information on subjects such as sales force connectivity that could be accessed by those willing to pay. "There's a market for stuff like this," Yang says. Brody, who is championing the company, says the killer apps for the technology include new game releases, software releases, and music. "You're investing here in a company that owns spectrum," he says, always a valuable resource as more and more content is beamed into cyberspace. The company, which has a number of well-connected strategic partners and investors, only wants one VC investor. But the price will be steep: an ownership share in the teens for close to a $100 million postmoney valuation. "I'm not crazy about that price," says Yang. Brody responds that he's reluctant to push on the deal unless everyone at the table is on board. "It will be a real sell to get it at a rational price," he admits. Yang sums up the approach: "We should move toward naming our price and then don't participate if we can't." Recognizing that that is more cautious than Redpoint's usual gung ho approach, Yang adds, "Maybe I'm getting pulled down by the psychology of a declining market."

There's a burst of laughter about the next company, which makes small, low-cost Internet devices that fit on a keychain and offer limited connectivity. Someone compares the product to Tamagotchi, the Japanese computerized pets. The idea is for companies to give the devices away as novelties. "The question is, is this a neat device or a real business?" says associate Josh Becker, who's done the research on the deal. "We're trying to figure out the recurring revenue stream." Brody insists that the idea is really cool. "You could see Nike ordering a million of these things and distributing them with their shoes." Other uses include using the device to plug into a computer and redeem a coupon for, say, a free cup of coffee at Starbucks. Brody and Becker will continue to meet with the company, which they think has real possibilities, but it's apparent that it will take some convincing to win over the rest of the group.

The partners go thumbs down on a Napster-like competitor because of questions about the business model and the market. "This company doesn't have the users that Napster does," says Yang. "Could they grow as quickly?" Brody says that the market is unfolding so unpredictably "that we could be blindsided and this company is worth nothing. It's also possible that Napster might go belly-up." The consensus: to pass.

The morning closes with a discussion of Redpoint's money-raising efforts on its next fund. Its first fund of $600 million was committed in less than a year, a pace that has been criticized by some of Redpoint's competitors, who felt that the firm invested too much too quickly. But Yang, in a private conversation, shakes off that criticism. You raise money when you can, he tells me, especially if there's concern that it will be more difficult in the future. At the time of the meeting, in May,

Redpoint had $250 million raised for its new fund. It closed the fund in August at $1.25 billion with a formal promise that it would last two years.

GROUP DYNAMICS

Evident from the three partnership meetings I attended is that experience holds the floor. The partners who have founded the firm and done the bulk of the investing dominate the meeting and make the decisions. This is not really a surprise, except that VC firms like to style themselves as egalitarian and open. That isn't wholly the case. In practice, the associates do the scut work, and the partners hold it up to the light and see if it flies. Even among the partners, definite hierarchies can be perceived. Still, compared with what goes on in the corporate world, the VC partnership meetings are definitely more free-flowing and inclusive.

Even in the best of times, it's a lot easier to shoot an idea down than to get one accepted by these guys. And it was no longer the best of times in mid-2000. Everybody had woken up with a hangover from the excesses of the previous era, some worse than others. In particular, many of the dot-coms funded in the unrestrained atmosphere of the late 1990s were being forced to slash their workforces or close their doors. In Chapter 11 we see how the herd mentality of the industry can drive an unwise stampede into unwanted, unneeded companies that then get shut down in the panic that inevitably follows.

CHAPTER ELEVEN

The Dark Side

Oone reason why venture capital has worked so well is that, à la Adam Smith's invisible hand, investors' interests are neatly aligned with those of the entrepreneurs, for the most part. The venture capitalist succeeds when the entrepreneurial company succeeds—in ramping up to a point where it can go public or be bought at a significant premium for investors—so it behooves the entrepreneur to draw as much as possible on the venture capitalist's skills to achieve all the goals: product launch, customer sales, initial public offering (IPO), and so on. Of course, conflict inevitably arises when the venture capitalist and the entrepreneur differ over how to achieve those goals. This conflict is exacerbated when external forces such as poor market conditions and excessive competition make the journey even tougher.

The dark side of the venture capital (VC) paradigm can be triggered by internal and external causes. Internal causes arise when the interests of entrepreneur and venture capitalist aren't so neatly aligned. For example, a promising start-up gets bounced from VC firm to VC firm, each one putting the founders on hold because the partners want one more indefinable piece of the puzzle put into place. Conversely, another start-up gets sucked into a bidding frenzy, with venture capitalists stabbing each other in the back to win the deal. Once the deal is done, the founders and venture capitalists may differ on strategy or execution, and the upshot might be a board vote that disposes of the former. As the Hummer Winblad partners' discussion on Gazoontite showed, the ultimate outcome can be abandoning a company that looks hopeless and forcing it to shut its doors. And let's not put all the burden on venture capitalists. Many an entrepreneur will say anything to get funding—inflating qualifications, lying on a résumé, making up customers that don't exist. Fact is, there's a lot of money to be made and glory to be wrung from entrepreneurial companies, which can bring out the worst even in people who already have hundreds of millions of dollars.

Sometimes you can do everything right, and the timing is just wrong. External forces come into play that no one can control. As in the recent bubble, public investors get too greedy and bid up the IPOs of companies that have no hope of profitability in sight. Venture capitalists, in turn, bring out too many mediocre companies to collect the easy pickings. This results in a massive fallout that shakes up the public markets so that even good companies can't get out. Private companies must stay private longer, requiring more venture capital to stay afloat. This dries up sources of cash for other start-ups. Eventually, as returns on investment drop, the limited partners start pulling back in the funds they give to venture capitalists. And a dry cycle is born.

Whichever portion of the venture capital cycle you're in—greed or fear—the dark side is always there, although it may manifest itself differently. Let's explore the various manifestations from both the entrepreneur and VC perspectives.

LOOKING FOR MR. GOODMONEY

Not every entrepreneur has the deal du jour that a venture capitalist will kill for. Yet, even when the feeling at the partnership meeting on a company is negative, it's hard for entrepreneurs to get a straight answer from venture capitalists. That's one of their greatest weaknesses and a source of irritation for many an entrepreneur who can't get a response to what seems like a simple question: "Are you in the deal or out?" That was the case with Alert1st, whose pitch to Highland Capital Partners was described in Chapter 7. Alert1st is trying to fill a hole in the customer relationship management (CRM) space by offering Internet-based software that allows companies to identify their best customers and solve their problems proactively. CEO Phil Beisel has a perfectly respectable record for an entrepreneur: He was a product manager at Apple Computer and then started another company, which was sold, before Alert1st. And his idea for differentiating among customers has merit, as many venture capitalists assure him. However, he can't get anyone to pull the trigger and give Alert1st a term sheet.

"The venture capitalist is looking for an unbridled opportunity, a huge market, a product that fills a gaping hole," Beisel tells me. "You've also got to convince them your friction is low; it's easy to get to the customer." Where he thinks Alert1st missed is that the product is a tough sell in a noisy, crowded space, so the friction in getting to the customer is high. Alert1st also hit two other, possibly fatal, barriers. The first was the friction in the VC industry itself. In mid-2000, when the company was searching for funding, the venture capitalists had funded so many start-ups over the past year or so that they were all overcommitted. "We got caught in the congestion," says Beisel. Sequoia Capital's Doug Leone "told me he takes home 30 business plans every night. Consider what you need in that plan to make it work for him. After that I took six pages of our plan and turned it into two."

The second barrier was the downturn in the public market, which made venture capitalists much more leery of leaping into a company like Alert1st, whose business strategy would take heavy up-front investment in customer sales and possibly a lengthy period of time to reach profitability. Alert1st's champion at Highland, Keith Benjamin, finally admitted to Beisel that the company probably wasn't going to get funding. "We did our nuclear winter scenario and asked, 'Can this company survive in a down market?'" Benjamin told him. The answer, at least from Highland's perspective, wasn't a positive one. Beisel turns to an Olympics scoring analogy to describe his dilemma. "Let's say we're 9.5 out of 10," he says. "But venture capitalists are now looking for 9.75 or 9.9 in this market."

Turned down by half a dozen other VC firms, Beisel worked hard to try to salvage the deal with Highland. At Benjamin's suggestion, he contacted several entrepreneurs whom the VC firm had funded in the past to see if he could work out a relationship with them that would make Alert1st more attractive to Highland. Yet the e-mail he got from

Benjamin was still negative: "I suspect we're not going to move forward." In phone conversations with Benjamin, the venture capitalist was increasingly noncommittal. "We'd lost momentum, hit the 95th percentile instead of 100," Beisel says. "Highland was freaked out about the market. They had to come up with reasons to say no." His e-mailed memo to another Highland partner never got a response, but Benjamin assured Beisel that the partnership respected him. "I got high marks even though I didn't pass the test," Beisel laughs bitterly.

Dan Plashkes, the CEO at San Diego–based eAssist, which provides Internet-based customer support and demand creation services, did pass the test. Of medium height and trim build, with short, graying hair, the native Canadian founded his first company, an interactive call center, in 1986. With eAssist, "we had very little trouble raising money," says Plashkes. That doesn't mean he's crazy about venture capitalists. A number of firms either turned him down or never bothered to return the calls. "With one firm, somebody called us back and said one partner's off for a month and everyone else is too busy. Another one said, 'I can't travel to your board meetings, so if you can get someone else to invest we're in.'" With the firms that were interested, the bargaining was cutthroat. The collegiality of the VC community, which Plashkes saw with his earlier company, is gone, he says. "They're all fighting each other for the good deals. It's gotten crazy." Indeed, one leading venture capitalist tells the story of a VC firm so eager to get in on a deal that it would close its own competitive company to do so. "They would go out and fire the CEO, fire the managers, and shut down the other company in order to get into this other deal. It's like, 'Well, you're prettier, so I'm going to go home and shoot my wife, so I can get married to someone else.'"[1]

If an entrepreneur does have a hot deal, the VC firm plays another game, sealing the company off from the world and insisting that it alone must be the early-round investor. This tactic often works when applied by a top-tier firm like Kleiner or Sequoia. Says Adam Boyden, the CEO of Autodaq (introduced in Chapter 7), "The games they play to get a hot deal are very off-putting. If it looks like they're going to lose out, they'll ring you up and say you're a dishonest person for not going with them. 'Your name will be mud in the Valley. You'll never do business again.' The negotiating styles can be very disheartening." Another tactic is to set a deadline of 12 or 24 hours before the VC firm pulls out. "They'll tell you, 'If you don't accept this offer in 12 hours, we're walking from the table. You'll get a worse offer from someone else,'" Boyden says. "Then when you walk away, the next day they call and offer you a better deal." What Boyden looked for in a venture capitalist was someone he could trust. "I didn't want to be looking over my shoulder for a knife in the back."

MAKING THE ROUNDS

In 1996, Sandeep Johri, the chairman and founder of Oblix in Cupertino, California, scraped together $600,000 in funding from friends and family to start the company. He was confident that the money would last at least six months, until he raised a formal VC round. Think again. Down to his last $10,000, Johri deferred salaries for himself and the other two founders and was forced to borrow money to make payroll for the rest of the employees. Venture capitalists can smell desperation; they sensed that Oblix, which made software for business-to-business (B2B) transactions, was running out of time. "We met with a lot of VCs," Johri says. "Some of them turned us down; some kept stringing us out. Some we didn't want because they weren't top tier. It was not one of those 'we made the presentation on Monday and had commitments by Friday' type of deals."

Through one of those tenuous connections that are the stuff of VC networking, Oblix got in to see Ted Schlein, a new partner at Kleiner Perkins, in mid-1997. One member of Oblix's management team had long ago dated Schlein's sister. Schlein referred the deal to Will Hearst, who had invested in a company whose technology Oblix was using. "We had a fairly lengthy courtship with Will," Johri recalls. It wasn't obvious that a deal with Kleiner would go through, so when a Boston-based VC firm put a term sheet on the table for Oblix, it was tempting. Then, "Will talked to them, and after that they refused to return our calls," Johri says. "Will told them, 'We've already done this deal; don't waste your time.' He hadn't told us that. [The other firm] went away, so we had less leverage." Kleiner wound up with 38 percent of the company in exchange for $3 million.

Johri gives Hearst credit for being up front about one thing: the need to bring in a veteran CEO (which turned out to be Gordon Eubanks, formerly of Symantec; see Chapter 4). "Will and I had the discussion about leadership even before they offered a term sheet," says

Johri. "Will was very open about it." Not all VC firms are as honest, he says. "Even though they have already determined that [they would replace the CEO], they don't necessarily share that with the entrepreneur because he might take the deal away." The better venture capitalists will have that discussion early in the process, he says. "Kleiner didn't really have to convince me [to name another CEO]. I just wanted to be involved in the selection process."

Another company that nearly ran out of money is zipRealty.com. It burst upon the scene in May 1999 as a finalist in the University of California at Berkeley business plan competition. The Berkeley, California–based company closed its first round of funding within two weeks of the competition, recounts Scott Kucirek, the MBA graduate student who is now president of zipRealty. Then it was on to the second round, in which zipRealty sought $16 million. "We targeted the top six funds and got lots of lukewarm responses," he says. In later rounds, with more money at stake, venture capitalists want coinvestors to share the risk. In November 1999 zipRealty was short on cash, and tempers were fraying. "We got a real lowball offer from a top-tier firm," says Kucirek. There was considerable internal debate over whether to take it. Instead, zipRealty managed to line up $2 million in bridge financing from current investors while it sought a better offer. It finally got one from Benchmark, just as it was about to sign the lowball term sheet from the other firm.

Raising a later round of funding, Peter Jackson, CEO of Orinda, California–based Intraware, also went through the "he loves me, he loves me not" stage with venture capitalists. The company, which provides an Internet marketplace for software and services aimed at information technology professionals, had a monthly revenue run rate of $1 million in late 1997 when it was seeking follow-on financing. "Phones were ringing off the hook" with calls from interested venture capitalists, Jackson says. He hooked up with Kleiner Perkins partner Doug Mackenzie and followed that with a presentation to the entire partnership, something like 18 people sitting around the table, including all the stars—Vinod Khosla, John Doerr, and Will Hearst. "I try to do the classic thing of visualizing my audience naked," recalls Jackson, "and I go through this presentation for about two hours, lots of Q&A." At the end Doerr came up and told him, "Good job, Tim." Jackson was convinced the deal wasn't going to happen, because, after two hours, Doerr didn't even remember his name.

But just presenting to Kleiner has its payoff. While that firm was doing its due diligence, "we were the prettiest girl in town—everyone called," says Jackson. One firm that had pulled out now wanted back in. "The day after I made the presentation, I was riding high." Getting ready to take his wife out to dinner on her birthday, November 4, he got a call from Mackenzie: "Hey, we wrestled until late in the night and we couldn't get a couple of the partners turned around." Over drinks at dinner, Jackson broke down and started crying when his father-in-law put an arm around him and asked how things were going. Jackson got up from the table to go check his voicemail messages. The word from Kleiner was evidently already out; several other firms had called to say they're no longer interested.

Later that night, unable to sleep, Jackson fashioned an e-mail to John Doerr asking him to reconsider. He told Doerr that any amount of money from Kleiner, even if it was only $1 million, would help, because the cachet alone would bring other investors on board. "When I finished typing I just stared at the message and wondered if I was being this sappy crybaby to the biggest, most powerful venture capitalist in the whole world," he says. He took a walk around the block to cool down, came back, and hit the send button. "That's it, you're toast," he told himself. The next day Jackson got an e-mail back from Doerr: "We changed our minds, we're in the deal."[2]

BELT-TIGHTENING, OR ELSE

The comments about nuclear winter that cropped up in the VC partnership meetings probably overstated the case, but the fact is that the industry is easily spooked by external events. It then undergoes a chameleon-like, virtually instantaneous change in attitude from either fear to greed, or vice versa. I witnessed one of these changes—in this case from greed to fear—as I was researching this book from early to late 2000. As the public appetite for dot-coms turned sour, stock prices plummeted, and companies that had depended on rising market capitalizations for financing suddenly had to rely on internal cash at hand. This resulted in (worst case) outright company failures and (best case) layoffs and hoarding of whatever cash the companies had left. When was the last time you saw a dot-com ad on TV? What this meant to venture capitalists, who rarely proffer funding to public companies, was that their still-private portfolio companies would stay private longer and possibly require more funding rounds before a liquidity event—an IPO or a merger. So the venture capitalists began advising their companies to conserve cash and get lean and mean, in effect reversing the spendthrift model that many late 1990s start-ups, particularly in the Internet space, had been built around. This was the VC pattern writ large, because venture capitalists have an inherent tendency to micromanage anyway. It is their investment, after all.

Jens Horstmann, the president of Santa Clara, California–based OpenGrid, has repositioned his company and altered the business strategy more than once in trying to comply with his investors' demands. Originally, in 1996 OpenGrid developed technology to do large-scale online trading. Then, when it lost its original funding source, individual investor Andy Bectolsheim (cofounder of Sun Microsystems, who decided to start another company), OpenGrid repositioned itself as a provider of B2B services for the travel industry. It picked up $900,000 in funding from Advanced Technology Ventures and Draper Fisher Jurvetson. "Our goal," says Horstmann, "was to put an infrastructure in place that would allow the travel business to collaborate." However, "what the VCs saw in us was not travel," he says. They saw bright people with good technology that could be used for a market much bigger than travel. "As a young entrepreneur, you look at VCs as the experts. You figure they must know what's happening out there," he says. "You do what they say."

Over the next couple of years, OpenGrid struggled to define its business strategy. "We tried too hard to make them happy," says Horstmann of the VC investors. "Later, we realized we should have pursued our own vision and not listened so much to the theme of the day." It wasn't that the venture capitalists tried to control the company, "it was that they kept changing their minds all the time." The executive staff would decide to pursue one strategy; then the board, which included venture capital as well as corporate and private investors, would direct it to do something else. "We decide we need to do A. The board said, 'You need to do B.' So we scrambled for a whole month to put together a new strategy to do B. We go to the board meeting, and they said, 'We've thought about what you said and we want to go back to A.' Then at the next board meeting they said, 'We've thought about it some more, and let's do elements of A and B and call it C.' So we chase after *C*. At the next board meeting new numbers come in, and we go back to *A*."

Today, OpenGrid is a wireless Internet solution provider, which means that it offers customers an interchange on which they can build customized applications. For instance, one early customer is Hilton Hotels, which will use OpenGrid's technology to allow travelers to check room availability and to book or update reservations from mobile devices. "The space was evolving so rapidly that we got distracted," Horstmann acknowledges. "What I learned is that you had to follow your gut, get something out, and if it doesn't work you take a new direction, but you don't keep constantly changing." He would take venture capital again, but with eyes wide open. "We had times when we hated the VCs," he says. "Just before you hit the wall, the VCs say, 'We'll give you a bridge [financing], but the terms are going to be ugly.' It's a game. Once you understand it's a game, it gets easier. It can even be fun."

In mid-2000 OpenGrid was raising a late round of $30 million, prior to a hoped-for IPO. "What we've seen in this last round is that [the investment world] has become a total black-and-white picture," says Horstmann. "You're either hot and everyone wants to invest, so they don't do any due diligence or even ask for product demos. Just, 'How do I get in?' If you're not hot, you can't raise any money." The hot/not-hot dichotomy extends beyond venture capitalists to real estate agents, lawyers, public relations (PR) people, and accountants. "We're looking for more office space, and they want to hear our investment pitch," he says.

In 1999 and early 2000, when optimism was still high, there might have been wiggle room for companies that fell on the not-hot side of the dichotomy. Not so by mid-2000, when being out in the cold could have dire consequences. Take eCurator.com, a San Francisco–based start-up aiming to provide appraisal, insurance, and other services to online buyers and sellers of art and antiques. Cofounders Chris Haigh and Guy Bristow raised $500,000 from friends and family to start the company in 1999. In April 2000 they were counting on a cash infusion of $750,000 from a New York VC firm to pay for expansion and marketing. Then came the market crash, and the funding offer was withdrawn. Haigh and Bristow laid off their staff of six and spent down to their last $5,000. "My children have more in their savings fund," says

Haigh. "We've reduced our burn rate to essentially zero and are talking to original investors to keep us alive."[3] When I tried to call eCurator a couple of months later, the phone line had been disconnected. Its onetime PR firm told me that the company had not been able to raise any venture capital despite a "last-ditch effort" and that the Website was now "just a hobby."

However, eCurator was far from alone in its misery. In August 2000 a survey of 238 Internet companies by Webmergers.com revealed the following: Since the beginning of the year, 41 had closed their doors, 29 had been sold (mainly at firesale prices), and 83 had withdrawn plans for an IPO. Retuning the business model was also commonplace: At least 17 of the firms had curtailed business-to-consumer (B2C) selling in favor of less costly B2B models, while 98 companies had laid off employees. Webmergers president Tim Miller said that companies were running into "brick walls" in trying to raise additional rounds of financing or to get to an IPO. "There's a huge middle class of Web properties that have no way to find a marketplace right now."[4] If those companies couldn't merge with someone else, usually another Internet company, the likely scenario was oblivion. One of the earliest victims was APBNews.com, a New York–based crime-reporting Website that ran out of money in June 2000 and abruptly laid off its 140 employees. Reel.com was another. Once one of the Web's largest DVD and video stores, the Emeryville, California–based company terminated its 230 employees in June 2000 after its IPO was canceled and funding dried up.[5] A March 2001 survey by outplacement specialist Challenger Gray & Christmas revealed that 75,000 dot-com workers had been terminated since December 1999.

Public companies were not exempt from the winnowing. In February 2000 the San Francisco–based e-tailer Pets.com had gone public at $11 a share. But by late 2000, the company was a penny stock, trading under a dollar. On November 7, when Pets.com informed its employees that it was shutting down, the share price stood at 22 cents. Pets.com had hired Merrill Lynch to help it sell itself, but of 50 prospective partners contacted, fewer than eight even wanted to visit the company. John Hummer, the Hummer Winblad partner who sat on Pets.com's board, says the VC firm lost about $20 million on the deal, yet he still defended the company. "This was a concept that worked, but you needed real scale to get profitable," he says. "You also needed a somewhat cheaper way to acquire customers." Amazon.com, an investor and partner, might have saved Pets.com, Hummer maintains, by either buying it or at least granting full access to Amazon's distribution channel and customer list. "Amazon was our partner, but we never really got the full benefit of their customer acquisition." The pullback from dot-com stocks, which caused Pets.com's price to tank, meant that the company couldn't do a secondary offering to raise more cash, expand its distribution, and bulk up on customers. Hummer denies that Pets.com's spending on an expensive ad campaign, including the Super Bowl, caused its demise. "An IPO won't get an e-tailer all the way home," says Hummer. "You have to do a secondary. You can't do that if the share price is 90 percent below its offering price." Unlike another Hummer Winblad dot-com, Gazoontite, which failed because the management team didn't execute properly, Pets.com was a matter of the public market losing confidence too soon, Hummer says. "You don't get 600,000 customers by not delivering." He would back Pets.com CEO Julie Wainwright again "in a heartbeat." The experience was a painful reminder: "When you have a terrific management team that meets a bad market, the bad market always wins."

Although it was one of the first publicly traded dot-coms to close, Pets.com would undoubtedly have plenty of company. At their peak in March 2000, Internet stocks had a combined market valuation of $1.4 trillion; by July, despite a partial recovery from the April crash, the stocks had lost 40 percent of that, erasing almost as much paper wealth as the 1987 stock market crash.[6] In November 2000 Goldman Sachs analyst Anthony Noto warned that only 12 to 14 of the 22 publicly traded e-tailers he follows would still be alive by mid-2001, compared with 28 in the previous year.[7] By early December 2000, during the presidential election turmoil, Nasdaq dropped below the level where it had opened the year. Dot-coms were left flailing for cash, and their employees' stock options were underwater—valueless. By March of 2001, the top 400 Internet stocks had lost $1 trillion in market valuation, and Nasdaq was in a profound bear market.

While VC investors may remain on the board of a newly public company, they will do so in a very different sense than when they were keenly involved with the private entity's day-to-day operations. They have made their money from the company, and their interests now begin to diverge. For the company, its very survival is at stake. For the venture capitalist, it's a more esoteric game: reputation versus resource (i.e., time). No self-respecting venture capitalist wants to see a company he or she funded go under, but time is inelastic. The venture capitalist must ultimately decide whether a public company can be saved and whether the time invested might be better spent on building a new start-up. Thus, venture capitalists will quietly bail out of companies that appear doomed, preferring to focus their efforts on the Next Big Thing.

THE OTHER SIDE OF THE MOUNTAIN

Entrepreneurs aren't the only ones with horror stories. Venture capitalists also have their share of founders who predict billion-dollar markets and call that a conservative projection, of start-ups that miss target after target and still have their hands out for more money, of entrepreneurs who lie about their qualifications, of founding teams that snipe at each other like spouses in a bad marriage, and of failing companies that expect the venture capitalist to step in and save the day (see "Flips and Flops"). "An experienced investor trusts nothing and nobody at first glance," sums up Sequoia Partners' Mike Moritz. When venture capitalists first invest in a company, "nothing about it is real. A thicket of claims, predictions, and projections always surrounds a new investment and makes the kernel of truth almost impossible to discern. . . . The company amounts to little more than a figment of someone's imagination."[8]

The hype generated by the tremendous successes of the last few years hasn't helped. Certain code words appear in every press release about a new start-up that I read: the "world-class" team, the "breakthrough" technology or service, the "huge and compelling new market." Just once I'd like to read a press release that describes a company with a "merely competent" team that has "modest but achievable goals" with a shot at becoming a "reasonably sized player" in a "decent but not overwhelming market." That's my fantasy as a journalist; it'll never happen. As Moritz puts it, "So much hot air rises from small companies in Silicon Valley that it must be a major contributor to global warming."

Thus, most venture capitalists, at least those in the top tier, professed to welcome the return to sanity resulting from public disenchantment with money burning, profitless Internet companies, and the corresponding drop in Nasdaq. Moritz's colleague, Don Valentine, told me bluntly, "We're funding too many bad companies because there's a too-much-money mentality." In the past, "we'd finance these companies with just enough money to frugally manage their business. Now if the amount of money you want is too little, we're not interested. Our checkbook is swollen, so we say, 'Why don't you expand the financing so we can put in more?'" Valentine, like his colleagues, also decries the dumb money pouring into the business, chasing the triple-digit returns that were about to disappear. "We're just waiting for the carnage to reap," he says.

The carnage started in mid-2000, a few months after my interview with Valentine. "We are in the fear cycle now," Kleiner Perkins' Vinod Khosla proclaimed in May 2000. For venture capitalists who were more interested in building companies than in generating exit events such as an IPO, this wasn't such a bad thing, he believes. For one thing, the unrealistic valuations that entrepreneurs placed on their companies started to drop, meaning that VC firms could get a greater stake in a company for a smaller investment. It's also a way for the top-tier firms to reassert their dominance. In a market where "it's fall out of the boat and hit the water time," anyone can do well. As times get tougher, the value of people like Khosla or Valentine becomes more evident. Says Khosla, "My [public] companies have had a much smaller decline in this down cycle. I did a personal analysis: Juniper hasn't declined, Cerent is part of Cisco, and Siara is part of Redback. I've been measuring it because I want to test myself. I have a burden to deliver returns."

Not everyone is as sanguine as Khosla. Integral Capital's Roger McNamee is normally one of the cheeriest guys in the investing industry. In his mid-forties, impish and boyish, McNamee resembles Paul McCartney with glasses, but don't tell him that because his real hero is the Grateful Dead's late Jerry Garcia. Dominating McNamee's office is a life-size papier-mâché figure of Garcia wearing a T-shirt with the name of McNamee's own band, Flying Other Brothers. (I'd hate to be a new cleaning person coming in there in the middle of the night.) On the wall are psychedelic posters of other great rock stars of the past, such as the Doors and Van Morrison. There's even a fake prospectus for the public offering of FOB (Flying Other Brothers). But when I talk to him in May 2000, McNamee's demeanor is intensely serious. "People are in denial," he says. "The emperor's buck naked

FLIPS AND FLOPS

Like the rest of us, venture capitalists don't like dwelling on their failures. However, in an industry that worships risks, failures are inevitable; indeed, they're an absolute necessity. For if there are no failures by a VC firm, there probably are no grand successes either, so thin is the dividing line between doomed obsession and dogged genius. Here are some of the answers I got when I asked venture capitalists to identify their biggest flops.

I invested in Gavilan Computers, a $4 million loss in the early 1980s. We just had too many moving parts. The operating system wasn't tied down. We were using a nonstandard disk drive. The semiconductor technology wasn't stabilized. The CEO got us into mass production before we were ready. I learned, don't try to do too many things at once.

Dick Kramlich, New Enterprise Associates

It was a semiconductor equipment company that was supposed to be the next Applied Materials. There were very major problems with the founder that we had no hint of. He was a religious fanatic; God was giving him directions. He drove the management team out, drove the company into the wall. It died in a huge flame.

Sam Colella, Institutional Venture Partners

There's only been one company I've lost money on in the last 10 years. That was OnLive [founded in 1994 with the goal of creating 3-D virtual-world software]. They had $30 million in cash, and I asked them to cut their burn rate. But we were the number three investor and I was the only naysayer. They were giving bonuses to these guys as they were driving the company into the ground.

Vinod Khosla, Kleiner Perkins Caufield & Byers

My biggest flop was not investing in Siebel Systems. The money you lose on a deal doesn't matter. Your biggest flop is what you didn't get into. Tom Siebel is a friend of mine. He's a killer salesman who doesn't like VCs. We were the only firm with an opportunity because of my friendship with him. He gave us the terms. The partnership couldn't gag it down. We could have gotten 10 percent of the company for $2.7 million. If you had 10 percent of Siebel today it would be worth billions.

Irwin Federman, U.S. Venture Partners

One company wanted to do a videophone in 1991. The company wasn't intellectually honest with itself. The marketplace was rejecting it, but they drank their own Kool-Aid and refused to believe their technology wasn't working. We lost about $3 million. I'm now very sensitive to making sure that as a VC I develop a good enough relationship with management to share sensitive information.

Kevin Fong, Mayfield Fund

We invested $500,000 in Pop Rocket, a CD-ROM company in the mid-nineties doing entertainment software. It had tremendous hype, but the product shipped a year late. By the time it got to market, it had lost its mind share. We now have a phrase: 'Saw it off and ship it.' If you do nothing else, get your product into the marketplace and gain customer traction. Not shipping product is like not swinging at strikes.

Mark Gorenberg, Hummer Winblad Venture Partners

My biggest failures have generally been investments in education business. I am passionate about education both personally and professionally. We have not lost money, but several have taken a very long time with a very small return, if any. I want to show Wall Street it's possible to build a very large successful [education] company.

Jim Breyer, Accel Partners

We missed Parametric Technology, one of the first billion-dollar cap software companies in the eighties. We were looking at this with a name-brand VC. We told Parametric we wanted to hire a CEO and raise $5 million instead of $10 million. The other VC watched us hang ourselves and then stepped in. We were the stalking horse. Sometimes it's best not to be the first one to deal with these entrepreneurs because they have fragile egos.

Bob Barrett, Battery Ventures

We lost on Chromatic Research, doing a media processor for PCs. We tried to boil the ocean. Instead of picking a couple of key things and doing those well, we tried to do everything. As a result we came late to market and consumed a lot of money.

Bill Davidow, Mohr Davidow Ventures

We did a biotech company in Maryland doing reproduction of stem cells for cancer treatment. We lost all our money, about $2 million. The lesson was, stick to your knitting. If you don't have any domain expertise, don't do it.

Promod Haque, Norwest Venture Partners

We passed on Compaq because it was in Houston. I went to visit them and decided it was too far to be on the board. Now I know, "Don't go to Houston; you may regret it." I went and decided not to do the deal and I regret it.

Pierre Lamond, Sequoia Capital

I've only had one company go out of business. It was my first and last foray into games: Rocket Science Games in the early nineties. I knew nothing about the game business. We ended up selling to Sega for nothing. All the people except a handful lost their jobs. It never went public. They couldn't even sell their games.

Kathryn Gould, Foundation Capital

and doesn't realize it. The attitude is, 'Everybody else is doing badly, but we're fine'." Here's how McNamee sees the situation: It's airplane rush hour in the New York metropolitan area, and somebody has removed all the airports. "There are a gazillion little companies up in the air, with no place to land, and they all need fuel."

THE CYCLE REPEATS

Experienced venture capitalists realize that the industry is bound to be cyclical, and both good times and bad will pass. "The land-rush perception of the Internet came about by degrees, and it's going to end by degrees," says McNamee. "Investors lowered their standards and got more aggressive. Entrepreneurs took advantage of that. In the last year we were in this environment where the venture business was pretty much out of control. Time will render its own judgment." Valentine agrees, comparing the recent boom era to the mid-1980s, "when the dam broke" on VC investing after the success of companies like Intel, Apple, and Sun Microsystems. "Money became very available, and all kinds of people got into the business because it was easy," he says. "Then a lot of them got their asses whipped when the correction came."

Another correction occurred in the last half of 2000, and for the first time in almost a decade, VC returns turned negative, according to anecdotal reports. Of course, the top-tier firms still expected to be top-tier, but just where that tier was would slip. It's kind of like grading on a curve. Average annual VC returns have historically been in the 20 percent to 30 percent range, and most VCs thought they'd wind up in that area again, after going lower for a time. "Average annual returns will fall to zero at least once in the next 10 years," McNamee predicts, similar to what happened in the late 1980s. Veteran New York venture capitalist Alan J. Patricof says that just as in the public markets, the psychology of private investing "can change overnight and dramatically. We don't know whether 90 percent of Internet companies will ever make money, and massive wholesale liquidation is possible." The loss ratio of venture capital in the late 1990s had dipped to about 2.5 percent, which was unnaturally low, says Patricof. In the past, the ratio was more like 10 percent to 15 percent, he adds, and he won't be surprised if it goes there again.

Here's the rest of the scenario in a down cycle: Massive consolidation occurs among both entrepreneurial companies and VC firms, especially those who aren't in the top tier. New firms will find it tough to raise money and will disappear. Meanwhile, companies that are raising venture capital can no longer expect an automatic step-up in valuation from one round to the next. Those companies that don't meet their targets and demonstrate a recognized path to profitability will find their VC investors driving increasingly hard bargains. There'll be questions about the staying power of venture capital as a legitimate asset class. On the plus side, swelled heads will be humbled. Sniffs veteran Bill Davidow, "Some VCs today actually think they're smart."

For what's it like in a down cycle, the best story I heard was from Irwin Federman, who took over U.S. Venture Partners (USVP) in the late 1980s and helped turn it around. Federman represents the old school of venture capital at its finest: he's a generalist, not a specialist, who is kind, candid, and humble. He and his partner spent nine months in 1989 going through the portfolio of USVP, whose founders were getting ready to retire. "We decided we should go in and make it our own firm," Federman says. "Well, we went in, and it was even worse than it looked." In the first three months of running the firm, three portfolio companies filed for bankruptcy. USVP's second fund was $25 million underwater, or below its original value, while the third fund was $20 million underwater.

"We had to re-establish the firm's presence in the community," says Federman, which meant taking whatever deals they could get. "We were late-stage investors in lousy deals with good VCs. We were early-stage-investors in lousy deals with second-rate VCs." He also hired an accountant from Ernst & Young to develop a portfolio tracking system and "systematize us." Eventually, the second fund managed to eke out a 4.5 percent annualized return, which for a fund at that time "was a pretty good return," Federman brags. The next fund, which had also been losing money, achieved a 15 percent return. Then USVP set out to raise a fourth fund, starting in 1991. It took two years to raise $135 million. But to date that fund has a 70 percent return and continues to produce. "It's the gift that keeps on giving," he says. In early 2000, USVP raised a $600 million fund in three days. "We went out for $500 million, and $850 million came in. We kept $600 million," says a satisfied Federman, who remembers the days when the knees of his pants were worn out from begging for money.

By late 2000, the venture capital and entrepreneurial worlds remained in a state of angst, unsure whether the public markets were ever coming back, whether we were headed for a nuclear winter, or whether we had gotten through the worst of it. Two things were certain: The golden era of 1999 to early 2000 was definitely over, but there was still a lot of steam left in the Internet revolution, which meant new ideas, new companies, and new investments. Once it happened, the sobering-up that occurred after the April 2000 Nasdaq crash was greeted with sighs of relief. "They were printing money at some of these firms, just hyping companies, pushing them out, who cares what happens. . . . It was a con game," says entrepreneur Beisel. "The game just changed."

Chapters 12 and 13 illuminate another consequence of the recent greed era: the tremendous influx of new money and new players into venture capital. Among the sources of capital are mutual funds, investment banks, corporations, and angel investors. We're also witnessing tweaks of the traditional VC model in incubators and publicly traded operating companies. It all adds up to a bewildering panorama of wanna-bes whose excesses threaten to undermine the very successes that lured them in the first place.

CHAPTER TWELVE

New Faces

Angels in America

I n some ways, the new faces introduced in this chapter and the next are very old faces indeed, for individual and corporate investors preceded the formalized venture capital (VC) structure by centuries. As noted in Chapter 3, it was wealthy people who helped finance the exploration of the New World and the Industrial Revolution. And corporations, of course, have long invested in their own R&D efforts. So why are this chapter and the next called "New Faces"? Because, like venture capital itself, the investors here are new in the sense that they are formal incarnations of previously existing trends. For example, what is called the *angel* investor—a wealthy individual with the wherewithal to provide risk capital—is now a recognized part of the fundraising process. In many VC strongholds, angels have banded together into identifiable entities that offer a much-needed source of very-early-stage capital. Likewise, moving away from occasional investing, some corporations and consulting firms have established designated funds to invest in innovative technologies. Incubators—designed to nurture start-ups—are sprouting by the day. It's all part of the institutionalization of venture investing, and once again has been spurred by the incredible successes of the professional venture capitalists.

The angel investor has now become an important stopgap for

those professionals. Because the sums available to VC firms are sharply accelerating, much more so than the number of partners who oversee investments, venture capitalists have boosted the amount of money they put into any one company and are more likely to do their funding at a level referred to as *first institutional money in*. The entrepreneurial company has already received at least one infusion of cash, a relatively small amount of around $1 million or so, which the founders have used to start hiring the team and developing a prototype. In the past, venture capitalists would provide this early funding (referred to as *seed* capital), and sometimes they still do, but more often they'll hand it off to angel investors, because general partners don't want to be bothered with a lot of small, labor-intensive start-ups.

"Venture capitalists have gotten very big and fat and happy," says Hans Severiens, coordinator and founder of the Band of Angels in Palo Alto, California. "They want to give so much money they wind up swamping the company. We offer a way around that." Severiens, in his sixties, is a Dutch immigrant who kicked around the edges of entrepreneurial funding for years before finding his niche as the head of an angel investing group. Companies who are initially financed by angel investors "get less money," he concedes, "but they can build up their business more slowly." Then, when they're ready, they go to venture capitalists for the next round of financing.

In areas like Silicon Valley, angel investors tend to be former entrepreneurs themselves and thus are knowledgeable enough to avoid being tarred with the "dumb money" label. Indeed, angels such as the well-known Ron Conway, whose list of participants includes such luminaries as Netscape cofounder Marc Andreessen and Sun Microsystems cofounder Bill Joy, have become a filtering mechanism for the VC industry. Conway will provide funding to companies that may need time to mature before they can prove themselves worthy of a top-tier venture capitalist. As Conway puts it, "We're the farm team for the venture community."

AN ANGEL *KEIRETSU*

One reason that Ron Conway is probably the most respected angel investor in Silicon Valley, which is saying a lot, is that his background would be perfectly suited to being a "real" venture capitalist or an entrepreneur. In the late 1970s, he was an executive with National Semi-conductor; he served as executive vice president and president of Al-tos Computer Systems through the 1980s; and then he was president and CEO of Personal Training Systems in the first half of the 1990s be-fore it was acquired by another company. Finally, in 1998, he started Angel Investors and persuaded many of the top entrepreneurs in Sili-con Valley and elsewhere, with affiliations ranging from eBay to Mor-gan Stanley to Microsoft to Cisco, to invest. In April 2000 Conway had raised two funds totaling $180 million and made investments in 178 companies.

With that many investments overseen by a small staff—only four general partners and two associates, plus six other support people—it's no wonder that the common rap against Conway is that he's way, way overextended. I found confirmation of that as I tried for weeks to set up an appointment. And when I got to his office in an obscure of-fice complex near the port of Redwood City, Conway showed up more than 20 minutes late. White-haired, with an unlined, young-looking face, Conway briskly shakes my hand and drops into a chair, remark-ing that he's not sure why he agreed to this interview at all. However, his answers to my questions, though brief, are thoughtful and articu-late.

Angel Investors is focused on early-stage technology and Internet companies in the San Francisco Bay Area. The only difference from a traditional VC firm, says Conway, is that his limited partners are all in-dividuals, whereas VC firms accept institutional money. The lineup of investors, which includes the likes of Andreessen and Joy, is the source of Conway's deal flow. "We ask each investor to show us all the deals coming to them," says Conway. Then Angel Investors selects the deals that fit into its portfolio, where it thinks it can add the most value. The first Angel Investors fund looked at 1,000 deals and picked 88 compa-nies; the second one plucked 90 out of a similar number. "It's like an index fund," he says. "The goal is to professionalize angel investing and offer predictable results."

The investor base "consists of very successful Internet entrepre-neurs who are willing to help new entrepreneurs," Conway adds. But these entrepreneurs were getting so many deals referred to them—much like a successful author becomes a lightning rod for that novel everybody has stashed somewhere—that they couldn't handle the flow. "Our fund gave this group of people a way of channeling their deal flow where they knew it would get taken care of," says Conway. "If we don't do the deal, we refer to other angels." He doesn't hesitate to compare his firm to the *crème de la crème* of venture investing. "We're the Kleiner Perkins of angel investing, and the [individual] investors are our *keiretsu*." Not only do the entrepreneurs refer deals, they also help with due diligence, critique the portfolio lineup, sit on advisory boards, and provide strategic and recruitment advice.

Angel Investors is particularly good, according to Conway, at helping start-ups find corporate partners and build out the team and then introducing them to top-tier venture capitalists. Early on, the partners in his fund quit taking board seats because there just isn't time. "We're an assembly line," says Conway. "We have 170-plus of these companies on the assembly line." At the time of the interview, 15 companies were already liquid or merged, and about 100 had been picked up by a VC firm, which then takes ownership. With the 50-plus remaining companies, Angel Investors was still the sole investor. It takes a 20 percent carry and charges a 3 percent management fee to its limited partners. The initial investment is typically $500,000 at a hoped-for $5 million postmoney valuation, which would give Angel Investors a 10 percent stake. If the company looks like it could be a winner after the seed round, Angel Investors will put in another $1 million in follow-on financing.

Conway acknowledges that running an angel fund has been a learning process. Originally, he figured he could take on such high volume because it would only be a short-term commitment before handing off to a VC firm. "At the beginning, our involvement is high," he says. "We're talking to an entrepreneur every day—that's where our activity level is monstrous. We start to train them on the skills of getting VC backing. Then we ramp down through the VC funding." He estimates that over the past couple of years, "we've done 20 percent of the deal flow that went into Sand Hill Road." But as the public appetite for new Internet companies began to wane, so too did VC enthusiasm for Conway's candidates, and many of his companies (one of which was Alert1st) couldn't get VC backing. By mid-2000, Conway was breaking his back trying to keep all his start-ups afloat. For companies that couldn't get venture funding, "we start moving them toward an M&A," he says. If the management team balks, "we're going to abandon the company." Looking toward a possible third Angel Investors fund, Conway says wearily, "we will invest in 50 companies, not 100."

One of Conway's individual investors is Hilary Valentine, the 30-something daughter of Sequoia Capital's cofounder. After she majored in psychology at St. Lawrence University in upstate New York, Valentine was hired by Conway to do marketing for Altos Computer. Then she joined a graphics design firm, Black & White, run by a female entrepreneur as a partner, and still spends two days a week there doing business development. When Conway started the angel fund, he persuaded Valentine to join as an investor. Like the other angels I talked to, Valentine has her own agenda. "My primary interest is in helping companies founded by women," she says. Black & White now handles design work for many of Angel Investors' portfolio companies. "I wanted to participate in angel investing with Ron Conway to learn the process," says Valentine. "People assume you know more than you do because of your name."

She is also involved with a San Francisco–based company called LevelEdge.com, which combines her interest in athletics—she played soccer, softball, and other sports in school—with her interest in female entrepreneurs. Founded by a largely female team, LevelEdge helps student athletes promote themselves online and secure college scholarships. Valentine brought the company to Angel Investors for early funding. In her angel investing, Valentine looks for companies that, like LevelEdge, have a societal aspect. "Those are hard to find," she says. "There are some very interesting ideas about how to make money, but you only rarely come across an Internet company that's original and community-oriented."

BANDING TOGETHER

Band of Angels' loose confederation is more typical of the genre than Conway's extremely structured approach is. Severiens, its founder, had a variety of jobs in Europe and on the East Coast from the 1950s through the 1970s. One of those was with the former Atomic Energy Commission, where he allocated funds to research in the early 1960s. "I began to appreciate the interaction of money with ideas," he says. "One without the other would fall flat on its face." In 1980 Severiens trekked west, working for a while with the Dean Witter investment bank [now part of Morgan Stanley]. "I started my own little venture fund in 1983, but we weren't successful," he says. "We came in at the top of the market and then watched it decline by 75 percent." The government of his native Holland hired him to do venture investing, but folded its fund in 1990. So Severiens, in his late fifties, had run two failed venture funds and was out of a job. It was difficult to get on with the VC firms, he says, because they were "very close partnerships" interested in very wealthy investors. "If you had $20 to $30 million, they would take you."

In the mid-1990s, after working with a couple of small investment banking firms in San Francisco, Severiens had his inspiration: "Wouldn't it be nice to have a little group of people who would invest together informally?" In a way, Band of Angels, formed in late 1994, was a return to the early days of venture capital as a collegial, noncompetitive group of people getting together to invest money in intriguing ideas. The difference is that the Band of Angels participants invest their own money and don't raise funds from limited partners. There are now 140 people in the group, not all of whom are active. Most are former high-tech executives, "but a couple of people have snuck in who are not of that mold, like lawyers and bankers," Severiens says. Generally, members like to invest together with at least several other people, offering confirmation that an idea is appealing. An individual investment ranges from $50,000 to $100,000, and each company might receive five to 10 of those. The typical deal is $600,000 at an average premoney valuation of $4 million to $5 million, Severiens says.

Band of Angels "is still doing deals the old-fashioned way," says Severiens, going after not only hot Internet companies but also businesses such as plastic recycling "where things don't move with the speed of light and the company will have liquidity in four to seven years." The bottom line is that the Band of Angels can provide start-up financing and some expertise from high-tech executives, without insisting on the same control that a VC firm has. The downside, though, is that the fragmented nature of the investing can leave a company with a dozen individuals or more all clamoring for information. For high-tech start-ups, Band of Angels is merely a beginning to the funding process. Most entrepreneurial companies funded this way must go on to get professional venture capital or close their doors if they can't.

One of Band of Angels' individual investors is another storied name: Lore Harp McGovern, who is married to Pat McGovern of International Data Group. She is also a former entrepreneur and one of the few women to have run a technology manufacturing company—cofounding Vector Graphic, a PC company, in 1976. As Vector's CEO she was chosen to serve on the board of the American Electronics Association: "I remember walking in there with 44 men and me," she says. In 1981 she and her husband started a venture fund, "but I decided I was more of an operating person. I wanted to be in the thick of things." So she got involved with a couple of entrepreneurial companies and then wound up with the Band of Angels in 1997. "I was quite fascinated by the concept of supporting start-ups from the point where they just had an idea," she says.

McGovern combines intuition with a sound business sense in making investments. Her criteria include the size of the market, whether the consumer really needs the product or service, what the start-up's long-term competitive advantage is, whether there is a sound financial strategy, and the founders' backgrounds. "How do they think? How intelligent are they? How committed are they, or are they just in it to make a quick buck and get out? I want people who believe passionately in what they're doing," she says, sounding just like the venture capitalists on Sand Hill Road. "In the end it is your gut feeling." At first she will invest a small amount, say $50,000 to $100,000, and increase that in subsequent rounds if the company progresses. When I spoke with her, she was an investor in 14 companies, working closely with five of those. With her connections, she can help companies to network, sometimes giving cocktail receptions at her house to introduce the founders to other potential investors. Out of the 14 companies in her portfolio, "three could be huge," she reports. "The other ones will be okay."

Her range of investments is eclectic. One is a Los Angeles–based company that aggregates Internet films, run "by a couple of 27-year-old kids who eat and drink their concept." Other investments include an Israeli-founded company that does workforce management software and a design company with a chip that reconfigures a cell phone to operate in varying locations. In another investment, a contractor that manages companies' information technology infrastructure, McGovern initially clashed with the chief executive, who seemed to her "an arrogant know-it-all." Their relationship improved after they worked together on obtaining more funding. "He knows that I'm extremely well connected and have a helpful way of looking at problems." Dealing with CEOs is one of her most exhausting tasks, she sighs, again sounding like her VC counterparts. "They haven't learned to grow with their company and to delegate. You need to work with them in a way that you don't insult them."

Why does she do it? It's obviously not for the money alone. "It keeps me sharp, on top of the technology curve," McGovern says. "I'm stimulated by working with very bright young people, so I'm doing this for my intellectual well-being." Nonetheless, being an angel investor does not mean merely scattering money to the winds and then watching what happens. McGovern is very hands-on with her investments. For example, on the day I met with her, she had started at 5 A.M. with an East Coast conference call, then participated via teleconference in a board meeting of a Los Angeles company. She had a couple of one-on-one conversations with founders of other companies, the interview with me, and later in the afternoon another entrepreneur was coming in for a strategy session, followed by a 5 P.M. meeting. After that McGovern was hopping on a plane for Boston. "I'm having a blast, but you work very hard," she says.

PLEADING THE CASE

Just like venture capitalists, angels must find a structured way to listen to all the entrepreneurial pitches for financing that pour in. Band of Angels hosts monthly dinners at the Los Altos Golf & Country Club, featuring several company presentations, with follow-up luncheons scheduled for anyone intrigued by the initial pitch. On February 16, 2000, I attend one of the dinners, after being told by Severiens to "wear a nice suit or dress." (Evidently, my usual journalistic trappings of slacks and a shirt don't meet the Los Altos Golf & Country Club standards.) Inside the country club's large communal room, set up with individual tables seating eight apiece, I find a group of some 40 mostly middle-aged men, with a couple of women among them. I talk to one of the latter, learning that she is attached to a company that will be presenting. As we finish the dinner of stuffed chicken, the presentations begin. Each entrepreneur must be sponsored by at least one member of the Band of Angels to get time before this elite group. Severiens reminds everyone to keep it tight, because the meeting is running late and there are four companies to present.

First up is Peter Levy, the CEO of San Jose–based Vyou.com, which enables Web publishers to protect intellectual property such as text or images from unauthorized use. Levy, a serial entrepreneur, says intellectual property rip-off was a big problem at his former company, IntelliChoice, an automotive research firm. "Another company was stealing our analysis, stripping off our logo, and posting it on the Web," he says. "Three months of legal maneuvers, many thousands of dollars, and a lot of heartache later, this firm was forced to stop. That got me to thinking, why wait until the horse is out of the barn?" As a result, he has founded Vyou to offer three services to Web publishers: security, traffic building, and pay-per-view pages. Vyou's technology allows Web content providers to section content so that you can look at it for $.50, print it for $1, and download and archive it for $3. Vyou has just launched its product, which earned a write-up in the *Wall Street Journal Interactive Edition,* and wants to raise a round of $7 million, including $2.5 million in angel financing, to accelerate product rollout.

Following him is Per Ljung of San Francisco–based Coyote Systems, who has none of Levy's experienced polish. Obviously a technologist, Ljung gives a dry recital about his arcane product, which improves chip design within a specific category called VLSI. "We can save $1 million a week for the VLSI companies," he says. "Most of our customers spend $100,000 per year per license." Although Ljung wants to build a direct sales and marketing team, it's clear that Coyote's future is to become part of another company. The investors don't evince much interest in this prospect, even though Ljung says it means a guaranteed return on the $1 million investment he's seeking. The company's burn rate is only $65,000 a month, and he expects to receive multiple takeover offers within the next year.

The next presentation generates more attention from the group of investors—who have by now finished their desserts—perhaps because it's done by one of their own: Sai-Wai Fu. Like many angel investors, he found a company that interested him and joined it. Yes Video is a five-month-old application service provider (ASP) that will edit home video and put it online. "People are shooting 100 million hours of tape a year," he says. "We want to help them share, organize, and preserve their video content. We're the first convenient video publishing service." You send your videotape to Yes Video, and the company edits it into CD or DVD format and also stores the material, charging $15 to $20 per CD. "Video is the killer app for broadband," Fu proclaims. Yes Video has already raised $1.3 million and is now seeking about $3 million to complete development and begin customer acquisition.

The final presenter is John Walsh, president of Intralect Solutions, founded by several refugees from Cisco Systems who are commercializing its tools for online management of human resource requirements. Cisco is one of the development partners, as is Apple Computer, which has also supplied part of the management team. With an impressive pedigree from two Silicon Valley icons, Intralect has raised $400,000 in seed capital and is seeking a follow-on round of $2 million. However, according to the information sheet Walsh supplies, the round is already oversubscribed, which means that his low-key presentation is relatively moot. The bottom line: Using the tools that Intralect is now commercializing, Cisco managed to keep its turnover at 7 percent versus a national average of 20 percent at technology firms. "Every 1 percent increase in turnover equals $150 million in costs," says Walsh.

(Seven months later, in the fall of 2000, all four companies are still alive, but, as expected, Coyote Systems has been acquired by a larger player in chip design, Microcosm Technologies. Intralect has changed its name to PureCarbon, although its mission is the same, and Vyou and Yes Video are both sailing along.)

After the meeting, Severiens tells me that the lineup was a typical mix, except that Coyote was unusual because of its highly technical nature. "Venture investing is an art, not a science," he says. "It's an art based on the intuition of people. What is the big unknown in the equation? People. You can analyze markets and technologies, you can analyze the competition, look at the balance sheets and costing models, but what's always left is the people." I decide that Band of Angels really is a mating service—between people with too much money and people who are eager to lay their hands on some of it.

WHAT ANGELS BRING

Most of the entrepreneurial companies in this book used at least some angel funding. The early angel round has become virtually as institutionalized as subsequent rounds done by professional venture capitalists, investment banks, and corporations. And with many companies unable to go public as the IPO market got harsher, angels were increasingly in favor for later rounds as well. Many a company that couldn't raise venture capital turned to angels. Just as with venture capital, with angel funding the trick is to get more than money. Companies want investors who are knowledgeable, committed, and connected, because the two biggest criticisms of angels are that they'll drop out at the first hint of trouble and that they're dumb money. Still, the growing numbers of angels can provide a ready source of funding, especially seed funding, as well as a welcome alternative to the sometimes stifling control imposed by venture capitalists.

Bo Holland, the founder and CEO of Works.com, the Austin, Texas–based Internet business purchasing service introduced in Chapter 8, sought angel rather than venture funding at first. "We wanted to build up gradually, and we wanted to get seasoned management," he says. For that reason, he went after angel investors who might be enticed to join the company. Holland tapped into Martin Neath, an executive vice president at Tivoli Systems who helped build that company from a start-up into a powerhouse technology management resource, later acquired by IBM. "We were his first and only angel investment," says Holland. "He put in $750,000, and then we brought him in as president and COO [chief operating officer]." He adds that the key with either angels or venture capitalists, for that matter, is to get "real value attached to the money."

Phil Beisel, the founder of Alert1st, which was still looking for its first VC round in late 2000, says his company was kept alive by funding from Ron Conway's Angel Investors. "They're awesome in getting you introductions," he says of Conway's group, but they don't take the place of experienced venture capitalists because resources are strained too thin. "Conway has taken on way too much," says Beisel.

One company pretty much made by angel investing was the nontechnological MBA Polymers, in gritty Richmond, California, just across the bay from Silicon Valley but a world away in terms of mindset. Mike Biddle, the president and CEO, founded the company in 1994 to figure out a better way to recycle growing amounts of discarded plastics, including those generated by computer and electronic companies. Initially, MBA Polymers was funded by research grants from the American Plastics Council and the federal government. The grants provided it with a total of $7 million, spread out over five years. By the late 1990s, however, the company required additional funding to finance construction of a manufacturing plant.

"We went to Sand Hill Road in the summer and fall of '99 and talked to a few venture capitalists, but we didn't fit their portfolios," recalls Biddle. "All they could see then were dot-coms." Later that year, Biddle hooked up with the Band of Angels and found a number of investors there, as well as two board members, David Bossen of Measurex and John Larson of the law firm Brobeck Phleger & Harrison. Angel money is "definitely expensive money," says Biddle. "If you're an entrepreneur who has put your heart and soul and all your savings into the company, you're going to give them a chunk of that," just as with venture capitalists. However, in the absence of VC interest, there aren't many other choices, he says. "If you don't have any operating history, not too many banks will invest in you." The Band of Angels board members did introduce MBA Polymers to American Industrial Partners, an investment firm that specializes in manufacturing and that became an investor in the plastics recycler.

By mid-2000, MBA Polymers had a 100,000 square-foot, state-of-the-art recycling facility, 50 employees, and a revenue stream in the "couple of million dollars range," reports Biddle. He's grateful to the Band of Angels, but says that having some 40 or 50 individual investors can be a "management challenge." On the downside, "I have to report what I'm doing to all these people." On the upside, "I have a lot of people I can ask questions." The value of experienced angels is similar to institutionalized venture capital. "The biggest thing the angels did for me is make introductions to prospective customers and suppliers," says Biddle. The angels were also helpful with advice, such as handling a contract issue or resolving a dispute with a supplier. "I think the Band of Angels is very smart money," he sums up, definitely a step above the old friends-and-family type of investment.

INTEL OUTSIDE

Corporate investing has been going on for years, as large entities have sought dominance by buying up suppliers and competitors. For instance, Andrew Carnegie acquired coal and iron ore companies to fuel his expanding steel business. John D. Rockefeller kept collecting oil companies until the government stopped him. But for New Economy technology companies, corporate investing has a different twist. Influenced by the success of the VC industry that enabled their creation, companies like Intel, Dell, and Oracle have used the recently styled *corporate venturing* as their chief tool for keeping in touch with the leading edge. Cisco Systems makes investments in innovative companies that it will later acquire and enfold in its formidable marketing and distribution channel. Microsoft seeks entrepreneurial companies that will enhance the Windows world. Likewise, Intel, one of the savviest and most dedicated corporate investors around, looks for technologies that will exploit the processing power of its chips. The deep pockets that these companies bring "radically altered the [investing] landscape," says Integral Capital's Roger McNamee, because corporate investors are not "price-disciplined." They will plow big bucks into start-ups to achieve nonfinancial goals, which has exacerbated the trend toward high valuations for early-stage companies.

By early 2000, corporate venturing had become significant enough to warrant its own newsletter, the *Corporate Venturing Report,* which in its premiere issue in January 2000 announced that "corporate venturing exploded in 1999."[1] Corporations committed $6.3 billion to funding VC programs that year, compared with $1.7 billion the previous year and $1.3 billion in 1997. And that $6.3 billion, the newsletter suggests, is only the tip of the iceberg, representing the 28 corporations that revealed the existence and size of their funds (including Intel, which was fourth at $450 million). Another 42 corporations that began venture programs in 1999 did not disclose the amount, among them such heavyweights as Chevron, Dell, and EMC.[2] By 2000 the announced commitments to corporate venturing programs had swollen past $10 billion, and 350 corporations had publicly disclosed their venture funds. Those numbers are probably quite low because there are no good measures of corporate venture programs, many of which are intentionally unpublicized and lumped under designations such as research and development.

For a specific example of the motivation and goals of corporate investors, I talked with Intel's former manager of strategic investments, Bruce A. Miller, who had just left the chip maker's finance arm after four years to join a start-up. Intel Capital, which started as a formal program in the early 1990s, has become one of the largest investors in the world, with more than 100 people devoted to it. In 1999 Intel invested $1.2 billion in 250 companies, compared with $830 million in 130 companies the previous year. In 2000 it invested $1.3 billion covering 300 transactions, about 80 percent of which were new investments and the rest follow-on financings. Even though its primary aim is strategic, not financial, Intel has done very well with its investing. In the second quarter of 2000 alone, it realized gains on investments of $2.1 billion, according to the company earnings report. In the third quarter, it realized $716 million in gains. However, with the decline of the public markets in late 2000, the value of Intel's equity portfolio of 550 companies decreased from $5.9 billion in September to $3.7 billion at year-end.

"In the early days [of Intel Capital] we were very focused on insuring our product line by accelerating technology," says Miller. As Intel's product lines grew beyond its cornerstone microprocessor technology, the investing also expanded, into areas such as services and Web software. Intel has two pillars of investing: The company must not only fit into its strategy but also have financial viability. "We want to make sure we're influencing where the market is going and ensuring that microprocessors continue to have a place," he says. Intel is not a lead investor, but it invests alongside venture capitalists, usually in a mid-level round of financing. Increasingly, it invests globally: In 1999, about one third of its VC investments were outside the United States, primarily in Asia, Europe, and Israel, compared with just 5 percent outside the United States in 1998. The typical investment is $3 million to $10 million in exchange for 5 percent to 19 percent of the company. Most of the investors at Intel Capital do about six to eight deals a year, according to Miller. Intel doesn't take board seats because of the potential for conflict of interest. "You don't want an Intel employee sitting on a board with fiduciary responsibility for another company," he notes. However, in many cases the Intel investors will take observer seats, which allows them to attend board meetings and offer advice, but not vote.

Compared to the venture capitalists, "we bring different things to the equation," says Miller. Intel's key value added is access to its technology. It will set up programs to license its own cutting-edge technology with companies in which it invests. It also allows the companies to use its labs to fine-tune their own products. And Intel's vast sales, marketing, and public relations machinery will also support its investments, one of which was Plumtree, the business portal software company introduced in Chapter 8. "We would bring their software into our labs and optimize the code so that it performs best on Intel architecture," says Miller. "We also want to evangelize Plumtree because their technology supports Intel." For example, Intel will sponsor marketing events with the message, "If you're looking for a corporate portal product, Plumtree is where we've bet our money." In short, Plumtree receives the highly regarded Intel seal of approval.

One problem for Intel Capital has been high turnover. As Intel employees, people like Miller can't take equity in the companies in which they invest, which prevents them from cashing in the way traditional venture capitalists do. "We're paid a salary, and we get a pat on the back," he says. "We're not even allowed to take 'friends and family' stock if it's offered to us." That may explain why he and several others from Intel Capital left in May 2000 to join iMediation, a business-to-business e-commerce company. (Intel was an investor.) "I left for the opportunity to get my hands dirty and experience growing a company myself," says Miller. "It had nothing to do with being discontented at Intel." But he acknowledges that the defection of people such as himself hurts the investment effort because it's so dependent on establishing working relationships with the companies. "The success of any investment strongly depends on the quality of the person in Intel managing it," Miller notes. "You need someone in Intel who serves as your champion. If you have someone who is your champion leave, the person who inherits the investment probably won't be as passionate."

The turnover also undermines the relationship with VC firms. "It's all done on the personal level," says Miller. "You have to cultivate certain venture capitalists to get your deal flow." One of his valuable connections has been with Sequoia's Pierre Lamond, the investor in Plumtree. "I learned a lot from him about how to manage boards and deal with tough situations," Miller reports. While the venture capitalists have an ongoing, day-to-day interaction with entrepreneurs, Intel's role is more transient. Rather than proffering advice on strategy and operations, "we get involved on a case-by-case basis, as needed." With the amount of money available for entrepreneurial investing, even Intel has to make its case. "We have to convince not only the entrepreneur but the venture capitalist leading the round that Intel will add value," says Miller. In Silicon Valley, "we often get pushed to the later rounds," rather than the more lucrative early rounds. Overseas, though, Intel's name alone is powerful. "In China or India they're flocking to us for the halo effect."

Two entrepreneurs, Plumtree CEO John Kunze and Homestead

CEO Justin Kitch, had contrasting views of Intel's value as an investor. Kunze was enthused because Intel led one of Plumtree's funding rounds and helped boost the valuation. Plumtree has also forged a partnership with Intel Online and has been involved in Intel marketing campaigns, all of which helped to put the company on the map. By contrast, Kitch characterizes the Intel investment in Homestead, which helps consumers design their own Websites, as a "huge mistake." For one thing, the Intel Capital representative who invested in Homestead has now left, so the chip maker's interest level is low. "Passive investors are bad because the only time they're not passive is when they want something completely against the interest of your company," says Kitch. "We took the investment just for the Intel name," which, he acknowledges, did help Homestead in its very early stages. But now that the company has gone through additional funding rounds, "no one cares about Intel any more."

PROFESSIONAL VERSUS AMATEUR

Although most venture capitalists will admit that the industry needs angel and corporate investors, that doesn't mean that they consider these sources to be on their level. The professional VC firms regard the angels as occasionally proficient amateurs who are likely to bail when times get tough. Says Hummer Winblad's Ann Winblad: "Every time I have come in as a venture investor after an angel round, it's like entering a pep rally." Enthusiasm is high, but competency is low. Angel investors don't push companies the way VC firms do, "so they've never quantified their business model. They're not covering the bases," she says. Adds Bob Barrett of Battery Ventures, "Most of the angels are doing so many deals they can't do the heavy lifting. If the shit hits the fan tomorrow, I don't think the venture business will go away. The angels might." Even Sequoia's Don Valentine, whose daughter Hilary invests with Conway's fund, doesn't have a kind word for angels, who he says make too many investments and then can't devote meaningful time to them. "Angels will come and go, but their expanse will be limited," he says. "Their value add will be limited. They will fund companies we will not fund."

Other venture capitalists are more tolerant of angels. Alan J. Patricof, of New York–based Patricof & Company, believes that angels are playing an appropriate role at the seed stage. "They've always been around," he says. "That's who gave me my start. You went to some person you knew with money." However, as the market worsens, he also foresees some fallout among angel investors. "I just hope there aren't too many casualties." Similarly, Tony Sun of Venrock Associates, which was originally set up as an angel fund by the Rockefeller family, thinks angels have a place. "They both partner and compete with us," he says. "They're usually coming from below with $1 to $2 million of funding, while we want to do $5 to $10 million." In good times, angels can be quite successful, "but when our returns go down to 20 percent, their returns are in trouble," he says.

Meanwhile, the rap on corporate investors is that their motivation isn't "pure," because they have their own agenda that doesn't necessarily match the start-up company's needs. "A corporate investor is always going to care most about its own stock price maximization," says Steve Jurvetson of Draper Fisher Jurvetson. "The success or failure of a young company isn't the corporate objective." Intel, he points out, is doing nearly a deal a day. "For Intel, anything that heats up MIPS [microprocessor speed] is good. They can just concentrate on growing their industry." There's also the potential for conflicts of interest. "If you take money from Oracle, can you sell to [database competitor] Sybase?" he asks. Then too, corporations, like angels, can be fickle. "In a corporate VC arm, people get fired. Investment managers get frustrated. Great deals get shot down because they're not strategic enough."

Despite the criticism, no one was forecasting that angels or corporate investors would disappear entirely. Corporations will select themselves out, predicts McNamee. "Those who are market-sensitive will pull out, but the strategic corporate investors like Intel will stay in." And with entrepreneurial activity at unprecedented levels, "angels have become part of the fabric," says Tim Haley of Redpoint Ventures. "They give a little bit of money to a company to see if the idea percolates. The ones that work they introduce to us." VC firms can no longer do that kind of filtering. "We can only see so many deals. We're going to see 22,000 business plans and fund 40," he says. Angel investor Lore Harp McGovern says that by doing the filtering for VC firms, "we're making the cost of entry a little more expensive." But it's also easier for the VC firms to invest in a company that has gone through "proof of concept." That's why angels will remain a complementary and vital part of the VC investing chain, she maintains. However, angel investing was expected to drop sharply in 2001, thanks to the public market doldrums.

Angels and corporations aren't the only ones jockeying for a place in the lucrative venture investing stream. Chapter 13 profiles several more of these adapters, including consulting firms who got tired of sitting on the sidelines as well as two new models: leveraged buyout (LBO) funds and incubators. Finally, Chapter 14 explores the future of traditional venture capital amid the ever-changing ecosystem of high-tech investment.

Ⓝew Faces

Incubators et al.

In the 1970s, after the Watergate scandal was broken open by two young *Washington Post* reporters, everybody coming out of school wanted to be a journalist and change the world. In the less idealistic 1980s, when "greed was good," everybody wanted to be an investment banker. Today, the entrepreneurial dream allows you to be greedy *and* change the world. That's why there's such an influx of renowned people into either start-ups or venture capital (VC) firms. Anyone who's made a ton of money, such as former San Francisco 49ers quarterback Steve Young, seems to turn to venture capital as a second career. In mid-2000, not long after his announcement that he was retiring from football, Young teamed up with former Novell senior vice president David Bradford to form FirstLight Venture Partners. The new firm was expected to benefit from Young's name recognition and connection with wealthy investors on and off the football field.

The existing members of the VC club—a very closely held organization indeed—are wary of the newcomers. "Everybody wants a piece of the action, whether you're a lawyer, banker, accountant, consultant, or LBO [leveraged buyout] fund," says Sam Colella, a longtime general partner with Institutional Venture Partners. With so many sources of cash, the valuations of entrepreneurial companies have been enormously inflated, increasing risk and lowering the potential payoff. "My personal view is that this [trend] may cook the golden goose," Colella adds. "Eventually, you've got to pay the piper. I have some real reservations about excesses in this business."

While the newcomers generally don't bring the same value added that the veteran venture capitalists do in terms of how to grow an entrepreneurial company, they bring unique values of their own. Take consultants like Geoff Moore, who spent years polishing a paradigm that describes the market life cycle and how to create a business model to exploit that life cycle. Many in Silicon Valley have bought into his notions of getting across the chasm of customer experimentation to mainstream acceptance or picking a market in which you can become the dominant gorilla. He's now applying that knowledge at Mohr Davidow Ventures. In an era when fresh sources of human capital are avidly sought, Steve Young and other athlete-investors provide ready contacts into a largely untapped world of bright, active talent. Maybe it's time that the solipsistic, insular world of Sand Hill Road and other VC capitals gets shaken up. This chapter will profile some of the entities trying to retool the VC model, some in incremental fashion, others with a more radical approach.

THE ANDERSEN FILE

As the new millennium dawned, the top consulting firms were wrestling with a brain drain as their brightest people went off to the entrepreneurial start-ups that offered much bigger dreams, and potentially much bigger rewards, than the dusty old world of consulting. Deciding that "if you can't beat 'em, join 'em," in late 1999 Andersen Consulting (since renamed Accenture) set up a VC arm—AC Ventures—and endowed it with $1 billion to invest in Internet start-ups over the next five years. AC Ventures is based in Palo Alto and headed by managing general partner Jack Wilson, who spent 16 years as a partner in the consulting firm. Wilson, who is on Andersen Consulting's executive committee, says the firm had considerable experience with VC investing before it established a formal fund. "About three years ago we did our first investment in a little software company while we were doing some implementation work for LSI Logic," Wilson recalls. The founder of the "little company" realized he would need someone like Andersen if he expected to sell his software to large enterprises. "We bought 10 percent of Siebel Systems that day" for $3 million, he says. That stake would now be worth some $3 billion. Today, Andersen's share of Siebel has dropped to less than 1 percent.

It wasn't just the spectacular monetary success of Siebel, which became the largest sales and customer relationship management software company, that encouraged Andersen's foray into venture capital. "What we learned is that when we got to know a company like Siebel in the early stages, we could bring a huge advantage to our own market," says Wilson. Another opportunity came along with Qpass, a Seattle-based company developing Internet-based micropayments. Andersen invested alongside Venrock, and Wilson had his first board seat as a venture capitalist. "We looked up last fall [1999], and we were doing an awful lot of this stuff [investing]," says Wilson. Then Andersen CEO George Shaheen jumped ship in September 1999 to run Webvan, a high-profile start-up. Andersen's new CEO, veteran Joe Forehand, told Wilson it was time to make venture investing into a real entity. "In a way we were in stealth mode for three years," says Wilson. Several months after having officially announced AC Ventures in December 1999, Andersen already had positions in 38 companies. About a quarter of those were equity stakes that Andersen Consulting took as compensation for services and are now grouped under AC Ventures. The rest were direct investments.

Andersen Consulting is the main limited partner for AC Ventures, providing half the capital. The other half comes from outsiders. AC Ventures will get a 2 percent management fee and a 25 percent carry. Andersen Consulting partners get to split the portion of the carry that goes back to the parent. "We were losing 15 to 17 percent of our people every year to dot-coms," says Wilson. "We wondered, 'Why can't they at least go to dot-coms that we've invested in?' We have now made it socially acceptable" for Andersen partners to join companies funded by AC Ventures. Besides Qpass, investments have included Covation, a joint venture with Bank of America to provide an e-commerce exchange for the health care industry; ChemConnect, an exchange for chemicals and plastics; and Blue Martini, which provides online merchandising software.

Wilson says there was heated internal debate about how to position AC Ventures. The VC industry "warned me, 'if this is about selling consulting, you can stand over there as a strategic partner like

Cisco or Intel. If you want to be a real player, you have to have no-shit profit maximation.'" AC Ventures' charter defines the number one objective as creating superior returns, not selling consulting services. "I wanted to create an image as a legitimate venture capital player," says Wilson. "Nowhere does it say we're going to sell consulting, although we can leverage our knowledge, our market channel, and our global brand." He acknowledges that AC Ventures is never going to be a pure VC play like Kleiner or Sequoia. But if you're going to be attached to one of the world's biggest consulting firms, take advantage of it. "I'd like to have them think of us where there are big plays or global reach involved," he says. "The deal flow and ideation that goes on in [Andersen] is amazing."

AC Ventures will invest in both early- and late-stage deals, particularly in cases where the start-up company makes information tools that could be leveraged through Andersen Consulting's potent distribution channel. Across the 38 investments that AC Ventures had done as of early 2000, the average ownership was 5 percent to 8 percent with a typical investment of $2 million, both low by today's VC standards. Wilson says that's because many of those investments were made when Andersen was still uncertain about whether it was going public with its venture investing and didn't want to make too much noise. He was ready to step up to investments in the range of $5 million to $10 million.

As of mid-2000, AC Ventures had 12 general partners in various locations, all of them drawn from Andersen Consulting itself. Wilson admits he'd like to draw in some new blood, because consultants tend to break everything down into small, digestible increments to meet established goals and deadlines. That approach doesn't work well in the risk-embracing VC world. "One of the things that made Andersen a great consulting firm is we try to take all the risk out of designing and implementing computer systems. When you go over to AC Ventures, you've got to throw all that away," he says. "At Andersen Consulting we like to argue something to death and then claim first-mover advantage. At AC Ventures, it's about thinking something is right, not being certain. It's about doing a business model on two pieces of paper, not a 100-slide PowerPoint presentation."

Wilson postulates that he can achieve returns that are at least at the VC average. "Let's assume we're only half as smart as the other guys," he says. Even so, the connection with Andersen Consulting makes up for the relative lack of VC experience. "Tom Siebel didn't come to us because we were brilliant. He wanted us because of the connection with Andersen Consulting." What Andersen Consulting gives AC ventures is "incredible content knowledge and global expertise." Wilson's biggest worry isn't finding investments or even generating acceptable returns. "We've got so many opportunities, it's very hard to stay focused. I worry about getting pulled in too many different directions."

Andersen is not flying solo in going into VC investing. Most consulting firms already take equity informally in exchange for their services, while others, such as PricewaterhouseCoopers and Electronic Data Systems (EDS), have formal funds like AC Ventures. The consulting firms certainly provide a significant new source of cash and a recognized fount of corporate expertise and connections to start-up companies. But whether they can fine-tune their expertise—which has usually been applied to remaking Fortune 500 giants—to help entrepreneurial ventures succeed in a far different milieu remains to be seen.

LEVERAGING THE VENTURE CAPITAL MODEL

In the 1980s, the LBO firm was synonymous with that decade's greed-driven mentality. As portrayed in movies like *Wall Street,* LBO firms would buy a publicly traded company and then ruthlessly carve it up into presumably more valuable pieces, using debt, or *leverage,* rather than equity as a source of financing. But despite their aggressiveness, leading LBO firms like Kohlberg Kravis Roberts, Forstmann Little, Hicks Muse, and the Texas Pacific Group stayed away from technology companies. The widely held view was that technology was too complicated, its employees too ready to change jobs, and its competitive landscape too fast-changing for LBO firms to be successful. But the maturing of the technology industry caused a rethinking of this view. With public investors flocking to every new Internet company, many older companies with established, *profitable* businesses saw their share prices plummet. Where undervalued companies exist, someone is bound to smell opportunity.

The first to do so was Integral Capital's Roger McNamee, who in 1999 helped create Silver Lake Partners, which the press heralded as the "first-ever technology buyout firm." Affiliated with Kleiner Perkins, Silver Lake invests in undervalued technology companies that may need to restructure themselves. One example is Seagate Technology, the largest disk drive company, which was taken private in March 2000 in a complex, $19 billion deal engineered by Silver Lake. In the same month, Silver Lake also invested $300 million in Gartner Group, the struggling technology research firm that wanted to strike out in new directions such as consulting. McNamee disdains the LBO comparison, which he says doesn't adequately describe Silver Lake. "We're the opposite of the old LBO model," which bought troubled companies at firesale prices, he says. "We call ourselves a technology private equity fund, until someone comes up with something better." Whatever you call it, Silver Lake aims to find hidden jewels that can be recut and revalued. But restructuring requires amounts of money that venture capital was not set up to provide. "Silver Lake assumes the technology markets are evolving in a way where venture won't meet their needs," says McNamee. "Technology has reached a scale where there are huge, growing businesses that are ignored by the public markets."

Silver Lake, headquartered on Sand Hill Road, is run by two experienced financiers: Jim Davidson, a securities lawyer who headed the old Hambrecht & Quist's mergers and acquisitions business, and David Roux, formerly vice president of corporate development at Oracle. "Historically, people treated VC and technology investing as one and the same," says Davidson. With the establishment of Silver Lake, "technology investing is more than VC. We're pioneers in large-scale private equity for technology companies." The characteristic that distinguishes Silver Lake from existing buyout funds, which have also moved into technology, is that it is a specialist. "Our belief is that technology requires a different skill set and focus," says Davidson. "The LBO world is the last bastion of generalists. They'll do a manufacturing company one day, a grocery story the next." By concentrating only on technology, he and Roux offer a more precise set of skills, similar to that of venture capitalists, even to the point of stepping in to run a company.

With a $2 billion fund, Silver Lake puts an average $200 million into each deal, with an investment horizon of six years. It takes high ownership stakes, so it will do fewer deals than a comparable VC fund and get more actively involved in each company. Out of six deals by late 2000, Silver Lake had majority ownership in three. With that level of investment and commitment to its companies, Silver Lake is more risk-averse than early-stage VC firms. "If you write a check for $200 million and the company blows up, you can't make that back," says Roux. "We have to field 80 to 90 percent of our tries successfully. In the venture world, if they hit on one fourth their deals, they've got a successful fund."

Silver Lake's target return is 30 percent, which is lower than what venture capital was getting in mid-2000 but far higher than what most mature companies aspire to. The average company that Silver Lake would consider as an investment is growing at around 10 percent to 15 percent, but has the potential to grow faster. "We refocus the business, get great managers, and let them grow the business," says Davidson. "We use all our relationships, networking, positioning, and customer sales skills to help." One of Silver Lake's earliest investments was Submitorder.com, which it pulled out of a distributor of storage products. Submitorder, which handles fulfillment for e-commerce companies, can take advantage of the huge Kleiner *keiretsu* in that arena. "But we're also talking to Accel and Softbank and other venture capitalists," Davidson notes.

Roux adds that technology is no longer just innovation at the fringes. "It's woven into the fabric of our economy, very much akin to what went on in steel, railroads, and cars," he says. Consequently, there's a role for a whole new business that applies the venture model to mature technology companies. "We're looking for a good business that's in the wrong place, where being able to operate independently would allow them to attract better management and pursue different opportunities," says Roux. "Our business will be contra-cyclical. We're the value investors in technology, as opposed to everyone else, who's momentum."

Sandy Robertson, who founded Robertson Stephens and then saw his namesake firm embroiled in the investment bank consolidation of the late 1990s, could easily have retired a wealthy man after all that turmoil. But when I caught up with him in April 2000, the avuncular, talkative Robertson was deeply engaged in his newest endeavor: raising a $1.5 billion to $2 billion technology LBO fund. Robertson's new firm, headquartered in San Francisco and appropriately called Francisco Partners, "is a fund for structured investments in technology companies that have reached inflection points," he explains. "We don't do

Internet companies because the values are inflated too much. We invest in the tired and the poor." The reason he's starting a new business at age 68 is pure excitement, like what he felt in 1970 at the start of the technology IPO boom. "Back then it was us and H&Q. Now it's going to be Francisco and Silver Lake." (McNamee, however, felt the field would have many competitors.)

Robertson acknowledges that Francisco Partners is patterned after Silver Lake. Francisco even has a partnership with Kleiner archrival Sequoia Capital, which will help with deal flow and recruitment. Robertson claims that his staff is much more seasoned than Silver Lake's, with more than 50 years of combined buyout and investment banking experience. Collectively, the group—which also includes Dave Stanton from Texas Pacific Group, Ben Ball from TA Associates, and Neil Garfinkel from Summit Partners—has evaluated 250 technology investment opportunities representing $15 billion in value. "We've cornered the market in people with technology and LBO experience," he says.

Francisco had already done one deal in early 2000, buying back a small firm that did remote management software after its parent was acquired. "We bought it back for 25 cents on the dollar," says Robertson, because the parent, Sterling Commerce, "didn't put any incentives for anybody to stay." The top leadership and most of the sales force left, while the growth rate plummeted from 30 percent to 6 percent. Francisco got the former CEO to buy into the deal and, using Sequoia's formidable network, recruited a new sales force. "We've already had an offer to sell the company at a nice profit," says Robertson, "but we'll ride it for a year or two. We might take it public or sell it." Francisco is looking for more hidden gems that can be rescued from troubled situations. Robertson anticipates returns in the 35 percent range. "The competition here isn't as great as in the VC world," he says. As the IPO market worsens, "we might do better than VCs. We have a lot less competition, and we're not doing dot-coms. We're contrarians. As the market comes down, our universe expands."

BABY ON BOARD

A model proliferating like kudzu in the late 1990s and early 2000s was the so-called *incubator*, designed to nurture start-up companies by providing such essentials as office space and services, recruitment help, access to equipment, management assistance, and, increasingly, financing. In some cases this overlaps with what early-stage venture capitalists do, but their overcommitment and arrogance have opened the door for what some regard as a kinder, gentler approach. Universities and government entities have operated incubators for years, but, sensing a profitable niche, the private sector has now created a stampede. Incubators have sprung up under the auspices of VC firms, consultants (Andersen Consulting, for one, has its dot-com launch centers), business groups, angel investors, office parks, and even publishers. In the Internet era, the idea is that incubators can accelerate (indeed, some are called *accelerators*) a start-up's growth by providing all the basics in one place. Once the company grows beyond a certain stage, it is then passed on to a professional VC firm.

Most VC firms will tell you that they incubate start-ups on an ad hoc, and usually very short-term, basis. Quips Ann Winblad of Hummer Winblad, "We have incubated three companies [in our office]. We have a rule: If you haven't hired enough people to leave in five days, you're out of the incubator." Winblad's jocular comment sums up the attitude that venture capitalists have had toward incubators: Those entrepreneurs who can get venture capital; those who can't incubate. Nonetheless, that attitude is softening because as incubators (like angels) proliferate, they're becoming an important source of deal flow, and no self-respecting venture capitalist is going to be left out. A few VC firms have established formal incubators themselves, such as Softbank's affiliate called HotBank, which runs incubators in several locations. Other VC firms are enveloping incubators within their formidable networks, such as Draper Fisher Jurvetson, which has a relationship with Cambridge Incubator in Cambridge, Massachusetts.

"Incubators are an evolutionary step in the VC process," maintains Ron Schreiber, a managing director of HotBank NE in Boston. He compares incubators to professional sports teams, which now scout at both the college and high school levels to get an early jump on the talent pool. "That's what we're doing in the incubation business: targeting very early opportunities," he says. "We want to turn great ideas into extraordinarily fast-growing companies at Internet speed." By providing a "turnkey infrastructure," HotBank frees entrepreneurs from spending a lot of time figuring out which phone system to buy or how to negotiate an office lease. To Schreiber, incubators are displacing not venture capitalists, but angels. "We are institutionalizing the start-up process."

The incubator model can encompass different types of entrepreneurial companies, Schreiber says. Most typical is a deal with a fairly seasoned entrepreneur who wants a place to test a new concept. In that case, "we're analogous to the angel round," providing funding of $500,000 to $2 million and winding up with a 20 percent to 30 percent stake in the company. On the other end of the spectrum is a rank neophyte with an interesting idea but no management team. An incubator in that case could build up the company, offering similar financing but taking a bigger stake, for example in the 40 percent range. Entrepreneurs-in-residence might also use an incubator to research ideas, and then join or create a company. "In that case we'll do a 50–50 [equity] split and put up the money," says Schreiber. Finally, the incubator itself hatches the idea, does the prototyping, and finds a management team to run the company. Under this scenario the incubator might own as much as 80 percent of the company early on.

Incubators are not designed to carry a company to an initial public offering. "In a period of about a year, we want the company to mature to the point where it appeals to outside financial forces," such as Softbank Venture Capital or another quality VC firm. "Every deal here has to continue to earn its stripes and build an argument for further financing. If a deal can't get financed, it goes away," Schreiber says.

Tim Rowe, who founded Cambridge Incubator in early 1999, left the Boston Consulting Group's e-commerce practice because he saw an unfilled need. "You don't want to leave the entrepreneur out on the field alone," he says. "In the previous generations you had the luxury of allowing a company to find its own way. In the Internet era you have to make the process happen as fast as possible." Enter incubators, which Rowe acknowledges still have to prove their merit. "We have to demonstrate the same kind of profitability and success as the big [venture] funds."

The difference from a VC firm, says Rowe, is the quality of attention that each of his companies gets. "On average all of the top venture capitalists have about five or six portfolio companies they monitor. They also spend about half their time looking for new investments. So maybe you get one tenth of one person's time." By contrast, in mid-2000 Cambridge Incubator had only five companies being incubated, with 35 people devoted to that. "That's an average of seven full-time equivalents per company," says Rowe. He works with a start-up that's little more than a concept in somebody's head. "We invest when there's no team, no track record, no proof of concept, and write a check for $1 million. For that we get half the company." Rowe and his team will help the company build to a point where it's attractive to venture capitalists, who, Rowe maintains, really want to invest after the hard work has been done.

An example of a stand-alone incubator is Techfarm, one of the earliest and most successful of its genre, founded by former entrepreneur Gordon Campbell in 1993. Techfarm is housed in Mountain View, California, in an industrial area next to a train station. Campbell, who founded pioneering companies such as Seeq Technology and Chips & Technologies, says he reinvented himself as an incubator because he wanted to work with start-ups, not run them. "I didn't want to be Jerry Sanders or Wilf Corrigan," he says, referring to two generational peers who are still heading technology companies. "But I wanted more structure than an angel."

When he started Techfarm in 1993, the incubator "wasn't a popular concept," but as VC funds have gotten bigger, there's more room under the radar for incubators. In addition, many venture capitalists are no longer former entrepreneurs but "financial guys" with MBAs. So there's room, Campbell says, for people like himself who can provide hands-on guidance to would-be entrepreneurs. "We work with these kids, helping them with structure and a business plan," he says. "Traditional venture has migrated toward the quick hit. You put the money in and see an IPO in six months to a year." It has also moved away from the labors required for a very early-stage company. "Venture capitalists today want to go to maybe half a dozen board meetings and then take the company out [public]."

Techfarm concentrates on certain segments, or clusters, that may be out of favor with traditional VC investors. For example, the Techfarm portfolio includes several companies in the mundane storage arena, especially very small devices that can be used in products like digital cameras. It also invests in things like semiconductor design, productivity software, and even game development. "What we look for is a good management team, good technology, good market opportunities," says Campbell. "I'm not as fussy about whether they're in a popular space." One portfolio company he singled out was Resonate, founded in 1996 to provide software that manages Websites. "The VCs I brought here then couldn't throw up on the idea fast enough," he says, "but today the popular sites like eBay and Schwab are getting a billion hits a day. You have to have software to manage those sites. The venture community four years ago was clueless because they were bidding up the dot-com deals." Resonate has since received funding from Kleiner, Intel, Flatiron, and Lehman Brothers.

Initially, Techfarm was purely an incubator with no funding capability, but "we found that one thing we were doing most was helping companies raise money." Campbell has since added venture funding to the mix, raising a first fund of $45 million, a second of $140 million, and a third of $400 million. He also acts like a venture capitalist by doing follow-on financing at declining levels of participation. "We believe that the value should be in the company and not in us." To that end, Techfarm receives its equity in a company on a vesting schedule just like the management team. "That had an amazing impact on founders because we put ourselves in the same circumstances as they are," he says. "We become part of the team."

OPERATING PREMIUM

In 2000 the most watched innovation in venture investing was combining incubating and investing with heavy ownership positions in operating companies, and then taking the whole shebang public. It sounds complicated, and it is, because it requires a rejiggering of securities laws to allow operating companies to coexist with an investment fund. Under the Investment Company Act of 1940, any firm that has more than 40 percent of its assets in nonownership positions in portfolio companies is declared a mutual fund, subject to strict reporting requirements. But the Securities and Exchange Commission granted an exemption to one of these incarnations, Internet Capital Group (ICG), which successfully argued that its active participation in its portfolio firms means that it is an operating company, not a passive mutual fund.[1] Another important player, CMGI, got around the rule by buying the Internet search firm AltaVista, a company of sufficient heft to offset CMGI's investment holdings.

The pioneer in this space is Pasadena, California–based Idealab, founded in 1996 by Bill Gross. The entrepreneur who started educational software standout Knowledge Adventure, Gross is a notable fount of innovative ideas. The concept behind Idealab was to put teams and infrastructure around his ideas, finance them in an incubator setting, and eventually see them go public. As of late 2000, five Idealab companies had achieved that goal: GoTo.com, eToys, CitySearch, NetZero, and Tickets.com. Another 50 Idealab companies were still private, in various stages of development. However, Idealab's own public offering was stalled by worsening conditions in the public markets and growing skepticism about incubators.

Idealab's VC arm, Idealab Capital Partners, has been doing early-stage investing, having raised a total of $450 million in two funds. "We'll be raising another fund next year [2001] that's bigger. There's some pressure to go to $1 billion, but I don't think we'll be doing that with just five partners," says Erik Lassila, a managing director of Idealab Capital Partners in Palo Alto. Although Gross is a general partner and investor in the VC fund, Lassila says that the decisions on where to invest are made independently of the incubator. "Most of our investments are in non-Idealab companies," he says, although there is a *keiretsu* effect between the incubated companies and the VC portfolio. Lassila believes Idealab is a step above most incubators, which provide space and "very basic" services, because it has executives with deep operating experience to help its companies. For example, former high-ranking AT&T executive Bob Kavner runs the Silicon Valley branch of Idealab.

CMGI, based in Andover, Massachusetts, can trace its ancestry way back to 1968 (ancient history in the Internet age), when it was founded as College Marketing Group, selling mailing lists and direct marketing services. Under the leadership of David Wetherell, it eventually transformed itself into an Internet incubator, going public in 1994. The following year it started an affiliated VC fund, CMGI @Ventures. With locations on both the East and West Coasts, and majority ownership of AltaVista, CMGI is the largest and most visible of the incubator/holding company combos. In mid-2000, CMGI's operating segment had ownership stakes in about 20 companies, while the VC arm had done roughly 75 investments. "@Ventures investments look like an index fund of the Internet," spanning content, community, business-to-consumer (B2C), business-to-business (B2B), technology, and infrastructure, notes associate Josh Daniels, who works out of West Coast headquarters in Menlo Park.

CMGI @Ventures, which started with a modest $50 million fund in 1995, was sitting on wads of money in 2000. It had a $1 billion fund that invests in Web services and B2C e-commerce, another $1 billion fund dedicated to B2B exchanges, and a third one for infrastructure, wireless, networking, and communications. The $3 billion total all came from CMGI. Finally, there was a $1.5 billion global fund, financed one third by CMGI and two thirds from the LBO fund Hicks Muse and the Asian investment group Pacific Century Cyberworks. With only one limited partner, CMGI itself, @Ventures is in no hurry to invest its billions. "We just do smart deals," says managing partner Peter Mills. With Nasdaq's malaise, he acknowledged that @Ventures' existing companies might not be able to go public as soon as expected. "If a company has a good scalable business model, an ability to get profitable in the foreseeable future, and the opportunity to be a dominant player in its category, we'd still want to fund it," he says. "The old model was to buy market share, and the world will wait for profits. The new model is to achieve dominance, scalable business, and profitability." All of @Ventures' companies are getting the same message: "Get real about your cost structure. Align it with your revenue outlook," Mills says.

ICG, founded in 1996 and based in Wayne, Pennsylvania, has ownership stakes in 60-plus companies, five of which were public in mid-2000, including the B2B exchange Vertical Net. Itself publicly traded and viewed somewhat as an Internet index fund, ICG proclaimed that it was different from competitors because of its focus. "Our objective is to build a B2B company that has dominant market share and is the most profitable in that sector," says Ken Fox, the ICG cofounder and managing director who operates out of the San Francisco office. "That's all we do. We're a holding company aggregating and consolidating a highly fragmented market." ICG will invest in infrastructure, service providers, or any type of technology that enables B2B. Like the top venture capitalists, Fox sees himself as building an industry. "You've got to decide whether you want to take part in the global economy or whether you just want to be a flipper."

ICG's average ownership stake in its operating companies is 37 percent, according to Fox. "We want to own big slugs of our companies." Although ICG acts like a VC investor in many ways, Fox says the difference is that his company will continue to hold portfolio companies after they go public, making profits from gains in the value of its assets. "We're not a mutual fund. We're not venture capitalists. We are a new breed of company, so it's hard to pigeonhole us." He attributed the steep drop in share price that ICG (along with CMGI) experienced in 2000 in part to Wall Street's failure to understand the new model. Although ICG is a pure play in the B2B space, "Wall Street's frustration is that our sector is extremely complex and involves multiple industries. They have never had the challenge of understanding multiple industries," says Fox.

In addition to its B2B holdings, ICG also runs an incubator called eColony to nurture new companies. Fox expected the initial group to consist of about 15 start-ups. "Our core competency is building businesses fast," Fox says. "The market slowdown forces everyone to prioritize, but our strategy has not changed one bit. We don't care whether companies are public or private. We just want to have dominant market share in B2B."

SUSTAINABLE MODELS OR FADS?

Traditional venture capitalists view both the pure incubators and the new incarnations like CMGI and ICG with suspicion. Are they competitors? Are they collaborators? Are they a new model that will force the intensely private VC firms to consider going public themselves? (See Chapter 14.) For an industry that cheers entrepreneurialism, venture capital can be extremely reactionary to anything new in its own field. "The definition of an incubator is to keep something alive that otherwise would never survive," proclaims Gill Cogan, a general partner with San Francisco–based Lightspeed Venture Partners, formerly Weiss Peck & Greer. "Eventually you have to push these companies out of the nest, and they crash. The incubator makes entrepreneurs feel too comfortable." Hummer Winblad's Mark Gorenberg sings the same chorus: "Incubators will lead to average companies," he maintains. "The great companies will stand on their own feet at the beginning."

The public market's distaste for the incubator incarnations seemed to bear out some of the venture capitalist's criticisms. In October 2000 the share prices of ICG and CMGI were both trading far below their 52-week highs: ICG was down 94 percent from $212 to $15, while CMGI was off 85 percent from $163 to $23. In the following month, ICG, reeling from a third-quarter loss totaling $264 million, compared with $15 million a year earlier, announced plans to lay off 35 percent of its workforce and take other cost-cutting measures. ICG also planned to make more information available about its private companies to help analysts and investors value the company. That didn't prevent its share price from slipping even further, to around $11. Later in November, CMGI had similar grim news. It closed two underperforming Web-based businesses—Icast, devoted to music and entertainment, and 1stUp.com, which provided free Internet service—resulting in the layoffs of more than 300 employees. And it intended to trim more of its operating companies to reduce losses. CMGI also forecast 2001 revenues of $1.65 billion, below analysts' expectations. By December, its share price had slipped to around $12, leaving its market cap at $3.8 billion, down sharply from a staggering $41 billion at the end of 1999.[2] The news was far worse by March 2001: CMGI was at $2.50 a share, while ICG had slipped below $2!

With its public peers struggling, Idealab put its IPO in limbo, withdrawing its registration in October, and concentrated on its own survival. Gross says that the company still plans to go public when market conditions improve, perhaps in 2001. Meanwhile, being out of the quiet period related to the pre-IPO stage allowed Gross to leap to Idealab's defense: The company has "plenty of operating cash" and strong support from investors and its board.[3] But not all of its holdings were as fortunate. Online beauty store Eve.com was poised between major layoffs and outright liquidation. Another Idealab company, entertainment site Z.com, was close to running out of money and had laid off about half its employees.[4] Idealab did have one piece of good news in late 2000: the SEC granted it a permanent exemption from the Investment Company Act.

Whether public or private, incubators thrive when there's a ready path for taking start-ups to IPOs. Since most of the incubators were formed in the heady days of the late 1990s, many will probably not survive a down cycle, with rare exceptions such as Campbell's Techfarm, which has proven its durability. However, proponents point out that VC firms have also endured up and down cycles. "I don't consider what we're doing a fad," insists CMGI's Peter Mills. "We were the first Internet-only fund. Our model has been in place since 1994; it is sustainable." He believes that CMGI's flexible model will be better able to adapt to change than will the traditional venture capital industry.

"What allowed us to emerge so rapidly is that we didn't come at this with the tried-and-true methodology of the venture industry," he says. "We aren't hidebound. We're able to evolve the way we have to." We'll see. Chapter 14 considers how the VC industry itself must evolve in order to survive its flaws.

CHAPTER FOURTEEN

The Future of Venture Capital

The year 2000 opened on a high note of jubilation: The economy was the best that it had ever been; the technology industry was minting millionaires daily; the United States was the lone and undisputed superpower both economically and militarily; the celebration of the new millennium was unmarred by any significant violence or terrorist activity; and despite dire warnings, computerized networks did not fall apart under the onslaught of Y2K (remember that?). As the year closed, we were at another of those turning points that have come to symbolize human history. We were on tenterhooks concerning the new U.S. president and the balance of power in Congress. A Middle East conflagration seemed perilously close. The vaunted U.S. economy was losing steam. And finally, the long boom predicted by technology edenists looked like it was about to blow up in our faces.

Because Nasdaq was poised to finish its worst year ever, the initial public offering (IPO) window was virtually closed, and venture capital (VC) investing was plummeting by more than half in the fourth quarter, critics of the VC industry were in full hand-wringing mode. Too many dot-coms with frivolous business plans, too much ridiculous spending on ads and promotions, too little consideration of profitability, lack of concern for consumers and businesses and what they want—all these charges flung at the overhyped industry were undoubtedly true. Curiously, however, the cauldron of criticism did reaffirm the point that venture capital has become so crucial to the New Economy, indeed the whole economy, that its missteps now warrant national attention.

Venture capital played a defining role in the emergence of many of the most innovative and important companies of the late twentieth century: Intel, Microsoft, Apple Computer, Sun Microsystems, Cisco Systems, America Online, Yahoo, eBay—the list could go on and on. As the twenty-first century dawned, venture capital was expanding its reach beyond technology into every corner of the economy: transforming old-line retailers such as Wal-Mart; forcing automakers and steelmakers to wake up to the Internet; and creating new models of financial transactions, information services, auctions, and business exchanges. With its capital in Silicon Valley, venture capital has become the icon carrying a lot of our hopes (and fears) about the future. Fred Hoar, a longtime observer of technology and chairman of the public relations (PR) firm Miller Shandwick Technologies in Redwood Shores, California, compares Silicon Valley to the fertile crescent in ancient Mesopotamia, once the cradle of civilization. Consultant and author Geoff Moore likens the Valley to Rome in its heyday. "The Roman roads were the Internet of their time, stretching all the way from England to Jerusalem and uniting the [known] world."

With those heady expectations heaped upon it, venture capital is staggering under the weight of its own successes. The VC practitioners who built the industry over several decades have watched with dismay as their structures were overrun by squatters and newcomers seeking a share of the wealth. "The change is not pleasing, but it's inevitable," says Hoar. He recalls the depression-era tale of a desperate farmer begging a banker for a loan. The banker told the farmer that he could have the loan if he could point out the banker's glass eye. The farmer picked it without hesitation: "In that eye there was the barest glimpse of human compassion and charity." Adds Hoar, "Today we have glass-eyed VCs who never made money the old-fashioned way. The DNA that drove the early VCs was the entrepreneurial risk culture. They fought the wars together. Now you're seeing come into the ranks not the people who fought the wars but the bean-counters and the MBAs."

However, some view it as a sign of progress and maturity when warriors give way to shopkeepers. It may not be as exciting or spontaneous, but it can be more effective. Even Hoar acknowledges that the discipline and focus brought by the bean-counters contributes to the long-term viability of venture capital. "We're finding a way to continue to mine in ever more efficient ways the tremendous potential of technology," he says. Not everyone agrees. Integral Capital's Roger McNamee proclaims that all the newcomers "have enhanced the amateur hour."

The VC industry itself is really conservative by nature and changes only when it has to. Sure, its practitioners take on risk as part of their jobs, but in their clubby little cubbyholes they savor the illusion of living on the edge without having to work quite so hard at it as the entrepreneurs who make them rich. It would be unfair to call venture capitalists cowards—many have put themselves on the line as founders or champions of companies with no other backers—but I would call them calculating. They have figured out a way to profit immensely from entrepreneurialism and still be able to walk away and say, "You didn't listen to me," when a company fails. Consequently, the seven trends that are shaping the future of venture capital are not revolutionary, but evolutionary, like incremental improvements to an existing, popular product rather than a wholesale rethinking of the model itself.

STAYING POWER IS BRANDING

Although Don Valentine rues the day that VC firms started to hire PR specialists, even his Sequoia Capital has jumped on the bandwagon. Increasingly, top-tier VC firms and wanna-bes either have an internal PR person or have retained an outside firm to handle the job. The intent is not merely to help publicize the portfolio companies, as some venture capitalists piously insist, but to attract attention for the VC firm itself. It's all about deal flow—getting the inside track on whatever new, hot thing is coming. Still, it's not PR people who build up the consistent track records that make for great VC firms. The next Marc Andreessen fooling around with tomorrow's breakthrough in the bowels of a college computer lab likely will take that invention to Kleiner or Sequoia or Greylock, not because they've issued bunches of press releases, but because they've already done legendary companies like Cisco and Netscape. In turn, the cachet of funding by such a firm will put this neophyte Andreessen on the fast track in the race for survival. Being a "Kleiner company," for example, aids in the recruitment of a high-quality team, attracts other investors (venture capitalists, angels, and corporations), and helps land a gold-standard investment bank for the IPO. Although top-tier firms must have the reliable track record laid out in Chapters 4 and 5, their future successes will be determined by their ability to invest in exciting new ideas. And it all starts with having access to deal flow.

Branding is inevitably bound up with the difference between top-tier firms and everyone else. When the magazine I work for, *Forbes ASAP*, published a list of the best venture capitalists, we were immediately besieged with the anguished cry, "Why wasn't I on your list?" That's because everyone knows that in venture capital, more than in any other investing category, the rich get richer. Building on their deal flow access and their ability to boost their companies' chances, the top-tier firms are able to deliver consistently better returns, which means that limited partners are more willing to invest and that the best entrepreneurs return time and again for funding. The definition of *top tier* thus becomes a self-fulfilling prophecy. Barring loss of a key rainmaker or a wholesale defection of personnel, the top-quality firms have enough momentum to stay there in the foreseeable future.

But even the super tier and those nearly there, as I described in Chapters 4 and 5, could be under stress in a prolonged down cycle. Sequoia, which clings to its generalist, invest-in-everything tradition (see the section on specialization), could find its lack of focus eroding its returns and, ultimately, its leadership. It must also cope with the gradual retirement of Don Valentine and Pierre Lamond. Meanwhile, what would happen to Kleiner if John Doerr goes into politics full-time? Certainly the firm has brought in a host of respected executives with operating experience, such as Ray Lane from Oracle and Tom Jermoluk from Excite@Home, but their abilities as venture capitalists have yet to be proven. Yet Kleiner probably has the deepest lineup in all of venture capital, with people like Vinod Khosla, Doug Mackenzie, Ted Schlein, and Kevin Compton. Finally, Benchmark came of age in the golden era and must demonstrate its staying power in tougher times. Super tier contender Accel may be too dependent on big deals like Wal-Mart.com, as well as on star partner Jim Breyer. Redpoint, the wanna-be, could have just the opposite of Sequoia's problem in being too narrowly focused, and it's still looking for the home run that would boost its claim to being at the very top. So even the mighty could fall.

FRAGMENTATION

The numbers of VC firms, angels, and corporate investors were each at an all-time high at the end of 2000. Since 1995, the number of professional VC firms has nearly doubled to 620. Angel investors are harder to count, but by one estimate they total one million![1] Worldwide, at least 350 corporations had acknowledged venture investing programs, compared with just 108 in 1998 and 203 in 1999, according to the *Corporate Venturing Report*. Then there were incubators, and accelerators, and universities, and government agencies, and not-for-profits—you name it, everyone wanted to get in on the venture investing trend.

In both direct and indirect ways, the fabulous success of the technology industry, especially in the past few years, has driven this fragmentation of the venture investing model. Directly, because entrepreneurial millionaires are, if you'll excuse the expression, now a dime a dozen. Scratch any self-respecting metropolitan area and you'll find young nouveaux riches entrepreneurs who are willing and able to invest in other start-ups. What to do with a hundred million dollars when you're 25 or 30 years old? It's not an academic question in Silicon Valley. They do more of the same: They become either a serial entrepreneur or a VC partner. Indirectly, because the VC model of entrepreneurial investing is rightly held up today as the cornerstone of the New Economy. Prestigious business schools have courses in how to be a venture capitalist. Vaunted magazines dissect the doings of John Doerr and Ann Winblad. The press seeks them out as pundits. Politicians vie for photo ops.

It was an orgy of adulation, and it inevitably reached its saturation point. As dot-com companies failed by the dozens in the second half of 2000, the investors who backed all these me-too start-ups faced a barrage of criticism. Venture capitalists practically trampled each other in the race to distance themselves from the piles of carcasses that their herd mentality had produced. The contrarian label was back in vogue, even though by definition it can only be applied to a rare few.

At the end of 2000, the fragmentation in venture investing appeared poised if not to reverse itself, at least to level off. Too much of anything, even investment capital, proved to be a prelude to calamity.

REMODELING VENTURE CAPITALISM

Closely related to fragmentation is the proliferation of reformulated models of venture investing, such as CMGI and Internet Capital Group (ICG), cited in Chapter 13. Less remarked upon, though, has been the internal tinkering by established VC firms. This has largely been subtle, because venture capitalists found a formula that works and are reluctant to mess with it too much. Still, change is happening. It's in the addition of venture partners with expertise in fields such as PR, executive search, law, accounting, and consulting. It's in the restructuring of the carry to give equal shares to every partner. It's in the implosion of established VC firms and the formation of new ones. It's also in outright experiments like Draper Fisher Jurvetson's meVC.

Tim Draper conceived the grand idea of opening up venture capital's tremendous returns to the "little guy," the general public. meVC, which began trading in June 2000 on the New York Stock Exchange, is a closed-end mutual fund devoted to VC investments. "Part of my mission is to bring VC to the masses," Draper says. Historically, he points out, VC returns have outperformed Standard & Poor's and other indexes, yet very few are able to benefit: "I've always thought it wasn't fair that you had to be a millionaire to be able to invest in private equities." Reflecting his libertarian philosophy, Draper decries government regulation that prevents nonwealthy individuals from investing in risky securities. "You educate people and then let them go and live with the consequences of their actions," he says. Draper concedes that meVC is a radical departure for the VC community. "We're the first major venture fund to break rank and try this," he says. "I just open it up and see if somebody follows."

Redpoint's Tim Haley agrees with Draper that experiments like meVC and ICG are needed. "Access to VC investments has been the domain of a select few individuals, foundations, and endowments," he notes. "The average person has no access until something like ICG comes along and opens the future value of their portfolio to the public markets." A few other firms offer ways for people who meet the wealthy investor requirements of the Securities and Exchange Commission to invest in venture capital for minimum outlays ranging from $5,000 to $1 million, including W. R. Hambrecht & Company, StoneGate Partners, Early Bird Capital, and J. P. Morgan. However, meVC is the broadest product, operating like a closed-end mutual fund.

While meVC raised $330 million in its public offering, its shares promptly dropped almost 50 percent by December, not an auspicious beginning.[2] Even Tim Draper's father, Bill, was skeptical. "Tim is a maverick all the way," says the senior Draper. "He's got the first VC fund that's a mutual fund, but I don't think venture capital was meant to be a public business. How do you determine the real value of a portfolio [of private companies]?" Draper Fisher competitors, all of whom were watching meVC with undisguised interest, thought that a few more private equity mutual funds might be formed. But few believed that established VC firms themselves would go public, since access to capital has not been a problem. "I can't imagine anyone who would want to stand up in front of shareholders," says Ted Schlein of Kleiner. However, Kleiner was involved in a joint venture (eVolution) to help Old Economy companies join the New Economy, which Schlein expected to become a public company eventually. While a wholesale conversion of venture capital from a private to a public industry is extremely unlikely, there will be more trials like meVC, eVolution, or CMGI, not necessarily because of pressure to open up venture capital to more investors but because venture capitalists love to find new ways of making money.

SPECIALIST TRUMPS GENERALIST

The first venture capitalists invested in anything that came their way, from industrial manufacturers to publishers to technology. Their value added was in the capital itself, as well as in general advice on how to run a business and what was needed to go public. In the 1980s, with the twin technology revolutions (biotech and high tech), which not coincidentally took off in the innovative corridors of Silicon Valley and Boston, VC investing became concentrated in those sectors. Many firms, including heavyweights like Kleiner, Mayfield, and Institutional Venture Partners (IVP), had thriving practices in both biotech and high technology. But with the Internet revolution of the mid-1990s, coupled with a very disappointing period for biotech, the two flows of technology investing diverged. The go-go model of the Internet age, with companies forming, growing, and going public as quickly as possible, produced unprecedented returns and opportunities, while biotech, with its endless regulatory hurdles, lagged far behind.

IVP's split into two entities—one of which became Redpoint and the other Palladium, continuing with biotech investing—personifies the specialization trend. "In the last three years we at IVP recognized that the life sciences and Internet businesses would require different skills and strategies," says Sam Colella, a longtime biotech investor at IVP. "Rather than continue as IVP, we joined with Brentwood and formed a focused technology fund, Redpoint, and a focused health care fund, Palladium." Some funds are even more intensely specialized than Redpoint, which concentrates on Internet investing. ICG takes it a step further and does only business-to-business. Kleiner's Java Fund invested solely in companies developing products based on the Sun Microsystems programming language. Sums up Colella, "Focused funds are the way of the future." In 1984, when he got into the venture business, "there were maybe five categories. I could do semiconductors one day, medical devices the next." Today, he says, there are probably two dozen categories in information technology and a dozen in health care: "You cannot be a generalist any more. You have to know your domain space."

Besides focusing on vertical sectors, VC firms are also dividing themselves up horizontally. That is, they're dedicated to seed, early-stage, or late-stage investing. Most of the firms portrayed in this book are early-stage investors: They want to be the first institutional money into a company, after a financing round raised from angels and "friends and family." They're not seed investors any more because they can't put enough money to work to justify the resources required at that level. Early stage is where the biggest returns have been and where star venture capitalists like John Doerr have made their names. During the Internet bubble, companies barely got beyond that stage before they went public and reaped a bonanza for their backers. But there is a need for the other types of investors. Menlo Park–based Onset Ventures, for instance, was formed in 1984 by Mayfield, Kleiner, and New Enterprise Associates to fill a gap in seed funding. Today, Onset finds itself competing with angels, but partner Susan A. Mason says the firm still has a niche. "Angels are bringing deals to us because we have the operating experience to give entrepreneurs the hand-holding they need," she says.

At the other end of the spectrum, late-stage firms like Technology Crossover Ventures, TA Associates, Meritech Capital Partners, and Integral Capital typically come into funding rounds just before a private company goes public. They also may continue to hold stakes and invest in public companies (hence the name *crossover*). Generally, there's less risk in late-stage investing because the business model has been proven, but that means that valuations of the entrepreneurial companies are much higher. Late-stage investors must buy in at some-times-inflated values, lowering their potential returns. However, as the public market withdrew its welcome mat, late-stage valuations, especially those for Internet content and exchange companies, declined precipitately. "Our primary emphasis is profitable-stage investing" is the way Kevin Landry of TA Associates in Boston puts it. "The companies are making money this month and, you think they're going to be making money thereafter." As for Internet companies, the standard is slightly different. "We try to get the ones with customers and proven products," even if they are not necessarily making a profit.

With the frantic attempt to get any possible advantage in an increasingly noisy space, both horizontal and vertical specialization among VC firms is here to stay, although this trend also leads to the consolidation mentioned next.

CONSOLIDATION AND SHAKE-OUT

The fragmentation and specialization just cited, combined with the enticing prosperity of the golden era, have created too many VC firms, so consolidation is inevitable. Firms that focus too narrowly on vertical niches may find themselves swept aside if their sector falls out of favor. Newcomer firms dependent on just one or two sources of funding will be jeopardized when those dry up in hard times. The horizontal funds at the tips of the spectrum are finding themselves cannibalized by angels formalizing their organizations and moving upmarket on the one end and public investors like the investment banks moving down on the other. Unproven models like the incubators and public operating companies, which haven't yet been tested in a prolonged down cycle, could fail the test. If Nasdaq's doldrums persist, watch for the dismantling of many incubators—along with their companies, which won't be able to raise more capital. If a rising tide lifts all boats, an ebbing tide strands quite a few in the sand.

As times get tougher, "we're going to see a wave of retirements in the VC firms because it won't be fun any more," predicts McNamee. "These guys are going to take their money, start foundations, and build their mansions." The number of VC firms could shrink by 20 to 25 percent over the next few years as marginal players disappear. McNamee also doubts the staying power of corporations, which will scurry to protect their own bottom lines as venture returns drop, as well as both angels and incubators, who haven't proven their value added or ability to stay in for the long term. "The established brands won't be nearly as affected," he says, "although the major players have spread themselves very thin and will have to retrench."

In October 2000, one sign of the coming consolidation was the announcement that eCompanies, an Internet incubator in Santa Monica, California, was going to combine its VC arm with a New York investment firm, Evercore Capital Partners. The move reflected eCompanies' inability to raise a follow-on round of financing after its $160 million first fund.[3] A month later, Stamford, Connecticut–based Walker Digital, an incubator for Internet start-ups founded by Priceline's Jay Walker, also found itself strapped for cash. It drastically slashed operations, laying off 100 of 125 employees and closing at least three of its funded companies. Expect a lot more of the same.

LIFE OUTSIDE SILICON VALLEY

For most of the industry's existence, venture capitalists have been satisfied to be parochial. "Why should I get on a plane to see a company when there are so many opportunities in my own backyard?" is a refrain that I heard in my interviews, predominantly along Sand Hill Road. As Silicon Valley solidified its position as leader of the technology revolution, East Coast VC firms opened offices and invested in companies on the other coast. The Sand Hill Road firms, beset with their regional prejudice, did not generally follow suit. What some have done instead is to go overseas. Sequoia has a long-standing fund devoted to investment in Israel. In May 2000 Benchmark raised a $750 million European fund, while Draper Fisher Jurvetson has dealt with entrepreneurs in Portugal, Russia, Czechoslovakia, Hungary, the United Kingdom, and Germany. Bill Draper's Draper International created a $55 million fund in 1995 with the intent to go global, and wound up investing in India. Notes Draper, "I wanted to prove that venture capital can be done internationally. We checked out China and Indonesia, but we picked India because they spoke English, were good on software, it's a democracy, and we liked the food better."

China and the Asia Pacific also attract interest from U.S. venture capitalists. "We're seeing a huge expansion of the U.S. venture industry into Asia," says Howard Chao, chair of the China practice for O'Melveny & Myers, a large law firm headquartered in Los Angeles. Chao has seen deals in China by Softbank, Kleiner, J. H. Whitney, and Robertson Stephens. "Part of the problem with a lot of these funds is that they don't have the knowledge and relationships in Asia—identifying who the local players are and how they think about things." On the other hand, the knowledge about VC investing resides in the United States. "It's not possible yet to be completely homegrown," says Chao. One of his clients, Chengwei Ventures, is run by two ethnic Chinese who got Stanford MBAs and returned to establish a fund in Shanghai.

Under its Japanese ownership, Softbank has been especially active globally. It has venture funds in China and Japan, and incubators in London, Paris, Munich, Bombay, Sydney, Auckland, Shanghai, Tokyo, and Buenos Aires. "These are facilities whose job it is to take the best ideas [Softbank has funded] and copy them," says Bill Burnham, a partner in Softbank's San Francisco office. "It's all driven by our success with Yahoo Japan." For instance, there are copies of eLoan and Buy.com in England, typically structured as 50–50 deals between the U.S. model and Softbank. "In the old days you could take two or three years to build a U.S. business, then go overseas," Burnham notes. "Now somebody will copy you instantly in China. So we're taking businesses around the world and replicating them. We can't wait."

American venture capitalists are slowly waking up to opportunities outside Silicon Valley and other traditional strongholds. As they do, they're going to find entrenched competition. Europe especially is starting to awaken to the power of venture capital. In the first half of 2000, private-equity firms there raised $22 billion, compared with $27 billion for all of 1999. About half that total was aimed at venture investing.[4] With the notion of entrepreneurialism taking root around the world, it's obvious that some of the great new companies will be created not in Palo Alto, Seattle, or Austin, but in Beijing, Stockholm, and Dublin.

IT'S STILL ABOUT MONEY

Money may be a commodity now for venture capitalists, but it's a commodity like gasoline—the industry wouldn't run without it. As 2000 drew to a close, there was more money than ever, but it seemed that there were fewer good ideas in which to invest it. New Enterprise Associates (NEA) may have hit the peak when it closed a $2 billion "gigafund," as *Redherring.com* called it, in September 2000.[5] Previously, $1 billion had been the hurdle that the largest firms aspired to. According to the VC tracking firm VentureOne, 17 VC firms raised funds of $1 billion or more, starting in late 1999, among them TA Associates, Accel, Softbank, CMGI@Ventures, Redpoint, Patricof, Meritech, TCV, Mayfield, and Benchmark. "VCs have become stars because of the M-word: 'money'," says Hoar. In *The Great Gatsby*, he notes, the title character describes Daisy's voice as being "full of money." Today the VCs' voices "are full of money, and they have enormous wealth and power as a result."

Despite these huge funds, most experts foresaw a leveling off of venture investing, a trend apparent in early 2001: VC firms raised only $16.1 billion in the first quarter, down 32 percent from the previous period. Even so, there were just not enough places to put that much money to work. In October 2000, Mohr Davidow Ventures' Greg Zachary moaned to the *Wall Street Journal* that he hadn't financed a new company in six months because there was just nothing out there.[6] The following month, Crosspoint Venture Partners took the almost unheard-of step of leaving $1 billion on the table. With commitments from limited partners for that amount, Crosspoint partners stated that they decided not to raise the fund because the environment for entrepreneurial companies was too tough to deliver high returns. (Insiders speculate that the underlying cause was difficulty with a generational transfer of power.) Following the public market's disapproval of spendthrift dot-coms with no profits in sight, venture capitalists were more demanding that start-ups have actual customers willing to pay for their products. "Money is going to get more concentrated in the good firms and not grow so much," predicts Kleiner's Ted Schlein. "We'll do fewer deals, and they will be more focused." The bad companies won't get funded at all or won't get as much funding, "and will disappear faster."

Another limitation on how much money can be put to work is an even more precious resource: time. The number of venture capitalists, although it has hit an all-time high, has not scaled to anywhere near the extent that the amount of money has. "The crisis in the Valley is people. VC firms have quadrupled their funds but not their people," says angel investor Ron Conway. "Everyone is choking on too many companies." VC partners who used to consider sitting on eight or nine company boards to be the upper limit have now stretched that to 10 or 12. But in a business that proclaims its value add as hands-on help in growing a company, venture capital may have expanded beyond the abilities of its practitioners. "VC is fundamentally nonscalable," proclaims Kevin Fong of the Mayfield Fund. "It's very people-intensive and relationship-oriented. If you try to turn it into a factory, it won't work."

Like Joseph Kennedy selling off his stocks when a shoe-shine boy gave him a tip just before the 1929 market crash, venture capitalists in late 2000 were contemplating the question, "When your barber or your real estate agent wants stock options, is the party over?" Late 2000 could have been the high point for VC fund-raising, at least for a time. The venture capitalists I interviewed universally conceded that returns were about to take a big tumble, from more than 100 percent at the top tier to low double digits. A sign of this was the 3.9 percent return that U.S. venture funds posted in the second quarter of 2000, which amounts to a 16.5 percent annual return. And it appeared that returns would go negative for late 2000 and early 2001. That compares to a 167 percent annual return in 1999! "No asset class in the history of the world has been able to sustain triple digit returns for an extended period of time," says Jay Hoag of Technology Crossover Ventures. The lavishly financed dot-com failures were bound to take their toll. There's a lag between lowered returns and a diminution in money flowing into venture capital, but the connection won't go away in the Internet era. One difference that will work toward keeping VC investment at historically high levels is the accumulation of wealth by venture capitalists and entrepreneurs, who can now afford to risk their own money. So the next down cycle for venture capital may be cushioned by the players themselves, but it is inevitable.

WHAT'S NEXT?

With the new millennium on the horizon, the venture capital industry was also at a crossroads. Like recovering drunks after a prolonged binge, venture capitalists swore they were going to invest more sanely, choose companies more carefully, and require more evidence of long-term viability. The trouble is, this pledge has been made and broken many times. The frequency of the VC industry's up-and-down cycles has speeded up in the Internet era, and those ups and downs are still with us. And most venture capitalists in the industry will continue to be caught up in the greed when it appears and in the panic when fear takes over. The great venture capitalists, who truly stand apart and make decisions based on their own inner convictions about potent new markets and the passion of entrepreneurs, will remain the exceptions.

What has changed are the speed and amplitude of these VC investment cycles. No one I spoke with could remember as breathtaking a switch from greed to fear as occurred in the second half of 2000. The tremendous profits of the 1999 to early 2000 era were the best in VC history. The downturn looked like it might be just as dramatic. But given the amount of money available, and the cap on venture capitalists' time, we're not going to return to the era in which a few million dollars and two funding rounds were enough for a company to achieve profitability—and then, after four or five quarters of being in the black, go public. The race is now to the companies that can attract top-tier VC firms, use higher levels of investment capital effectively, and execute on their business plans to reach an IPO. The markets in the Internet era do not wait for the laggard or the perfectionist; they still reward the one who gets there fast. "Our industry is continuously in a two-minute drill now," says Jon Feiber of Mohr Davidow. "If you can't do this, you'll lose."

Along with that, venture capital has grown meaner, more cutthroat. Like two dogs who once got into a fight and now snarl at each other every time they meet, this can't be undone. The mind-set is too ingrained, the potential rewards too huge, for venture capitalists to return to the collegiality of the early years. Collaborating on early-stage deals—*syndication*—could become more common among second- and third-tier firms struggling to survive, but the top tier will retain and hone its edge by swallowing all of a promising deal in the early stage. In later funding rounds, they will continue to syndicate, because validation of a deal by peers is the VC industry's own proof of concept.

The drop in Nasdaq that signaled the end of the golden era was a welcome relief to many in the VC industry. "It resets the public markets to a more rational environment, where fundamentals matter and valuation matters," says Hoag. On the private equity side, "you are likely to see a rippling effect," with entrepreneurial companies either closing their doors or getting sharply written down in value. Significant numbers of start-ups will beg in vain for funding, or they'll get it from second-tier investors who won't last in the trenches. Says Conway of his angel investing, "We're taking a breath right now. We're telling companies 'sorry, no vacancy.'"

However, we're not at an end but merely at a pause. The Internet Revolution has only just started to transform virtually all human interaction, social and financial. A common theme that ran through my interviews was the comparison of our own era to the Industrial Revolution in long-term impact. "We're on the verge of a technology revolution similar to the assembly line in 1900," says Mark Yusko, who handles venture investments for the University of North Carolina. "It took 80 years for that assembly line to get around the world. We're in year two of the Internet. It will probably be a 40-year cycle." While the speculative bubble of 1999 and 2000 burst in April, "this is a bubble on a wave," says Feiber. "The Internet is a fundamental shifting that will go on."

Don Valentine likes the wave analogy too: "In surfing, the waves always come in a set. The ninth wave will be the perfect gigantic wave. If you hit that, you ride forever." There will be more ninth waves. We just don't know quite when.

NOTES

CHAPTER ONE

1. Staff report, "Money Magnets: The Top Money-Raisers in Venture Capital," *Forbes ASAP,* May 29, 2000, pp. 121–132.
2. CNNfn, "ONI Sparkles in its Debut," online story, June 1, 2000.
3. Ibid.
4. Kelly Zito, "Fiber-Optics Companies at Forefront of IPO Pack," *San Francisco Chronicle,* June 2, 2000, p. B2.

CHAPTER TWO

1. David Leonhardt, "Harvard Targets Tech: Prestigious Business School Switches Focus to Silicon Valley," *New York Times,* June 18, 2000, pp. D-1, D-4.
2. Neil King Jr., "With a Nod to 007, the CIA Sets Up Firm to Invest in High Tech," *Wall Street Journal,* April 3, 2000, pp. A1, A8.
3. Kara Swisher, "A Contract with America.Com: Ex-Speaker Gingrich Wants the Government to Act More Like a Tech Firm," *Wall Street Journal,* June 19, 2000, p. B1.
4. Margaret Carlson, "Now Comes Venture-Capital Politics: Do Voters Really Care If a Millionaire Spends His Own Money To Win?" *Time,* June 19, 2000, p. 41.
5. Staff report, "The New Establishment 1998," *Vanity Fair,* October 1998, p. 218.

6. *Business Week* staff, "The Top 25 Power Brokers," *Business Week,* August 25, 1997, pp. 87–90.

7. Donald Katz, "Rise of the Silicon Patriots," *Worth Online,* January 1996.

8. Staff report, "Forbes 400: The Richest People in America," *Forbes,* October 9, 2000, pp. 168, 176.

CHAPTER THREE

1. John W. Wilson, *The New Venturers: Inside the High-Stakes World of Venture Capital,* Addison-Wesley, pp. 16–18.

2. Paul A. Gompers, "The Rise and Fall of Venture Capital," *Business and Economic History,* vol. 23, no. 2, 1992, pp. 1–26.

3. Wilson, *The New Venturers,* pp. 19–20.

4. Gompers, op cit.

5. Wilson, op cit.

6. Wilson, *The New Venturers,* pp. 26–27.

7. Gompers, op cit.

8. Rodes Fishburne and Michael S. Malone, "The Founding Documents," *Forbes ASAP,* May 29, 2000, pp. 139–142.

CHAPTER FOUR

1. Deborah Lohse, "VC Firms Press for Good PR," *San Jose Mercury News,* September 29, 2000, pp. 1C, 6C.

2. Staff report, "The Money Men: Venture Capitalists Don Valentine and Michael Moritz," *Asian Wall Street Journal,* September 23, 1996, p. S11.

3. Staff report, "The Best VCs," *Forbes ASAP,* May 29, 2000, pp. 98–105.

4. Laura M. Holson, "Feeding a Frenzy: Why Internet Investors Are Still Ravenous," *New York Times Online,* June 7, 1999.

5. Staff report, *Forbes ASAP,* op cit.

6. Linda Himelstein, "Benchmark's Venture Capitalists Take the Valley by Storm," *BusinessWeek Online,* June 1999.

7. Gracian Mack, "Ariba Perfects the Modern IPO," *Redherring.com,* June 25, 1999.

8. Mike Veverka, "Plugged in Venture Firms Are Coming Back for More Cash," *Barron's,* July 3, 2000, p. 36.

CHAPTER FIVE

1. Kara Swisher, "A Matchmaker for 'Bricks' and 'Clicks,'" *Wall Street Journal,* March 13, 2000, p. B9.
2. Staff report, "The Best VCs," *Forbes ASAP,* May 29, 2000, pp. 98–105.
3. Om Malik, "A Networked Matrix," *Forbes.com,* January 26, 2000.
4. Staff report, "The Best VCs," *Forbes ASAP,* op cit.
5. George Anders, "Japan's Softbank Strikes It Rich on the Internet," *Wall Street Journal Europe,* February 4, 1999, p. 7.

CHAPTER SIX

1. Neil Weinberg, "Damn the Torpedoes," *Forbes,* July 24, 2000, p. 116.

CHAPTER NINE

1. Susan Pulliam and Randall Smith, "Linux Deal Is Focus of IPO-Commission Probe," *Wall Street Journal,* December 12, 2000, p. C1.

CHAPTER ELEVEN

1. Toni Logan, "Killing Your Wife," *Forbes ASAP,* May 29, 2000, p. 112.
2. Rodes Fishburne, "Sobbing on the Roadside," *Forbes ASAP,* May 29, 2000, pp. 110–111.
3. Peter Sinton, "Fighting for Survival," *San Francisco Chronicle,* June 14, 2000, pp. C1, C4.
4. Carolyn Said, "Dot-Coms Struggle to Survive," *San Francisco Chronicle,* August 10, 2000, pp. C1, C2.
5. Chris Taylor, "Is This the End.com?" *Time,* July 3, 2000, pp. 43–45.
6. Greg Ip, Susan Pulliam, Scott Thurm, and Ruth Simon, "The Internet Bubble Broke Records, Rules, and Bank Accounts," *Wall Street Journal,* July 14, 2000, pp. A1, A8.
7. Carol Emert, "Analysts See Dot-Com Death," *San Francisco Chronicle,* November 28, 2000, p. C2.
8. Michael Moritz, "Many Are Called But Few Are Believed," *Forbes ASAP,* October 2, 2000, pp. 41–42.

CHAPTER TWELVE

1. David G. Barry, "Corporate Venture Capital Soars, As Funding Hits Record $6.3 Billion," *Corporate Venturing Report,* premiere issue, January 2000, p. 1.
2. Ibid., pp. 1, 24.

CHAPTER THIRTEEN

1. Peter D. Henig, "And Now, Econets: Some Internet Incubators Are Morphing into Economic Networks," *Red Herring,* February 2000, pp. 96–108.
2. Saul Hansell, "CMGI Can Defy Gravity Only So Long," *New York Times,* December 10, 2000, Section 3, pp. 1 and 15.
3. Anna Wilde Mathews and Lisa Bransten, "Idealab Postpones Its Initial Offering Amid Nasdaq's Fall," *Wall Street Journal,* October 19, 2000, pp. C1, C22.
4. Ibid.

CHAPTER FOURTEEN

1. Scott Lajoie, "Cities of Angels," *Forbes ASAP,* April 3, 2000, pp. 146–150.
2. Lynnley Browning, "The Mass Marketing of Venture Capital," *New York Times,* December 17, 2000, Section 3, p. 10.
3. Laura M. Holson, "Ecompanies in a Venture Merger Plan," *New York Times,* October 2, 2000, p. C2.
4. David Woodruff, "European Start-ups Revel in a Deluge of Venture Capital," *Wall Street Journal,* November 29, 2000, p. A23.
5. Matthew A. DeBellis, "NEA Catches a $2 billion Gigafund," *Redherring.com,* September 12, 2000.
6. Lisa Bransten, "Venture Capitalists Find Cash, but Few Great Ideas," *Wall Street Journal,* October 2, 2000, p. C18.

INDEX